THE MAKING OF A
ROYAL
ROMANCE

Katie Nicholl has been writing about the British Royal Family for nearly a decade. She is the royal correspondent for the *Mail on Sunday* where she also edits her incredibly popular and respected eponymous weekly column of which Prince Harry is a regular reader. In conjunction with her successful print career Katie works as a commentator on Sky News, the BBC and ITV. She also reports on the Royal Family for ABC's *Good Morning America* programme, CNN and *Entertainment Tonight* in the United States. She lives with her husband in North London.

'Nicholl delves into the secret lives of William and Harry . . . [and] uncovers what makes the two young Windsors tick' *USA Today*

'A great inside look at growing up royal' Larry King

'Full of insight and juicy details about both young men, it's a must for any fan of the royals' *Life & Style*

'Using her unrivalled sources [Katie Nicholl] has written the most revealing book ever about Princes William and Harry . . . the most vivid and engaging study yet of our future King' *Mail on Sunday*

'*William and Harry* is the perfect tell-all tome with impeccable sources. With Nicholl's help, we broke the engagement exclusive the world wanted' Omid Scobie, European Bureau Chief, *US Weekly*

'Katie Nicholl is the Bob Woodward of royal reporting' George Stephanopoulos, *Good Morning America*, ABC

THE MAKING OF A
ROYAL ROMANCE

WILLIAM, KATE, AND HARRY—A LOOK BEHIND THE PALACE WALLS

A revised and expanded edition of
William and Harry: Behind the Palace Walls

KATIE NICHOLL

WEINSTEIN
BOOKS

Previously published in hardcover as *William and Harry*, this paperback
edition includes updated and expanded material, as well as new photographs.

ISBN: 978-1-60286-153-4

First Edition

10 9 8 7 6 5 4 3 2 1

This book is dedicated to my husband for his uncompromising love and support, and to my family, especially my mother, for showing me what true courage is.

Contents

Preface

Modernisation is quite a strong word to use with the monarchy because it's something that's been around for many hundreds of years. But I think it's important that people feel the monarchy can keep up with them and is relevant to their lives. We are all human and inevitably mistakes are made. But in the end there is a great sense of loyalty and dedication among the family and it rubs off on me. Ever since I was very small, it's something that's been very much impressed on me, in a good way.

Prince William on his twenty-first birthday

It was an unexpected encounter with Prince Harry at the Kensington Roof Gardens in London in April 2003 that lit the touch paper for my career as a royal writer. At the time I was working as the showbusiness correspondent for the *Mail on Sunday* and I just happened to be in the right place at the right time. Prince Harry was enjoying a private party in the VIP room and invited me to join him. He should have been revising for his A-levels, instead the prince was drinking vodka Red Bulls and enjoying the company of a group of pretty young girls. Gregarious, vivacious and most of all normal, I was struck by how warm and charming the handsome young prince was. When I met his brother at a polo match shortly afterwards I was equally impressed. These are two young men born into extraordinary lives, with no choice but to live under the scrutiny of the public eye. Having overcome the greatest tragedy – the loss of their beloved mother, Diana, Princess of Wales, at such a tender age – they are now forging their own lives and careers.

Over the course of my career I have spent many nights in Boujis, once William and Harry's favourite club, attending polo matches and travelling on official royal tours and engagements, getting to know the princes. In my book *William and Harry*, which I have updated, refined and retitled as *The Making of a Royal Romance* ahead of the royal wedding, my unrivalled sources told me that Prince William would finally marry his university sweetheart Kate Middleton in 2011. According to the couple's inner circle they were already 'as good as engaged' and had made a secret pact to be together while on holiday in the Seychelles in 2007. William promised Kate she was the one, but he wanted to complete his military training before they got married. Kate put her trust in William and waited. The press may have dubbed her 'Waity Katie' but Catherine Middleton, as she prefers to be known, knew better.

It was on the slopes of Klosters on 1 April 2004 when the world was first introduced to the girl who had captured Prince William's heart at St Andrews University in Scotland. 'Finally . . . Wills Gets A Girl' was the headline in the *Sun* newspaper. The truth was William and Kate had been dating for months but because of an agreement between the press and the palace to leave William in peace, the romance was known to only their closest friends. Ever since that day we have been intrigued, mystified and captivated in equal measure by William's beautiful and beguiling brunette. I have been chronicling Prince William and

Kate Middleton's romance ever since it began when they were students living in a modest top-floor flat in Hope Street in St Andrews. To the public it may seem like a fairytale but this is a story of true love, companionship, compromise and sacrifice. It is in every aspect a modern royal romance which has experienced the same ups and downs as every love affair.

A normal middle-class girl from the home counties who descends from a coal-mining ancestry, it was this sporty yet quiet and unassuming girl who caught William's eye when she shimmied down the catwalk in their second semester at university in a see-through dress and her lingerie. 'Wow,' William whispered to his friend Fergus Boyd. 'Kate's hot!' After one of the longest courtships in royal history William and Kate are to be married on Friday 29 April 2011 at Westminster Abbey and history will be made. It will be the first time an heir apparent has married a commoner in 350 years.

William, who like his late mother continually pushes at royal boundaries, is determined do things his way from his wedding day and beyond. When the couple announced they were to be married, it was on their own terms. They kept their engagement secret for nearly a month before taking the palace and the rest of the world by surprise on 16 November 2010.

So who is this young woman who has been a part of William's life for the past eight years and who waited so patiently for him to finally propose? To truly understand Kate, one must try to understand William. I spent more than a year trying to uncover just that in *William and Harry*. I discovered a sensitive, thoughtful and sometimes misunderstood young man who more than anything wants to be ordinary. It was something the Princess of

Wales, whose legacy lives on today through both her sons, had desperately wanted. I discovered that just like all great love stories, the genesis of William and Kate's romance lies in the character and the upbringing of the individuals involved.

William is a young man who will one day be the King of England. His future has been mapped out since the day he was born and it is exactly because of this that he refuses to be rail-roaded into anything. As a young boy he was known for being stubborn and sometimes spoilt, and as a teenager he was deeply sensitive and resented the attention he attracted far more than his robust and more extrovert younger brother. Like their father, William and Harry still struggle with the idea that their lives are pre-destined. While they recognise the unique privileges their royal titles bring, they both still crave normality. It is why William loves to ride his motorbike around the streets of London, safe in the knowledge that in his leather and helmet he is anony-mous. And it is the reason Harry has admitted he often wishes he wasn't a prince. It is more than a decade since William and Harry walked behind their mother's funeral cortege. The single white envelope bearing the word 'Mummy' written in Harry's hand is still probably the most powerful and moving image of these two extraordinary princes. Today they are young men – they are soldiers – trying to carve meaningful careers and earn the respect of their public. Ultimately it will be William and Harry who re-shape the future of the great British monarchy and they are working hard to shoulder their responsibilities. It is not simply a case of William being the heir and Harry the spare. The bond between them runs far deeper.

Since graduating from Sandhurst Harry has gone to war and

fought on the front line for Queen and country in Afghanistan. He is determined to go back and is training to fly the Apache attack helicopter in order to do so. It has meant sacrifices for the young prince and over the years his on/off relationship with Zimbabwean born Chelsy Davy has suffered.

Now a fully qualified search and rescue helicopter pilot, William has finally found a sense of purpose as well as embracing his duty. When he pulled the student Kate in towards him on those snowy slopes to kiss her, neither could have predicted the making of this remarkable royal romance. In this book I trace the true story of how Catherine Middleton met and fell in love with the future King. It was over breakfast in the canteen at St Andrews that the pair became friends before they fell in love. Over the years they have weathered two separations, both instigated by William. But he always came back to Kate.

Some royal observers have been quick to compare Kate to the young Diana Spencer, but the truth is they could not be more different. While Kate is just as glamorous and intriguing as the late princess, she is headstrong and confident. Lest we forget, this is the young woman who when told she was lucky to be dating William retorted, 'He's lucky to be going out with me.'

As they prepare for their future as man and wife William and Catherine are, many believe, the future of the House of Windsor. Harry, who has always proved to be much more than just 'the spare', defined his role when he was in Africa with his brother on their first overseas tour. On a cold mountainside in Lesotho where he works tirelessly for his charity Sentebale he declared, for the first time, that his job is to support his older brother.

Male primogeniture dictates that we will have King Charles

and possibly Queen Camilla before we have King William V and Queen Catherine. But many believe, myself included, that it will be William, with Catherine at his side, who will be the standard bearer for a new twenty-first century royal family.

Chapter 1

An heir and a spare

I want to bring them security. I hug my children to death and get into bed with them at night. I always feed them love and affection.

Diana, Princess of Wales

Princess Diana peered through the floral curtains of her room at St Mary's Hospital in Paddington and watched the rain trickle down the Georgian sash windows. Below, the crowds snaked along the street, sheltering beneath a canopy of umbrellas. Among the sea of soggy cellophane-wrapped flowers, Union Jack flags and congratulatory banners, Diana could make out the press pack, some of who were on ladders, their lenses trained on the hospital entrance, eagerly awaiting the first glimpse of the baby prince. Very soon all eyes would be on the royal baby sleeping peacefully in his new cot oblivious to the fact that his first photocall was awaiting him.

Wrapped in swaddling blankets the future king of the United Kingdom of Great Britain and Northern Ireland had already been assigned a full-time bodyguard from Scotland Yard's Royalty and Diplomatic Protection Squad, who now stood guard outside the private hospital room. While Diana had wanted nothing more than for her son to be 'normal', this child would grow up in palaces. He was only a day old, but the young prince's life had already been mapped out, his destiny shaped by a thousand years of royal history.

Outside, the mood was of anticipation and growing excitement. The Queen, jubilant and immaculate in a purple dress coat, had been to visit that morning. They had not always seen eye to eye, but today Diana could do no wrong in the eyes of her mother-in-law. She had produced a healthy heir to the House of Windsor, and in keeping with tradition a notice had been posted on the gates of Buckingham Palace announcing the happy news. The prince and princess had yet to decide on a name: Charles had wanted Arthur, but Diana preferred William and would get her way. It had been a long labour and she was desperate to get home to Kensington Palace, where more well-wishers awaited the couple's arrival.

Diana had written royal history when on Monday 21 June 1982, the summer solstice, Prince William Arthur Philip Louis of Wales was born in the private Lindo Wing of St Mary's Hospital. Like generations of royals before him, his father Charles had been delivered in the Belgian Suite at Buckingham Palace, but Diana, as the royal family quickly discovered, wanted to do things differently. She had endured a difficult pregnancy and terrible morning sickness – which had been the subject of daily press articles to add to the indignity of it all – and when the time came, she was determined to give birth in a modern hospital, not a palace.

The prince and princess had arrived at St Mary's in the early hours of Monday morning, following Diana's first contractions. The princess later recalled she had been 'sick as a parrot' during the sixteen-hour labour. Charles had been there throughout, offering words of comfort and sips of water to revive her. At one point he had dozed off in an armchair but he was at Diana's side when her gynaecologist George Pinker and his team of nurses safely delivered their son at exactly three minutes past nine that evening. The prince had blue eyes and a wisp of blond hair and weighed in at a healthy seven pounds, one and a half ounces. Only when he was content that Diana was asleep did Charles leave his wife's side to address the public. The little boy, he announced, was beautiful, and mother and child were doing well. 'We're very proud.' He beamed. 'It's been thirty hours, a long time.' 'Does he look like you, sir?' a royal reporter enquired. 'No, he's lucky enough not to,' joked Charles, adding that he was relieved and delighted, if a little exhausted from the birth. He couldn't stop smiling, and when a female fan squeezed under the police barrier to plant a kiss on his cheek he blushed furiously. 'You're very kind,' he spluttered before bidding the crowd farewell and returning to Kensington Palace for a nightcap.

The prince was the first to arrive at the hospital the next morning, followed shortly by Diana's sister Lady Jane Fellowes and her mother Frances Shand Kydd, who had travelled from her home in Scotland to see her daughter and new grandson. As world leaders sent congratulatory telegrams, landlords at pubs around the country served rounds on the house. Even football fans managed to prise themselves away from the World Cup to celebrate the joyous news. Britain had been on high alert following Argentina's invasion of the Falklands in April, but on 14 June the Argentinian forces on the islands had surrendered and within days the war was declared over. Now the people of Britain had another reason to celebrate: a future king had been born. It was a momentous occasion and the great British public planned to celebrate.

The spring sunshine had dispersed the rainclouds when Diana and Charles walked down the steps of the Lindo Wing holding their newborn son. Dressed in a green and white spotted maternity dress adorned with an oversized white collar, Diana blinked against the exploding flashbulbs. 'Over here, Diana! Look this way! Show us his face!' the press men shouted above the clicking of their shutters. The crowds, cordoned off behind police barriers, called out their congratulations and waved at the happy couple. It was less than a year since they had lined the streets of the Mall to watch the newly-weds kiss on the balcony of Buckingham Palace. The wedding at St Paul's Cathedral was the celebration of the decade and not since the Queen's coronation had there been such a street party. The British public had their fairy-tale prince and princess and the royal succession was secured.

It was almost too much for Diana, still fragile and exhausted from the birth, to take in. Life had been a whirlwind ever since the Palace confirmed that the Prince of Wales was to marry Lady Diana Spencer. When she gave birth to William she was still navigating the maze of royal life and coming to terms with the fact that home was no longer a flat in west London but a grand palace. It was a steep learning curve and she had yet to master the confidence and sophistication she would acquire in later life. She was still painfully shy in public and turned to her husband, who was well practised in his public role, for support. While Diana had wanted to blend into the background, the British public positioned her centre stage, a role the baby prince would later also struggle with. The minutiae of her daily life was now public consumption. Every outfit she wore was pored over in the pages of glossy magazines as Charles and Di mania gripped Britain. It had not escaped Charles's notice, nor the Queen and the Duke of Edinburgh's, that around the world the princess was being referred to as a 'breath of fresh air' in the House of Windsor. It was Diana the papers seemed most interested in, and before long the retiring and camera-shy princess would eclipse her husband entirely.

The couple had embarked on a whistle-stop tour of Australia and New Zealand following their wedding and Diana had been an instant hit on the other side of the world. Women demanded a 'Lady Di' cut and blow dry at their local salons while her signature spotted frocks and frilly Victorian-style collars were copied on the high street. While it was all rather flattering and laughable at times, privately Diana struggled with her new fame. Married life was not everything she had expected, and, she later complained, in the transition from her uncomplicated life as the unknown Lady Diana Spencer to that of Princess of Wales she had been largely unaided. However, she should have been well prepared for royal life. The youngest daughter of Earl Spencer and Frances Shand Kydd, Diana came from an aristocratic family which had been linked to royalty for over three centuries. Her father had served as an equerry to King George VI and later the Queen, while her mother was the daughter of the fourth Baron Fermoy. Both her grandparents served the royal family: her paternal grandmother Countess Spencer was a lady of the bedchamber to Queen Elizabeth the Queen Mother, while her maternal grandmother Lady Ruth Fermoy had worked for the royal family for more than thirty years. As a child Diana and her siblings would play with Prince Andrew, who would visit the

Spencer family at their home Park House, an impressive mansion nestled amid great oak trees in the sprawling royal estate a short drive from Sandringham, the Queen's Norfolk home.

As a teenager Diana dreaded trips to the royal residence, which she found 'strange', but she got along with Andrew, who was close to her in age, and they would spend hours watching films together in Sandringham's home cinema. Charles had been paired off with Diana's older sister Sarah and they had enjoyed a skiing trip to Klosters, but it was the lissome and gamine Diana who caught the prince's eye at a friend's barbecue in the autumn of 1980. At the time Diana was a nineteen-year-old nursery school teacher living with three girlfriends in Earl's Court. The attentions of the prince, who had been linked with numerous aristocratic suitors known as 'Charlie's Angels' in the British press, was a novel experience for Diana, who had not yet had a serious boyfriend. She immediately fell in love with Charles and was deemed the perfect virgin bride. For several months they managed to keep their courtship clandestine, but the newspapers eventually picked up on the romance. For the hitherto unknown Diana, life changed overnight. Her flat was suddenly besieged by reporters all desperate for nuggets of information about the beautiful aristocrat who had finally won the Prince of Wales. As she sped off in her battered Mini Metro, photographers clinging to the car, the strain showed on her beautiful face. 'It's been very difficult,' her concerned father Earl Spencer remarked.

Incredibly, the couple managed to keep their engagement a secret for three weeks while Diana was in Australia for a holiday, but when she returned there was little option but to make it official. At 11 a.m. on 24 February 1981 Buckingham Palace announced they were to wed. While the prince was largely protected by Palace mandarins, Diana was left to cope with her new celebrity status alone. Her dignified silence won the royal family's approval and Diana moved out of her flat and into the nanny's quarters at Buckingham Palace on the second floor. There Diana complained she felt cut off and isolated and started to have second thoughts. While those around her put her doubts and anxieties down to pre-wedding nerves, it was apparent from the start that Diana and Charles had entered into the marriage with polarised expectations. The princess had dreamed of a romantic escape following their wedding; instead they honey-mooned at Balmoral, the royal family's Scottish retreat, together with the Queen, the Duke of Edinburgh, Princess Margaret, Princess Anne and her children Peter and Zara Phillips. It was not the honeymoon Diana had hoped for, and she was flum-moxed by the family's strict timetable, which was meticulous even when on holiday.

The Queen's cousin Lady Elizabeth Anson recalled that Diana found the rituals of royal life hard to grasp. By now the princess was suffering from bulimia and could not tolerate the heavy three-course meals which were served at lunch and supper, nor could she fathom having to change for every meal and occasion.

Diana found her holidays to Sandringham and Balmoral tedious right from the start. She could not get to grips with the etiquette of changing her clothes sometimes as many as four or five times a day. The palaces work to their own timetables and Diana found them impossible. It is rather daunting as no one actually tells you when to change between breakfast, lunch, high tea and supper; you just learn. Diana's grandmother was a lady-in-waiting for years so she really should have known the drill.

As Diana wrestled with the royal regime, Charles became increasingly perplexed by what he perceived as his wife's strange behaviour. He could not understand why Diana would shut herself away in their bedroom for hours at a time. The Queen, more astute in such matters, was aware that the transition from carefree young woman to the goldfish bowl of royalty was taking its toll on the sensitive young princess. Amid growing concerns for her health she summoned a doctor to visit Diana, who was by then suffering from depression, but it did little good. The strain showed when the newly-weds posed for their first photo-call on the banks of the River Dee. Against a backdrop of rolling hills and wild heather, Diana said she 'highly recommended' married life as her husband tenderly kissed her hand, but she was unconvincing and looked uncomfortable in the presence of the assembled press pack. It was only many years later that she admitted she had found her wedding day, which was watched by 500 million people around the world, 'terrifying' and that the pressure of becoming the Princess of Wales was 'enormous'. There had been little time to master the assorted ceremonies and rituals of state she was expected to carry out as consort to the Prince of Wales and she lacked confidence. As Diana struggled to retain her identity behind the mask of royal protocol, rumours of her misery seeped into the newspaper gossip columns, which were obsessed with every twist and turn of the royal marriage. For those watching closely, the strains and tensions were already beginning to pull at this union of two fundamentally different people.

However, when she discovered she was pregnant less than a year into their marriage Diana was overjoyed and busily set about preparing the top-floor nursery in Kensington Palace. A former kindergarten teacher, she loved children and longed to start a family. Her parents' marriage had broken down when she was just six years old, and Diana vividly recalled her parents fighting when her mother Frances produced three daughters but no heir to the Spencer estate. Eventually a son, Charles, was born, but it was not enough to hold the Spencers' marriage together and eventually Frances left the earl for her lover Peter Shand Kydd. Diana recalled the awfulness of listening to her brother sob himself to sleep as her cuckolded father padded sleeplessly through the house. She did not want the same fate for her own children. 'I want my children to have as normal a life as possible,' she remarked, recognising that it was within her power to shape the future of the monarchy. Diana was determined to do things her way, even if it meant going against the grain, which it invariably did. 'I want to bring them up with security, not to anticipate things because they will be disappointed. I hug my children to death and get into bed with them at night. I feed them love and affection. It's so important.' Like Charles, Diana had been raised by a governess, but for her security meant being hands on. She was determined that she alone would raise their firstborn and insisted on breast-feeding William. However, with a packed timetable of royal duties and engagements it was soon apparent that a nanny was required.

Diana immediately dismissed Charles's suggestion that his former governess Mabel Anderson should take up the post. She did not want an old-fashioned nanny with outdated ideas looking after her son. After many arguments it was decided that forty-two-year-old Barbara Barnes would join the royal nursery. Miss Barnes believed that children should be allowed to develop at their own pace, which immediately endeared her to Diana. She had come highly recommended by her former employer Lord Glenconner, a close friend of the Queen's sister Princess Margaret, who lived next door to Charles and Diana at Kensington Palace, and during the early years the appointment was a success. It was made clear to Nanny Barnes that she was there to assist rather than take over. Diana was in charge of the nursery and she and Charles made all the important decisions. Nanny Barnes was told to dispense with her uniform and informed, as were all the staff, that she would be called Barbara. For a shy and demure young woman who had initially found the palace so daunting, Diana's changes were fast taking effect in the royal household.

For the first time since their wedding Diana seemed happy, as did Charles, who wrote to his godmother Lady Mountbatten of his elation at becoming a father. 'The arrival of our small son has been an astonishing experience and one that has meant more to me than I could ever have imagined.' It was not just Diana who enjoyed spending time with William in the nursery. Charles loved being with her son, and at bath time he would jump into the tub and splash around with William's favourite plastic whale toy. At bedtime he would often give William his bottle before retiring to his study to catch up on his paperwork.

On 4 August 1982, the Queen Mother's eighty-second birthday, William was christened in the Music Room at Buckingham Palace by the Archbishop of Canterbury. He was baptised in the same gown that Charles had worn as a baby. Diana, who kept William from crying with a soothing finger in his mouth during the ceremony, was still upset that Charles had chosen such mature godparents, among them his close friend and adviser Laurens van der Post. She had wanted younger guardians, but Charles refused to change his mind. Another source of friction was their state visit to Australia and New Zealand the following spring. Diana had been inconsolable at the prospect of leaving William behind for six weeks, and in a further breach of precedent it was agreed that they would take the nine-month-old William with them.

It was the first time a working member of the royal family had ever undertaken an official engagement with a baby and a far cry from Charles's childhood, when he had been left in the care of his governess while the Queen and Prince Philip embarked on a tour of the Commonwealth. During Charles's early years his parents were often overseas. Prince Philip was serving in the Royal Navy in Malta, which meant he barely saw his son for the first year of his life and missed Charles's first two birthdays. Neither Charles nor Diana wanted such an upbringing for William. Times had changed, and with the speed and ease of air travel there was no reason to leave him behind. When Barbara Barnes descended the steps of the Queen's Flight aircraft tightly cradling the baby prince there was no contest over who was the star of the show. William delighted the crowds and revelled in every second of his fame, happily crawling across the lawn in front of Government House in New Zealand for his first official photocall.

It was just two years before Diana discovered she was pregnant again, which was as surprising as it was joyful. Publicly the Waleses had put on a united front, but behind the wrought-iron gates of Kensington Palace the tears in the fabric of their marriage were beginning to show. The couple had not stopped crisscrossing the world, and eighteen months of tours and state visits on top of motherhood had left the vulnerable Diana tired and drained. She later admitted that Harry's conception at Sandringham was 'as if by a miracle' but secretly hoped that the pregnancy would be the glue that would repair the fractures in their marriage. There was a glimmer of hope when she returned from a trip to Norway. On the desk in her study was a note from her husband. 'We were so proud of you,' he had written and signed it 'Willie Wombat and I'. Her joy was to be short-lived, and on top of suffering from morning sickness Diana was convinced that Charles was seeing his ex-girlfriend Camilla Parker Bowles.

Charles had first met Camilla in 1970 at a polo match in Windsor. He had been immediately smitten with the attractive and gregarious aristocrat but the following year had joined the navy and was sent on an eight-month naval tour of the Caribbean. By the time he returned Camilla was engaged to Andrew Parker Bowles, a captain in the Household Cavalry. Charles was crushed but determined to keep Camilla as a friend, and they remained close, moving in the same social circles and sharing a passion for fox-hunting. Diana, who was aware of their friendship when she first met Charles, became increasingly paranoid about Camilla during her marriage. When Charles disappeared, she would anxiously question their staff on his whereabouts. While the public only saw her smile, behind closed doors she was miserable and later conceded that her second son was born into the end of their marriage.

On Saturday 15 September 1984 Diana gave birth to another healthy boy at the same hospital where William was born. Prince Henry Charles Albert David – to be known as Harry – was delivered at 4.30 p.m., and weighed six pounds, fourteen ounces. Charles, who had fed his wife ice cubes during the nine-hour labour, left Diana's side to tell the waiting crowds the good news before returning to the Palace for a Martini. 'The delivery couldn't have been much better: it was much quicker this time,' he said. According to Diana, who had known from an early scan that she was expecting a boy, her husband's comments were rather more crushing. 'Oh, it's a boy, and he's even got rusty hair,' Charles is understood to have commented. To compound Diana's distress, she was devastated when upon returning home to Kensington Palace, Charles sped off in his Aston Martin to play polo in Windsor Great Park. 'Something inside of me died,' Diana later admitted. The fairy-tale marriage was falling apart.

Chapter 2

The early years

William is very much an organiser which probably might be useful in future years . . . Harry is more quiet. He's certainly a different character altogether.

Diana, Princess of Wales

William had earned his nickname 'Basher Wills' with good reason. As he furiously pedalled his bright-yellow plastic truck along the upstairs corridor of Craigowan Lodge he let out a squeal of delight before crashing the toy into the wall for the umpteenth time. Harry, who had learned to walk and was quickly copying everything his older brother did, clapped his hands in glee and beeped the horn of his red tractor. His Christmas present from Granny was smaller but capable of doing just as much damage, and he raced from one end of the long narrow corridor to the other as fast as his little legs could pedal. The boys had been playing for over an hour under the eye of Nanny Barnes, and the evidence of their afternoon of fun was etched all over the wallpaper and skirting boards, which had been badly scuffed. As Nanny Barnes swept up chips of paint from the floor, Diana, dressed in jeans and a warm roll-neck jumper, for it was always cold at Balmoral, came upstairs. 'Whatever will your grandmother say?' Diana exclaimed as she scooped Harry into her arms and planted a kiss on William's head.

Outside it was raining, and while the Queen had spent the afternoon riding across the moors Diana kept the children inside. William had a sniffle, and while the Queen's advice for a common cold was to wrap up warm and brace the elements, Diana had insisted that both boys stayed indoors. Downstairs in her bedroom Diana had been flicking through the collection of magazines she had brought with her from London. She had spent most of the morning on the phone regaling her friends with the utter boredom of the New Year holiday while Charles had spent the morning salmon-fishing. Yet another barbecue had been planned for dinner that night, and Diana was not sure if she could think up a new excuse not to be there. Barbecues were the Duke of Edinburgh's forte, and the weather, no matter how inclement, never put the Windsors off their picnics, which were either enjoyed outside in the summer months or in front of a roaring fire in one of the outhouses on the royal estate during Scotland's wet and windy winters. It never ceased to amaze Diana that with a staff of hundreds the Queen would insist on washing up every plate and utensil before returning to the main house after dinner, having given the household the night off.

The princess had spent the last few evenings having supper with the boys in the nursery, but the Queen and Prince Philip were desperate to spend some time with their grandchildren and had insisted they all ate together that night. They adored the time they got to spend with William and Harry, and when Diana had insisted on moving out of the main house into Craigowan Lodge a mile away the Queen had been crestfallen. Diana, who privately complained to Charles that she felt suffocated at Balmoral, had needed some space. Knowing it was best not to antagonise her daughter-in-law, the Queen obliged and had offered the couple the use of Craigowan, where she resides when Balmoral is open to the public. When Princess Anne and her children Zara and Peter came to visit, which was at least twice a year, they always stayed in the main house, but Diana was different, and now that they had left, the house was suddenly terribly quiet. 'The Queen was so upset when Diana and the boys moved to the lodge,' recalled her cousin Lady Elizabeth Anson. 'She said, "Why did they have to move? There are so many corridors for them to race down here and it's so quiet now they have gone."'

While the Queen had noticed that William had become quite a handful, she adored her grandsons and encouraged them to let off steam at Balmoral. The boys were free to roam and explore every nook and cranny of the house so loved by Queen Victoria, who bought the estate in 1854. The turrets and sinuous corridors provided hours of fun for the young princes, who loved to play hide-and-seek with their father. When they got older their grandfather taught them how to salmon-fish, and the boys would spend hours yomping with him through the wild Scottish countryside, Harry atop Charles's shoulders and William working hard to keep up with Prince Philip's brisk pace. They were happy days and an extension of William and Harry's life at Highgrove, where they escaped the hustle and bustle of London at the weekends.

Charles had bought the 347-acre estate in Gloucestershire in 1980 for over £750,000 from Maurice Macmillan the Conservative MP and son of the former Prime Minister Harold Macmillan, and he adored the Georgian house. It was just 120 miles from the centre of London and had the added bonus of a working farm. Conveniently for Charles, as Diana later acknowledged, Highgrove was just a stone's throw from the Parker Bowleses' residence in the town of Allington, near Chippenham.

The prince and princess would arrive in their chauffeur-driven cars – Charles alone and Diana with the nursery – on Friday night. During the early days life at Highgrove was happy enough. The princess pottered around in the house with the children while Charles would spend hours in the gardens, tending his impressive beds of hydrangeas, sweet peas and roses, and while away afternoons wandering among the pear and plum trees discovering new herbs for his chefs Mervyn Wycherley and Chris Barber to incorporate in their recipes. Although a traditional country house, Highgrove is less grand and much smaller than you might expect for a royal residence. The cream-coloured property comprises two studies, a drawing room, dining room and kitchens on the ground floor, with two floors, primarily living quarters, upstairs.

The impressive grounds, opened to the public every summer, are a mixture of landscaped gardens and overgrown wilderness, reflecting the Prince's taste. Charles once said he had put his 'heart and soul' into Highgrove, and accompanied by his beloved Jack Russell terrier Tigger and her puppy Roo, he was at peace. He desperately hoped both of his sons would inherit his passion for gardening. 'I've yet to see which child will take to gardening,' he once said. Thoughtfully he had reserved two small plots of land for William and Harry and invested in child-size tools so that they could tend the garden with him. While Harry loved to dig, as they grew up both boys were more interested in playing war games in their miniature military fatigues than becoming gardeners. While Charles gardened the boys would play army games in their tree house, which had a real thatched roof and windows that opened and shut. They kept rabbits and guinea pigs, which they fed with carrots their mother had chopped, and the highlight of many weekends was diving into a special play pit full of plastic balls that Charles had created in one of the sheds on the estate. When they played hide-and-seek or big bad wolf this was the most popular hiding place, and the boys would shriek with excitement as their father dived into the colourful sea of balls to pluck them out in time for tea.

When they were tucked up in bed on the top-floor nursery, Charles liked to entertain. Diana, who was a good decade younger than most of Charles's friends, found she had little in common with his country set. She liked his skiing companions Charles and Patti Palmer-Tomkinson and his old friend from Cambridge Hugh Van Cutsem, a millionaire farmer and pedigree bloodstock breeder, and his Dutch-born wife Emilie, but given the choice preferred to share informal suppers with Charles in front of the television. She did however look forward to visits from her future sister-in-law Sarah Ferguson and Charles's younger brother Andrew.

William and Harry adored their uncle, who was a real-life navy pilot and had fought in the Falklands War. He would entertain them for hours with his war stories and Harry especially was mesmerised. During the summer holidays their cousins Zara and Peter would come to visit, as would their maternal grandmother, 'Granny Frances', who William and Harry adored. Diana was at her happiest when she and her mother could take tea on the terrace and watch the children playing by the swimming pool soaking the royal detectives with their long-range water pistols. They were happy days.

While she claimed to love the countryside, Diana was in truth far happier shopping on Sloane Street. She once confided to Highgrove's housekeeper Wendy Berry, 'It's constantly raining there and Highgrove can be such a chore. The thing is that the children enjoy it, and I go because of them. It's important that they can have somewhere like that to go at weekends.' Instead of joining her husband in the gardens she would stay inside and watch her favourite soaps on the television or chat on the telephone for hours on end to her girlfriends back in London. If the weather was fine she would take the boys into Tetbury with her protection officer Sergeant Barry Mannakee for company. To outsiders it was a picture of domestic bliss, but to those who knew Charles and Diana it was apparent that the twelve-year age gap between them was beginning to cause problems.

Everything about their personalities was different, and they clashed over the simplest things. Diana wanted to listen to pop music and watch movies with her sons, while Charles preferred listening to classical music and being outdoors. While Diana loved nothing more than flicking through *Vogue* magazine and coming up with new ideas for her wardrobe, Charles would be poring over a philosophical tome in his untidy study, where magazine cuttings and half-finished letters littered the carpet. By 1986 the prince and princess were sleeping in separate bedrooms. Diana blamed Charles's snoring and said she got a better night's sleep in her own room, which was littered with soft toys and photographs of William and Harry. To the millions of royalists who still wanted to believe in the fairy tale all seemed well, but behind the scenes the marriage was in serious trouble.

* * *

Summer hung on into September and it was warm enough for shorts when Prince William arrived for his first day of nursery on the morning of Tuesday 24 September 1985. As he tottered up the stairs, the three-year-old prince clasped his Postman Pat flask in one hand and his mother's hand in the other. It was William's first day at Mrs Mynors' nursery school, situated in a pretty tree-lined avenue in west London a stone's throw from Kensington Palace. The Queen had expected William to be educated at home in keeping with tradition, but Diana wanted both her sons to mix with children their own age. It was all a part of her plan to raise the princes as ordinary boys and show the House of Windsor that it could be done successfully. On this occasion Charles was in agreement that William, who could be spoilt and difficult, would benefit from mixing with his peers – known as Cygnets, Little Swans and Big Swans at the school.

Diana had allowed William to choose his own outfit, and they had arrived on time, as had the hundreds of photographers who had gathered outside the school gates to take pictures. Diana's wish to integrate her sons in modern society had disadvantages as well as advantages and it was with growing concern that the Queen noted that every stage of her grandsons' young lives was now chronicled in the media. If William had a new haircut or Harry acquired a tooth, it would somehow find its way into the papers. By now William was accustomed to the omnipresent cameras. Unlike Harry, who shied away from the long lenses, William relished the attention and played up to the 'tographers', as he called them. With a wave he had already mastered, the prince smiled broadly before boldly marching through the front door.

Diana would drop William off each morning and collect him in the afternoon, having rearranged her diary around the school run. 'He was so excited about it all,' she recalled. 'He just adored other children. He's very much an organiser, which probably might be useful in future years.' Like any mother, she had been anxious about William settling in, but the prince was popular with his new friends, who had no idea that their fellow Cygnet would one day be king and barely noticed the protection officer who accompanied William twenty-four hours a day and sat quietly at the back of the classroom keeping a close eye on his young charge.

When it came to playtime, William, already aware of his princely status, left his fellow pupils in no doubt as to who was in charge. When he got into a scrap, a common event for the boisterous youngster, he would draw his play sword and challenge his opponent: 'My daddy's a real prince, and my daddy can beat up your daddy,' he would shout.

Diana and Charles became alarmed that the rumbustious William needed more discipline. At home he often misbehaved. Mealtimes were an ordeal and would frequently end up with William throwing his supper across the table and being banished to the nursery by his exasperated parents. When it came to bedtime he would always demand another story, which had to be read by Papa. The Queen was increasingly aware that her grandson, now four, misbehaved and reminded Nanny Barnes that it was her job to instil discipline.

The real test came in July 1986, when William was a page at Andrew and Sarah's wedding at Westminster Abbey. Diana and Charles were both anxious that he would not sit still and Diana had stitched up the pockets of his starched sailor's outfit to stop him from fidgeting. Instead William rolled the order of service into a trumpet and stuck his tongue out at his cousin Laura Fellowes, who was a bridesmaid.

Meanwhile Harry was growing quickly, and on a warm summer's morning in September 1987, a day after his third birthday, he too enrolled as a Cygnet. William had thrived at the kindergarten and his latest report read, 'Prince William was very popular with other children, and was known for his kindness, sense of fun and quality of thoughtfulness.' Harry, as his father remarked, was the quieter of the two, and having grown accustomed to being bossed around by his older brother, was a follower rather than a natural leader like William. When he arrived at Mrs Mynors' he had not wanted to get out of the car, but after a few days he settled in and busily set about making a pair of binoculars with two loo roll tubes, which he hid behind when photographers tried to take his picture.

'Harry was always more sensitive than William when they were little,' recalled Simone Simmons, a close friend of the princess who spent time with William and Harry when they were growing up. 'William loved being the centre of attention but Harry was quieter. It was not uncommon for him to have a day off from school because he wasn't feeling well. He used to go down with more coughs and colds than William, but it was nothing serious and most of the time I think he just wanted to be at home with his mummy. He loved having her to himself and not having to compete with William.' Harry had had to get used to William being the 'special one' from the start and from a young age was aware of the pecking order. When they were little William would often be invited to Clarence House to see his great-grandmother without Harry. 'I'm off to see Gran Gran,' he would announce, leaving Harry to play alone in the nursery.

Diana was aware that Harry felt left out and doted on him. With his red hair and close-set eyes the little prince was the spitting image of her sister Sarah when she was a child. Diana called him 'my little Spencer' and despite rumours that later surfaced about Harry's paternity (some suggested following Diana's affair with James Hewitt that he could be the father), he was a Spencer through and through. He had also inherited his mother's quick wit. When William announced that he wanted to be a policeman 'and look after mummy', Harry astutely observed that for once the hierarchy of royalty worked in his favour: 'Oh no you can't, you've got to be king!'

Throughout their childhood William was always one rung of the ladder ahead of Harry. On 15 January 1987 he trotted up the steps of Wetherby School under the watchful eye of his new headmistress Frederika Blair-Turner and hundreds of cameras all there to capture his first day. It was bitterly cold and the four-and-a-half-year-old prince was a bundle of nerves as he stepped out of the chauffeur-driven car tightly clasping his mother's hand. Diana had told him not to wave at the cameras and for once he did as he was told. Dressed in his brand-new school uniform, a grey wool blazer with red piping, black shorts and a grey woollen cap, all from Harrods, the young prince seemed far less confident than when he had enrolled at Mrs Mynors', and there was good reason. Back at Kensington Palace it had been an unsettling few days with William in tears after being told that Nanny Barnes was leaving. Diana had decided that after five years it was time for Barbara to move on. Her relationship with her boss had become increasingly fractious, and Diana had observed how strong the bond was between her sons and their nanny. While Diana was travelling the world with her husband, Nanny Barnes had been their surrogate mother. She took them to the Scilly Isles for summer holidays and spoiled them with hamburgers and chips for dinner and chocolate ice cream for dessert. With Barbara, William and Harry were as good as gold, and they adored her. If William woke from a nightmare he would go to 'Baba', and Harry still crept into her bed first thing in the morning before thundering downstairs to jump into bed with his mother.

When he was told Barbara was leaving, William had been inconsolable. Diana had explained that she would be looking after William with Olga Powell, Barbara's assistant, until they found a new nanny. Secretly she had hoped that by coinciding the dismissal with William's first day at Wetherby it would go unnoticed, but of course the press found out and his nanny's sudden departure was an even bigger story than William's first day at school.

The households at Highgrove and Kensington Palace were not altogether surprised by the news. Over the years the nursery at Highgrove, which had its own kitchen and bathroom, had become Barbara's domain, and the princess had begun to feel excluded. There were tantrums from Diana when she returned home and tried to reassert her authority, only for the boys to listen to their nanny instead of their mother. While she never criticised her boss, Nanny Barnes complained on occasions that Diana was 'downright rude' and once remarked to Wendy Berry of William, 'It's no good Diana pretending he can have a completely normal life because he can't.' There was a great deal of wisdom in this warning.

*　*　*

It was a Saturday afternoon, and instead of travelling to Highgrove William and Harry were with their mother shopping in WH Smith on Kensington High Street. It was a rare treat and so far no one had noticed the royal trio disguised in caps and scarves. Much to William and Harry's delight, their mother had opted for a long brown wig and oversized sunglasses, and they giggled as they strolled hand in hand down the busy high street, which was a five-minute walk from Kensington Palace.

Diana revelled in the fun of it all as she guided William and Harry down the aisles of stationery, books and magazines. Harry headed straight for the comics with brightly coloured covers featuring his favourite action heroes while William set about choosing some new stationery. Very soon he would be starting boarding school and he needed everything from a geometry set to a new pencil case. They had been given their pocket money, which they handed over to the lady at the till, but not before they had each been allowed to choose a packet of sweets. Their eyes lit up as they surveyed the rows of shiny packets and tubes in front of them. Harry being Harry wanted a chocolate bar *and* a packet of chewy sweets, but his mother reminded him that he would only have enough money for one.

While none of the royal family generally carried cash, Diana believed it was important that William and Harry understood that the rest of the world survived through hard work and salaries, and she wanted them to understand the value of money from a young age. 'Diana always gave them pocket money, something Charles never did, not because he was mean but because he never understood why the boys needed money,' recalled Simone Simmons. 'They were always accompanied by protection officers, who paid for them, but when they were out with their friends it embarrassed them and they wanted to pay for things themselves.'

'Diana and the boys were ecstatically happy,' recalled Dickie Arbiter, who handled the prince and princess's media relations. 'It was important for Diana to take her children shopping and do normal things with them. Their favourite day out would include a visit to Smiths followed by a trip to the Odeon cinema, which was just down the road. If they were really lucky, Diana would take them to McDonald's as well.'

On this occasion the boys had behaved so well that Diana decided they deserved a cheeseburger and chips, each of them delighting in personally giving their order to the uniformed sales assistant who didn't have a clue that the well-spoken customers were in fact the Princess of Wales and her two sons. At a round table in a rear corner of the restaurant the boys wolfed down their Happy Meals and played with the cheap plastic toys that had come with the meal. At the next table their protection officers polished off their own hamburgers. For anyone else it would have been the most normal lunch in the world, but for Diana and the boys it was a special treat made all the more exhilarating by the fact that they were incognito. Such happy times were becoming increasingly rare.

At home the situation between Charles and Diana had become unbearable. The boys' games and laughter dispersed much of the tension, and Charles and Diana tried their hardest to keep their quarrels from William and Harry, but Diana, who craved her husband's attention, was breaking down in tears almost every day. When she came down to Highgrove Charles would speed off to the nearby Beaufort Polo Club in his pristine white breeches. He had inherited his father's love of polo and was in turn to pass the family passion and talent on to the young princes, who would both grow into accomplished players.

Diana found the sport tedious even though she had claimed in a television interview that she adored it. She was not, however, altogether uninterested in polo. She had taken something of a shine to a young red-headed cavalry officer called James Hewitt, who was quite something on the polo pitch. They had met after Diana decided she wanted to learn to ride. She had never been a horsewoman, but after seeing how much pleasure it brought her sons decided to have a go. The handsome Hewitt became her instructor and soon became a regular visitor to Highgrove, where he would help William and Harry improve their trotting and cantering. The staff noticed that when Charles was away the dashing officer became a more regular visitor, and his arrival was always guaranteed to lift Diana's spirits. It would be another year before the British press exposed their secret friendship.

Chapter 3

Off to school

It's quite something, putting one's eldest into school.

Diana, Princess of Wales

Prince William charged into the garden slamming the door behind him. He could not bear to hear his parents bicker any longer. 'I hate you, Papa. I hate you so much. Why do you make Mummy cry all the time?' he had shouted angrily as Diana broke down again. William had been aware for some time that his parents were not happy. The princess had become increasingly dependent on her elder son, who she regularly confided in, and it was William who would pass his mother tissues through the bedroom door as she sobbed on the other side.

It was a heavy burden for a young boy, and there was a great sense of relief, among the staff at Kensington Palace at least, when William went away to school. Charles and Diana agreed that the boys-only boarding school Ludgrove in Berkshire would be perfect for their elder son. Set in 130 acres of unspoilt countryside, it had an excellent reputation for sport as well as an impressive academic record. William had been worried and apprehensive about leaving home for the first time. It was 10 September 1990, and as the chauffeur-driven Bentley pulled up at the £2,350-a term school Diana blinked back tears. William, who was eight years old, was dressed in his new uniform of corduroy trousers and tweed jacket.

This time it was Diana who clasped her boy's hand. Her elder son was leaving the nest and things would never be the same again.

Meanwhile in the front passenger seat Charles was also in reflective mood. His school days had been the unhappiest of his life, and he desperately hoped his son would not be subjected to the bullying he had endured at Cheam School in Surrey. He had cleared his diary to be with William after the criticism he had faced in the newspapers for not turning up for his first day of prep school. By now Charles and Diana's private lives were headline news, and the prince suspected that the source of many of the stories was his wife. When Charles was on a painting holiday in Italy in May 1988 Harry had been rushed to Great Ormond Street Hospital to have an emergency hernia operation. The British press had again noted Charles's absence even though he had made half-hour checks via the telephone. This time he was not going to give his wife any ammunition.

Diana had spent the morning double-checking William's trunk, which had been carefully packed by his new nanny Ruth Wallace. It contained his favourite wombat toy, which she always placed next to his pillow, and everything else he would need for his first term. At Ludgrove, once William was settled, Diana sped up the M4 back to Apartments 9 and 10 of Kensington Palace while Charles returned to Highgrove. By now the Waleses were living separate lives.

For William, who had matured from a boisterous child into a sensitive boy, school proved to be a relief from the turmoil at home. William and Harry had only just got used to Nanny Ruth, who whisked them upstairs when discussions became heated between their parents, but now she was leaving and would be replaced by Jessie Webbe.

William found comfort in the routine at Ludgrove. The day began shortly after seven o'clock, when he would wash and dress for breakfast. Lessons did not start until 9 a.m., and William liked to fit in a quick game of football before the first class. Lessons continued until 5.20 p.m., when the boys were free to play more sport before supper, and after chapel it was lights out at 8 p.m. The school's amiable headmaster Gerald Barber had been quietly informed by Diana about the complicated situation at home and had promised to keep a close eye on William. Both he and his wife Janet would become key figures in William and Harry's lives as their parents' marriage finally fell apart.

Despite his initial nerves, William had at least one familiar face at his side at all times. His protection officers were Sergeant Reg Spinney, a former marine, and Graham Cracker, known as 'Crackers' to the boys and all the staff at Kensington Palace. They lived in private accommodation on the perimeter of the school grounds next to the tennis courts and the art school. Both had been told to keep their distance from William and allow him space and time with his peers. If anything, having the avuncular detectives around made William immediately popular with his dorm-mates, who found the high-tech tracking devices they used to keep an eye on their royal charge fascinating.

Aware that the Waleses increasingly fraught domestic situation was making the front pages of the daily newspapers, the Barbers sensibly banned them from the school library, and television was restricted and supervised. By now nearly every row appeared to be catalogued in the daily press and on the princess's thirtieth birthday the *Daily Mail*'s gossip columnist Nigel Dempster broke a story about the couple rowing over a birthday party.

CHARLES AND DIANA: CAUSE FOR CONCERN ran the headline. Charles had apparently wanted to throw a party for his wife, but Diana, knowing it was a facade, was having none of it and insisted that she would not be celebrating.

By now both sides were leaking stories to the press and this particular piece of propaganda appeared to have emanated from Charles's court. The staff at Highgrove and Kensington Palace were also split, with Diana's household, which included her private chef Darren McGrady and butler Paul Burrell, based at Kensington, and Charles's team of aides in Gloucestershire. As a member of staff you were either with the prince or the princess, and there was a great deal of mistrust between the two camps. Diana claimed she was always careful of what she said at Highgrove as information in unsympathetic hands could be used against her. According to the prince and princess's spokesman Dickie Arbiter, who was vainly trying to stem the torrent of stories pouring out of the royal household at the time, Ludgrove helped to shelter the boys from their troubled home life.

The boys had access to the newspapers at Kensington Palace because Diana used to read them. It was very easy for them to see the front pages. Given what was going on in William's life at the time, Ludgrove was extremely good at protecting him and later Harry. It took them out of troubled waters. The media couldn't get onto the grounds. It was very sheltered apart from a public footpath between the school and the playing fields which could be accessed by photographers.

'The Barbers were more than equipped to deal with the princes. William and Harry weren't the only members of a royal family to attend the school and they certainly weren't the only children to come from dysfunctional homes,' recalled a former pupil. 'The Barbers made it their sole mission to shield William and Harry from what was going on at home.' At weekends William would return home but the constant rowing was a reminder of just how unhappy his parents were. Diana tried her hardest to make William feel settled and comfortable and had the larder stocked with his favourite treats. She encouraged him to bring his new schoolfriends home, and their next-door neighbours Lord Freddie and Lady Ella Windsor, the children of Prince and Princess Michael of Kent, would often come over to ride their BMX bikes through the palace gardens.

Both Diana and Charles were delighted with how well William settled in at Ludgrove. He was in the top stream for most of his subjects and one of the best swimmers at the school. He also captained the rugby and hockey teams. Despite their feuding, Diana and Charles made an effort to visit William. 'Diana would often drive to Ludgrove to watch football and rugby matches,' said a former pupil. 'She would sit on the bench and watch William play. I remember one time I was sitting out because I was injured and Diana was very concerned about how I'd hurt myself. There was never a big deal when she showed up at the school and she seemed to like that. For us boys she was just William and Harry's pretty mummy, not a princess.'

On sports days William and his father would compete in the clay pigeon shooting competition, which they won in 1995. William was just four when he accompanied his father to Sandringham to watch his first shoot, and like Charles he was an impressive shot from a young age. At Christmas Charles and Diana would attend the school's annual carol service and watch William when he was in school plays. He loved dressing up and appearing on the stage and became the head of Ludgrove's dramatic society, much to his parents' delight. Kitty Dimbleby, daughter of Prince Charles's official biographer Jonathan Dimbleby, recalled that Charles would arrange theatre trips for his sons during the school holidays:

> Charles invited us to a production of *A Midsummer Night's Dream* in Stratford-upon-Avon one Easter, and William and Harry loved it. Charles was incredibly proud of them and they had so much fun together that day. We all met at Highgrove and I remember being in the car with William and Harry who was blowing raspberries at his dad through the window. There was a lot of joking around and it was a very normal and lovely family day out. Charles seemed so happy to be with his boys and they with him. I do remember William being distracted by what was going on at home. At the time there was a lot in the newspapers about Charles and Diana's marriage being in trouble and William told me 'Papa never embarrasses me but Mummy sometimes does.'

Publicly the prince and princess put their troubles behind them and when William was injured in a freak playground accident in June 1991 they both rushed to be with him. William had been playing with a friend on the school's putting green when he was accidentally struck on the head with a golf club. Diana, who had been lunching at San Lorenzo, her favourite Knightsbridge restaurant, went white according to her bodyguard Ken Wharfe, who received the news on his pager, and it was an agonising journey from London to the Royal Berkshire Hospital in Reading. When she arrived it was decided that William should be transferred from Reading to Great Ormond Street so that he could be checked over by a brain specialist. While Charles, who had driven from Highgrove to Reading, followed in convoy, Diana sat in the ambulance with her son holding his hand. At Great Ormond Street he was diagnosed with a depressed fracture and underwent a seventy-minute corrective operation which left him with twenty-four stitches. Charles and Diana waited anxiously at the hospital, but when they were informed that the operation had been successful and William was fine, Charles sped off to the Royal Opera House for an official engagement. Diana was used to her husband's habit of putting duty before family, but the press turned on the prince. WHAT KIND OF A DAD ARE YOU? asked the *Sun* on its front page. Fortunately William made a speedy recovery, and although he was advised not to ride his pony, he was back at school within days showing off his war wound. Today he still bears a reminder of the accident, which he calls his Harry Potter scar.

Harry hurled a pillow with all his might. It hit his target on the head, and as his latest victim toppled from his bed the prince let out a jubilant shout. It was after lights out, and the boys knew there would be trouble if Mr Barber discovered they were still up. Harry had only been at Ludgrove a matter of weeks but he was loving it. He had got off to a wobbly start and been terribly homesick when he started in September 1992, but William soon helped him settle in, and matron, who had taken an immediate shine to the cheeky little redhead, had allowed him to sit in her room and watch *Star Trek* with a cup of cocoa. It was not long before Harry had persuaded her to allow his dorm-mates to join him. Charles had once remarked that his younger son was the one 'with the more gentle nature', but in his final year at Wetherby, once William had left, Harry had come out of his shell. He was more talkative and confident in class, and at home his parents noticed a change in the brothers' characters. William, who was deeply affected by the breakdown of his parents' marriage because he was more aware of what was going on, had become quieter and more sensitive. He preferred to curl up on the sofa and watch movies with his mother, while Harry would be in the paddock showing off his latest tricks on his pony Smokey. He had grown into an accomplished horseman, and Marion Cox, who had taught both boys to ride from the age of two, had long dispensed with her rein. Now Harry was cantering and jumping fences, and it was not just on horseback that he was beginning to emerge as a daredevil. When their mother took them skiing to Lech during a half-term vacation in March 1991, it was Harry, then only six, who was the first to race down the slopes with his instructor.

When he arrived at Ludgrove, the troublesome streak that would later see him crowned the rebel of the family began to emerge. While William had grown out of childish pranks and immersed himself in his studies, Harry earned a reputation for being the class clown. One former pupil recalled that his favourite trick involved using a ruler to remove the contents of his unsuspecting victim's pocket or pencil case. The prince would watch in glee as the classmate fumbled around trying to find the missing items, which were always returned with an impish grin at the end of the lesson. When Charles and Diana came to visit him at Ludgrove for his first sports day, Harry decided to get his own back on the photographers who had gathered on the public footpath ahead of his parents' arrival. At his instigation, four school leavers mooned at the press, some of who were hiding in the undergrowth. 'Harry didn't actually moon at anyone. He dared the school leavers to do it and they did,' recalled one school contemporary. 'He didn't want to get caught. I do remember that he wasn't very flattering about the photographers. He was very aware of them and didn't like them being there.'

On Sunday evenings when it was time to go back to school, Harry couldn't wait. William was reluctant to leave his mother alone in the palace, but Harry had already packed his bags and was desperate to see his friends at Ludgrove, where he would be rewarded with a Cremola Foam, which was similar to a cream soda with ice cream in it and served to all the returning boys. Sunday nights were also typically when Harry and his friends would instigate dorm raids, but on one occasion, not realising his own strength, Harry sent a victim crashing to the floor as he jumped from bed to bed. Hearing the child's wails, the housemaster burst into the dormitory and switched on the lights. While the boy was taken to the school nurse for a check-up, Harry was taken aside for a stern talking-to. When his friend's concerned mother came up to the school the next day, the prince was made to apologise.

'Harry wasn't given any special treatment and neither was

William, which is probably why they liked it so much,' one of their friends recalled. There were, however, occasions when the boys were granted certain privileges, and when their father announced that he had tickets for the FA Cup final in May 1995 they were allowed special leave. Everton won, and the boys returned to Ludgrove dressed in the winning team's kit with a signed football. 'They kept us all up way past lights out that night,' recalled one of their friends. 'It was so exciting and we wanted to know every detail of the day over and over again.' Their privileges won them more friends than foes, and when the alarms at the nearby Broadmoor High Security Hospital were tested, Harry would assure his friends, 'Don't worry! Our policemen will protect us all from any baddies.' It was Harry who triggered a security alert at the school when he lost his GPS satellite security tag one evening. Both he and William had been instructed to wear the tags every day so that their protection officers could track them even if they weren't actually with them, and there was chaos when Harry lost his. After several frantic minutes, the device was located beneath the dirty clothes in Harry's laundry bin.

The routine of Ludgrove distracted both William and Harry from the troubles at home, as did holidays. More often than not Charles and Diana took separate vacations with the children. Tara Palmer-Tomkinson, daughter of Charles's dear friends Patti and Charles, recalls holidaying with the princes one summer on the *Alexander*, a luxury yacht owned by John Latsis.

We never discussed the problems at home. William and Harry would make calls home to their mother, but the breakdown of the marriage wasn't ever talked about. The boys were going through a difficult time so we tried to make holidays as fun as possible. There were lots of silly games and both William and Harry were obsessed with seeing me and my sister Santa without clothes on. I'd be downstairs changing in one of the cabins when I'd hear a snigger from the wardrobe and Harry would suddenly burst out. He was always the naughtiest one. I got so fed up of them giving me a fright that one day I just took my top off and said, 'If you want to see them, here they are!' They thought it was hilarious. I was only young at the time and so flat-chested there was really nothing to see. It was all innocent fun and there were so many comedy moments. They were great kids and we were just like a big family albeit with the police back-up and everything else.

When the Waleses did go away together as a family – to Canada in October 1991 on an official visit – it seemed to be a points-scoring exercise more than anything else. Diana, elated to be reunited with her sons, made a great show of embracing William and then Harry as they ran across the deck of the royal yacht *Britannia* to greet her. The cameras clicked away, but it was only the photographs of Diana with the boys which made the papers the next day. 'It was a great pity that they didn't also show the pictures of Charles embracing the boys,' recalled Dickie Arbiter, who accompanied them on the trip. 'These were two compassionate parents who adored their sons and would do anything for them but didn't get equal billing.'

By now the strains in the marriage had taken their toll on William. He was at a difficult age and stormed off when his mother asked him to pose for a photograph with *Britannia*'s crew. Diana had a habit of sending mixed signals when it came to cameras, and William had had enough. Eventually Charles persuaded William to come out from his cabin to wave at the crowds as the yacht pulled out of the harbour, but he was in a mood for the rest of that day. Harry, in contrast, was in high spirits and brought some much-needed light relief to an otherwise oppressive situation. When he started an impromptu game of deck hockey with the crew his mother happily joined in. While Harry tore around the deck delivering sharp smacks to the shins of anyone that dared get in his way, William, who was still sulking, watched from the sidelines.

He resented being part of what he knew was a sham, and there was more drama the following summer when the family went on a Mediterranean cruise with Charles's friends Lord and Lady Romsey aboard the *Alexander*. When Diana discovered that Charles was telephoning Camilla she threatened to go home, and when they did eventually return to the UK after much upset, the situation worsened. On 24 August 1992 taped conversations of Diana speaking intimately to her friend James Gilbey found their way into the newspapers in an embarrassing episode dubbed 'Squidgygate' in the press.

Nevertheless the Queen was determined that Charles and Diana should give their marriage one final chance. Andrew and Sarah had separated in January after the Duchess of York was photographed in a compromising situation with the Texan financier John Bryan, and in the sovereign's eyes, enough embarrassment had been caused. Diana agreed to accompany Charles to Korea in November 1992, but their final official tour as husband and wife was a disaster. They could hardly stand to be in one another's company, and the newspapers focused on nothing else other than the state of their marriage. It was a disaster for the British monarchy, which was still recovering from the shock of Andrew Morton's book about the princess, published that June.

Diana – Her True Story had shaken the House of Windsor to its foundations and ensured the princess's exclusion from the circle of the royal family for good. Across 174 pages the fairy-tale myth of Diana's marriage to Charles was shattered, while the monarchy was portrayed as a cruel and outdated institution. 'Friends' revealed that Diana had suffered from bulimia ever since she and Charles were engaged and that she had tried to commit suicide five times during their marriage. For the first time Camilla Parker Bowles's name emerged as the catalyst for the Waleses' failed marriage. Charles read the pages of the *Sunday Times*, which serialised the book, with horror. Diana denied ever speaking to the author, but the truth was she had secretly collaborated on the explosive biography via her friend Dr James Coldhurst – she would never be forgiven for doing so.

The Queen, who would later refer to 1992 as her '*annus horribilis*', was furious at the embarrassment and damage the book caused. That November Windsor Castle caught fire, adding to the Queen's woes, and by Christmas she had given her permission for Charles and Diana to separate. As 'Defender of the Faith', the Queen had been staunchly against separation – the ghost of Wallis Simpson, the American divorcee at the heart of King Edward's abdication in 1936, still cast a cloud over the House of Windsor – but she recognised there was no alternative. The marriage was over and the situation was as dangerous as it was untenable.

On 9 December 1992 Prime Minister John Major announced the news in the House of Commons. William and Harry already knew. Diana had driven to see them several weeks earlier, and as her red Mercedes crunched up the gravel drive, they surely knew her visit was not good news. In the comfort of Mr Barber's living room Diana sat William and Harry down and explained that she still loved Papa, but they couldn't live under the same roof. Harry burst into tears but William put his bravest face on and told his mother, 'I hope you will both be happier now.' In the corridors of Buckingham Palace the news was also met with relief. 'It didn't come as any great shock. It was obvious that a separation was going to happen after Charles and Diana's trip to Korea,' recalled Dickie Arbiter.

I was on the ground for three days before they arrived. When the door of the aircraft opened and they emerged I thought, Oh God, we've lost it. The body language said it all, it was non-existent. You could have driven a fleet of tanks through them. There was a total lack of any connection. The press picked up on it immediately. Diana looked so distant and Charles had a look of total resignation on his face. When we returned from Korea there were discussions with the private secretaries in each household as to how the announcement should be made. Of course it was sad. We all wanted to believe in this golden couple who would make the monarchy great.

Although the initial shock of their parents' separation hit the boys hard, their lives changed very little. For several years they had divided their weekends between Highgrove and London, and if anything their holidays were even more fun now that their parents had separated. Diana and Charles competed to give them the best vacations, and because they were not together, there were no more arguments. Diana treated the boys to magical holidays at Disney World in Florida and on the island of Nevis in the Caribbean, and twice they were guests on Sir Richard Branson's private island of Necker; with their father, the boys whiled away long summers at Balmoral with their grandparents. In keeping with royal tradition, Christmases were spent at Sandringham, although Diana refused to go. 'They're always out killing things,' she complained to her friends, but the boys were in their element and loved following the guns on the traditional Boxing Day shoot. They also had a new nanny, the thirty-year-old Tiggy Legge-Bourke, who Charles had employed to help look after them during their half-terms and holidays. Young, energetic and attractive, Tiggy, who had grown up in Wales and was a close friend of Charles, loved shooting, hunting and fishing, more than enough to secure the affection and trust of the young princes.

Chapter 4

The Eton years

Eton was not like Ludgrove. At Ludgrove everyone had been protected.

Charles, Prince of Wales

William had just finished unpacking his ottoman at Eton College and his room was beginning to look less like a cell and more like the home it would be for the next five years. Above his desk, the thirteen-year-old prince straightened the picture of Cindy Crawford which took pride of place on the wall. It was not so long ago that he had met the American supermodel when his mother invited her for tea at the palace. William had blushed with embarrassment but he still couldn't decide who was more beautiful, Cindy or Claudia Schiffer, so he decided to hang them both above his study desk to brighten up his room.

As he sat down on his fold-up metal bed and looked around, he was pleased with the transformation. His mother and father had helped settle him in, and while Charles chatted with William's housemaster Dr Andrew Gailey downstairs, Diana helped him put up a new set of curtains. Like his housemates, he been allowed to bring his own duvet and covers to make him feel at home, but this time he had chosen to leave his cuddly wombat behind. Like his mother he loved pop music, and he had also brought his CD player and video games to play once he had finished his evening study period. He also kept a framed photograph of his parents by his bedside, which was the last thing he looked at before lights out at 9.30 p.m.

His uncle Earl Spencer, who had once been a pupil at the famous British boarding school tucked away in the shadow of Windsor Castle, had told William what to expect. The uniform was actually rather comfortable once you got used to it, and the trickiest thing was getting to grips with the timetable, which changed from week to week. On top of finding his way around the different buildings and departments dotted around the small town, which overlooks the River Thames, William also had centuries-old traditions to master and a new vocabulary to get used to. At Eton teachers are known as 'beaks', lessons are 'divs', food is 'sock' and William, like his other first-year housemates, was known as an 'F-tit'. He was delighted to get into Manor House, his top choice. It is the elite of the school's twenty-five houses and situated on a busy lane next to the library and opposite the chapel. The school, which dates back to 1440 when it was founded by King Henry VI, has produced eighteen British prime ministers and educated members of royal families the world over, so William was only the latest in a long list of illustrious names to arrive at the college. As his uncle had warned, there would be initiation rites to pass, and William's title would not prevent him being picked on.

It could not have been easy for the prince when his parents dropped him off on 6 September 1995. While Ludgrove had been protected from the main road by acres of lush countryside, William's new boarding house was so exposed he could see the bright green Windsor Hopalong sightseeing bus pass from his bedroom window. It was not uncommon for him to wake up and find a gaggle of American tourists standing on the street pointing up at the building, trying to discern which bedroom was that of the future king. When he played sport, which he often did, William would have to ignore the crowds which gathered on the public road for a glimpse of him. Of course, the necessary security arrangements were in place, and William's bedroom windows had been refitted with bulletproof glass ahead of his arrival. The turquoise lacquered door to his study was also reinforced, and should there be any problem his protection officers Trevor Bettles and Graham Cracker were just down the corridor.

Both Charles and Diana had been delighted when William passed his Common Entrance. No concessions were made for the royal applicant, who had had a further series of tests and exams to pass before he was granted a place at the prestigious school. Charles, who had been miserable at Gordonstoun, the boarding school in Scotland to which he (and subsequently his brothers Andrew and Edward) had been packed off when he was thirteen, was particularly pleased. While the Duke of Edinburgh had been keen for William to follow in his father's footsteps, Charles and Diana were adamant that both William and later Harry would be educated at Eton.

They had momentarily forgotten their marriage woes that morning and posed as a family in front of the wooden gate that led up to Manor House's imposing black door. Charles, his hand in his pocket, was on one side of William and Harry; Diana, resplendent in a cobalt-blue jacket, on the other. It had not been the low-key arrival William had hoped for. Dressed in a smart checked blazer, grey trousers and shiny black shoes, he managed a smile for the 300-strong press pack which flooded onto the street and held up the traffic leaving Windsor. As they jostled on the pavement behind a police barrier it looked as though they were enjoying their very own version of Eton's famous wall game. William was nervous, signed his name in the wrong place in the entrance book and had to be reminded by his father which religion he should enter.

Inevitably his arrival had sparked a flurry of gossip among pupils including rumours that a nuclear bunker had been built ahead of his arrival. 'The morning that William arrived we were all a-buzz with the news that a bomb shelter had been built at Manor House,' recalled a boarder. 'Of course it was probably just a wild tale, but it was all very exciting and a lot more security was installed when William started. Every corner of the school, especially Manor House, was fitted with a CCTV camera.' Eton did indeed have a nuclear shelter, but it was constructed beneath the college in 1959 to house the college's provost and fellows and is now used for storage. At Manor House little fanfare was made about the royal arrival at William's request. He was deeply embarrassed by the attention and wanted nothing more than to slip seamlessly into the background.

Sadly it was not to be the case. Despite the Press Complaints Commission warning that William was a private individual who should be left alone at school, he was rarely out of the newspapers. After his high-profile arrival at Eton, Sky Television aired two documentaries, *The Making of a King* and *Inside Eton*. William was mortified and begged his new schoolfriends not to watch the programmes. He had grown increasingly resentful of public interest in his life and the cameras that seemed to follow him everywhere. He also had to suffer the indignity of having every aspect of his parents' lives played out in the press. Within weeks of William enrolling at the school it was reported that his mother was having an affair with the married England rugby player Will Carling. Before long Diana was linked with another man, Oliver Hoare, a London-based art dealer.

Unlike at Ludgrove, where the Barbers had banned newspapers, Eton's library was well stocked, and William was exposed to the front-page stories and cruel playground taunts that inevitably followed. Fortunately he had a small group of dependable allies to protect him. His father's godson, Lord and Lady Romsey's son Nicholas Knatchbull, promised the Prince of Wales he would keep an eye on William. Meanwhile, his cousin Freddie Windsor, who was just down the road in Aitkinson's House, would often pop into see William. Dr Gailey, an amiable Irishman and a respected historian who loved music, was also to become a confidant. Appreciating that many of his charges were away from home for the first time, the door that linked his own house to the pupils' living quarters was always open. The boys would all breakfast and take lunch and dinner in the wooden-floored dining room which smelt of furniture polish, and William was often invited to sit with Dr Gailey at the head table, which looked onto the well-manicured lawn and colourful flower beds.

Having always had his clothes laundered and ironed for him at home, William had to get used to getting himself ready in the mornings. He was required to wear a pressed uniform including a tailed morning coat, a waistcoat and white shirt. Fortunately he struck up a warm rapport with Elizabeth Heathcote, matron of the house, who taught him how to iron his shirts. He also had his own personal tutor, Christopher Stuart-Clark, who spent two hours a week with the prince and made sure he was keeping up in class. It took William several months before he could confidently navigate the school and its maze of corridors, but he managed to cope academically. He was also popular with his peers, according to one of his housemates. 'At first he alienated himself by spending time with some of the older boys who were his protectors, but William did come out of his shell and he definitely had a presence at Eton. When you got to know him he was a great guy and utterly normal. He wasn't at all arrogant and he was an outstanding sportsman. One person you always wanted batting for your team was William Wales.'

William sat nervously in Dr Gailey's study. His housemates were all working in their bedrooms upstairs but William had been given special leave. It was a cold November's night and the young prince was just one of 20 million people in the country who had sat down to watch Diana, Princess of Wales give her first sit-down interview. For weeks the newspapers had been filled with speculation about the *Panorama* documentary which would see the recently separated princess talk candidly for the first time to journalist Martin Bashir about her marriage.

Diana had been to see William ahead of the programme being aired to assure him that he had nothing to worry about, but as he sat watching the interview his eyes filled with tears of fury and frustration. He could simply not believe that his mother had invited the television cameras into the home he had grown up in and loved, to betray his father and their family in such a public way.

As Diana welled up and spoke about her bulimia, the breakdown of her marriage, her husband's infidelity and her own adultery, William was in shock. She had never before spoken about her affair with James Hewitt, the amiable Life Guards officer who had come to teach Diana to ride when the boys were still children at Highgrove. The affair had started in 1986, when William was four and Harry just two. At the time Diana suspected Charles was back with Camilla and claimed to have sought comfort with Hewitt. It was speculated in the press that the timing of their relationship was so close to Harry's birth that he could in fact be Hewitt's son. The rumours appalled Diana, and in the end Hewitt was forced to declare, 'There is really no possibility whatsoever that I am Harry's father. Harry was twenty months old when I first exchanged pleasantries with his mother, and past his second birthday when the affair started.' It was eventually Diana who called off the affair, when Hewitt, whose regiment took part in the First Gulf War in 1991, left for Iraq. Ultimately he would breach her trust and the confidence she had placed in him by writing a book about their love affair and selling her love letters. 'Yes, I adored him. Yes, I was in love with him, but I was very let down,' she said. Her revelations were shocking and sensational. This was Diana's most public move in her war against the Windsors, and her most damaging yet. 'There were three of us in this marriage, so it was a bit crowded,' she said, famously referring to Camilla Parker Bowles.

When William returned to Kensington Palace he refused to speak to his mother. He had always sprung to her defence, but this time she had gone too far. William, who was older now and capable of forming his own opinions, never entirely forgave

Diana. According to Simone Simmons, the *Panorama* interview led to their first major falling-out.

> William was absolutely livid. It wasn't until after she'd done the interview and it was too late that she actually told him about it. Of course it was in all the papers and William told me he was teased at school because of it. He felt really bad for his mum because of what she had gone through, but he was furious with her. People at school were calling her all sorts of names. He wanted to defend her, but it was very confusing and hard for him. The weekend after it went out they had a big row at Kensington Palace. William was furious, and Diana was distraught. I was there the day after she'd spoken to him and Diana was in a terrible way. Eventually William said he forgave her when she promised him she would never do anything like that again. It was the most angry I had seen him at his mother.

Harry was still being shielded by the Barbers in the safety of Ludgrove, but William, out in the open at Eton and exposed to the press, was painfully embarrassed by his feuding parents. Fed up with their public war, he refused to allow either of them to attend Founder's Day. This annual event, which is held in July, commemorates the birthday of King George III, who resided at Windsor for much of his reign and took an active interest in the school, and is the highlight of Eton's social calendar. William, still reeling from his mother's interview, knew that having his parents there would put him under the spotlight. He had become quite stubborn, and despite his mother's pleas invited Tiggy and his close friend William Van Cutsem, who he regularly shot with, to accompany him. Diana was devastated, particularly because William had invited Tiggy over her.

By now Charles had collaborated with Jonathan Dimbleby on his only ever authorised biography, *Private Man*, in which he admitted he had resumed his love affair with Camilla. Their secret was out and the infamous 'Camillagate' tapes, which contained explicit conversations between the lovers, had been published in the British press, causing further humiliation and ridicule for the royal family. The reputation of the British monarchy was at its lowest ebb for decades, and it was not just William who could take no more of this farcical and public warring. Polls in national newspapers questioned the need for a monarchy that didn't pay taxes and a tide of republicanism washed over the country. The Queen finally conceded there was no solution but for the Waleses to divorce; her aides at Buckingham Palace were in agreement, and Charles, by now desperate for an end to his marriage, breathed a sigh of relief. It was to the Queen's eternal regret that the mystery that had shrouded the royal family and ensured the fascination and respect of her subjects had been blown apart by one woman.

As 1995 drew to a close the Queen wrote to her son and daughter in-law and insisted that they get a divorce. The letters were hand-delivered to Kensington Palace and St James's Palace, the prince's London offices. Their decree nisi was rubber-stamped on 28 August 1996 in a dingy room at Somerset House. Diana, the Queen had decided, would be stripped of her HRH title, something William promised he would return to her when he was king. It was unsettling and upsetting for him to watch his mother suffer such a humiliation. She had already retired from public life at her own instigation, but had wanted to retain her royal status so that she could continue her charity work. She had realised early on that it was a key not only to a life of privilege, but to raising awareness of the causes she passionately believed in. Diana had not been afraid to confront taboo issues like Aids and landmines; she believed everyone who suffered deserved compassion. It was a belief she instilled in William and Harry, who she took to hospices and shelters in London so that they could see for themselves the reality of poverty. William was twelve and Harry nine when Diana took them to visit The Passage, a shelter near Vauxhall Bridge in London. They spent ninety minutes chatting with volunteers and playing cards with the homeless, and went back many times. Those midnight visits had a lasting effect on her sons.

As he turned right out of Manor House and headed for the High Street, William stopped off at Tudor Stores, the local newsagent always overrun with Eton boys. He purchased a small bag of his favourite boiled sweets and slipped them in his pocket before heading over the bridge. It was a Sunday; he had been to chapel and had the rest of the day free. He had announced to his friends that he was 'off to the WC' much to their amusement. The sun was shining, and as he walked across the pretty bridge he could see a swan and her cygnets gliding over the River Thames. Ahead of him stood Windsor Castle in all its glory. From this distance William could just make out the scaffolding where work was still being carried out to repair the damage caused by the fire. Followed at a discreet distance by his protection officer, William was waved through security with a friendly salute from the duty police officer. Through the labyrinth of stone corridors he made his way to the Oak Drawing Room, where his grandmother was waiting for him. Often the Duke of Edinburgh would accompany them at their weekly lunch date and quiz his eldest grandson on what he had learned at school that week, but as tea was served he would retire to his study, leaving the Queen and her grandson alone together. William looked forward to these meetings all week. He shared a close bond with his grandmother, who could see Diana's sensitivity in the teenage boy. Not only did he physically resemble his mother, with his doe eyes, blond hair and lean athletic frame, he had inherited Diana's capacity for empathy. The Queen recognised these as qualities that would endear William to his public in years to come, and rather than advising William to keep a stiff upper lip, urged him to express his concerns. Emotionally William had been bounced from pillar to post in the years following his parents' separation. During these hardest of times, in the privacy of the castle crying was allowed, even encouraged. According to Elizabeth Anson, his grandmother desperately wanted to help William.

Charles had complained that he had never shared a close bond with his mother. When he was growing up they saw little of one another, and in times of need he had turned to his beloved grandmother for advice and support. The Queen was determined to learn from the mistakes of her past. While her grandson regaled her with stories from the classroom, she would tell William about the official engagements she had carried out that week. She considered it vital preparation for his future role as king. Her father King George VI had seen it as his duty to ensure that she was capable and ready to lead the United Kingdom when she succeeded to the throne on 6 February 1952 at the age of just twenty-five on his death. Her father's counsel had strengthened and prepared the young Elizabeth, and as reigning monarch she intended to do the same for William. Part of the training had been her introduction to public life at an early age. On her twenty-first birthday she had addressed the Commonwealth from South Africa, displaying a confidence beyond her years. During that historic speech she made a pledge that she still swears by today: 'I declare before you all that my whole life, whether it be long or short, shall be devoted to your service and the service of our great imperial family to which we all belong.'

Both Charles and Diana, however, were reluctant for William to embark on official engagements too soon. Diana had taken him to Cardiff on St David's Day when he was eight years old, and the crowds had adored him. As he collected armfuls of daffodils William waved happily at the cameras. Now he was a teenager he was uncomfortable in the media glare and hid awkwardly beneath his floppy fringe. His grandmother understood better than anyone else his fears for the future, and she was in a unique position to help guide him. Those long afternoon teas, however, were not solely for tutelage. Aware of the emotional turmoil William was going through, the Queen encouraged him to talk about his worries. During those private and relaxed tête-à-têtes the Queen offered her grandson practical advice which William found invaluable. According to Lady Elizabeth Anson, such meetings were hugely cathartic for William and gave him the strength to return to Eton with his head held high ready for the next week. 'The Queen spent a huge amount of time with William, and she often used to bring him out of Eton to spend time with him. They are exceptionally close and the Queen has been a wonderful mentor for William over the years.'

It is to William's great credit that he never once turned against his family. While he adored his mother, he recognised his position within the royal family – it had been instilled in him since the day he could speak. His sense of duty and his place in history is in his blood, and there was no question that he would ever turn against the system like his mother had.

Diana, who had secured a £17 million divorce settlement, knew that she would never get sole custody of her sons. One was heir to the throne, the other the spare, and their lives would always be dictated by their position. As their mother she had achieved more than she imagined possible in her quest to raise her boys as 'normal', but now they were on the brink of adulthood the future of their identities would be shaped by the formidable House of Windsor.

While he was deeply loyal and fiercely protective of his mother, William was beginning to see for himself how difficult Diana could be. Now grown to over six feet in height, he towered over her and was old enough to make his own decisions. At his confirmation in March 1997 he was upset when Diana insisted Tiggy Legge-Bourke could not attend the ceremony. Diana was convinced she was having an affair with Charles and refused to invite her. She had also had an argument with her own mother and banned her from the service, which upset William. Both he and Harry adored their Granny Frances and had spent many summers as children holidaying at her home on the distant Isle of Seil near Oban on the west coast of

Scotland. But to invite her would risk their mother's wrath and spoil the day. Frances was struck off the guest list, and tragically mother and daughter were never to reconcile their differences before their deaths.

Chapter 5

Goodbye, Mummy

She was our guardian, friend and protector . . . quite simply the best mother in the world.

Prince Harry, 31 August 2007

As Harry lay sleeping, his head rested heavily on his mother's lap. It was a cold afternoon in November 1996 and Diana was with her friend Simone Simmons in the second-floor living room of Kensington Palace. Dressed casually in jeans and a pale blue cashmere sweater, her long legs tucked beneath her, the princess leaned in trying her hardest not to wake her son from his nap. 'What do you mean an accident? Who is in the car, Simone? You have to tell me,' she whispered urgently as the little boy stirred in his sleep. 'I don't know, Diana. I see four people in a car and a terrible crash. I don't know who they are.'

It was a Saturday, and according to the princess's chef Darren McGrady, one of the few staff she had retained following her divorce from the Prince of Wales, a typical weekend at Kensington Palace. Harry was home from Ludgrove while William was still at Eton. Simone had dropped over for tea, as she often did, and the three of them had spent the afternoon watching James Bond movies. Exhausted by their day out, which had comprised one of Diana's famous shopping trips, the twelve-year-old prince had dozed off as his mother and her friend chatted. It was dark outside by now, and Diana and Simone had worked their way through two pots of herbal tea. Over the past four years Simone had become one of Diana's closest friends and years later would give evidence at the inquest into the princess's untimely death. They had met at the Hale Clinic in London's Regent's Park, where Simone worked as a healer, and had immediately got on. They spoke on the phone daily and Simone was always in and out of Kensington Palace. 'Simone would come over to Kensington Palace most weekends. I was in the kitchens preparing food and they would be upstairs in the sitting room. The boys were often home from school and would sit chatting with them,' recalled Mr McGrady. Although some of the staff viewed Simone with scepticism, Diana adored her and instructed her to 'cleanse' the house after her divorce. She also asked her friend to teach her 'healing', which, according to Simone, Diana practised on her children when they were ill.

Diana had an established coterie of spiritualists and astrologers whom she depended on for guidance and instruction including a psychic called Rita Rogers. William was also fascinated by the notion that people could see into the future, and when he was younger would often make secret calls to his mother's psychic, begging her for a reading. Rita told him he was too young, but this did not dispel the young prince's curiosity. Harry was also intrigued by the idea that some people were 'gifted'. At this particular afternoon session this 'special lady', as Diana called Simone, had a premonition of an event that would change Harry's life for ever. Less than a year on he would walk by his brother's side, their heads bowed in grief, behind their mother's coffin. It was the greyest day of their lives after the most wonderful summer.

The bedroom door slammed shut. 'It's my room and no, you can't stay in it,' Omar Al Fayed shouted from inside the locked cabin. Harry banged his fist on the door. 'Don't you say that. Your mummy said we can stay wherever we want and I want this room.' Aboard the five-star yacht there was no shortage of space. The boat had a crew of sixteen, a master bedroom with a king-size bed and its own jet skis, and everything was in place for the royal party. But according to Mohamed Al Fayed's daughter Camilla, her younger brother Omar wanted his own bed that night and there was no way he was going to give it up for Harry. Upstairs Diana stretched out on her towel and turned the music up on her Walkman. The boys had been bickering for the best part of an hour, and still no solution had been reached to the problem of where Harry would be sleeping. William was on the upper deck quietly reading with Camilla and her sister Jasmine. They giggled about the fight going on downstairs, although it would be a whole day before their younger brother spoke to Harry again after being made to give up his room. The row aside, it had been a wonderful holiday so far, and Diana, William and Harry had wanted for nothing as the guests of Mohamed Al Fayed, the Egyptian-born billionaire owner of Harrods in London.

While the royal family's relationship with the Fayed family has always been frosty, Diana enjoyed the company of the flamboyant store owner. With money no object, Mohamed Al Fayed had purchased the *Jonikal*, a luxury £15 million yacht, as soon as Diana had accepted his invitation to join his family in St-Tropez. It was Mohamed's way of safeguarding his royal guests and ensuring they had maximum privacy, his ulterior motive was to play Cupid between the princess and his eldest son Dodi, a divorced forty-one-year-old film producer. Diana was single, having recently broken off her romance with Hasnat Khan, the heart surgeon who she had fallen in love with in the summer of 1996, and Mohamed, who they all referred to as 'Mo', was convinced Dodi was the man to make Diana happy.

Keen to put her troubles behind her and desperate for some Mediterranean sun, Diana and her sons flew to the south of France on Al Fayed's private Gulfstream jet on 11 July 1997. William and Harry always looked forward to holidays with their mother, and as they touched down on the sun-baked tarmac in Nice, Diana had promised them the holiday of their lives. Stripped of her HRH title, Diana had decided to part with her long-serving bodyguard Ken Wharfe, but the boys were accompanied by their two protection officers. Al Fayed also had his own team of security at the Villa Castel Ste-Therese, the family's pink-painted villa set high above the mountains of St-Tropez, where they enjoyed the first days of the holiday.

William and Harry had known Jasmine, Camilla and Omar for several years, and they had already spent some of that summer together in London. According to Camilla, she and her siblings had been invited to the newly refurbished games room at Kensington Palace to play computer games with the princes. Harry was the self-proclaimed king of Sonic the Hedgehog, and his mother could barely keep him away from the screen. Before the divorce Diana had spent a fortune redecorating the palace, stripping the walls of their traditional patterned wallpaper and painting them vibrant yellow. William's bedroom was painted blue while Harry's room was papered in fresh lemon and white, a contrast to the green military paraphernalia that littered the newly installed cream carpet. Camilla, the youngest of Mohamed and his wife Heini Wathen's four children, recalled how they would spend hours playing games that her father had sent to the palace from the toy department of Harrods: 'That summer we all became a team. I was eleven at the time and my sister was fifteen. We used to hang out with William and Harry all the time at the palace. We were all so excited about spending the summer together and it was wonderful. We adored each other and we did everything together.'

The boys did not know Dodi, but he now charmed them with his stories of Hollywood and won their mother over with compliments and expensive gifts. According to Camilla, the holiday was an adventure from start to finish.

There were reports that we children didn't get along but that wasn't true. I have nothing but happy memories of that summer. I will never forget the time we spent together in France, it was wonderful. It was great fun being with Diana, she was so beautiful and kind and she doted on us all. She would come and tuck us up in bed like we were her own children. We were all very close, it's just no one really knew about our friendship. You have to remember we weren't star-struck by having the princes and Diana around. We'd have Michael Jackson to tea, so for us it was very normal to have famous people around. I remember that Harry was very much a mummy's boy and he always wanted Diana's attention. He and Omar did have an argument but there was no fight as was reported in the newspapers. The truth is they fell out over a bed! Our mother told Omar to give up his bed for Harry, because he was our guest but Omar didn't want to. He wasn't having any of it and I remember there was a lot of shouting and door slamming but no fisticuffs. We were all laughing about it, especially Diana, who thought it was so funny. Omar and Harry didn't speak for a whole day because of it and we laughed about the whole thing until we had tears streaming down our faces. William was quieter than Harry and a real gentleman. I always remember he had impeccable manners and you could tell even then that he had been groomed for the top job. He would always open doors for his mother and make sure she was comfortable and happy. He was the perfect little prince.

While the holiday was just what Diana and the boys needed, it was hard to relax on the yacht. Pictures of the holidaymakers were being sold to newspapers for tens of thousands of pounds, with the press based on a nearby mooring day and night, their long lenses constantly trained on the *Jonikal*. Diana, tanned and stunning in an eye-catching swimsuit, had tried to reason with the paparazzi but to no avail. Without a protection officer to help, she decided to take a tender across to the press to ask them to leave her family alone. 'William is freaked out,' she shouted at the photographers. 'My sons are always urging me to live abroad and be less in the public eye, and maybe that's what I should do – go and live abroad.' It was typical Diana, and of course her comments were front-page news the next day. Did she plan to move to the States, as had been widely speculated, and would she take William and Harry with her? There would be another crisis for the royal family if that was her intention. By now William deeply resented the media circus that accompanied his mother, and he spent much of his time below deck, where the lenses could not reach him.

It was with some relief that they flew home on Saturday 20 July. The boys attended the Queen Mother's ninety-seventh birthday lunch at Clarence House before joining the royal family aboard the *Britannia* for the royal yacht's last ever cruise of the Western Isles. They left the yacht early to spend the rest of the summer with their father at Balmoral. Since Charles and Diana's separation, the Queen had insisted on her grandchildren spending more time in the privacy of the royal estates, and Charles had agreed. There were concerns that whenever the boys holidayed with their mother, the vacation, whether it be Disney World or the south of France, was news. For the Queen, who believed in keeping her family life private, this was alarming to say the least. On the royal estate in Scotland the boys were safe from prying lenses.

Ironically, after their divorce relations between Diana and Charles were smoother than they had been for years. With their marriage now a closed chapter, Diana was determined to enjoy her summer, and Dodi provided a welcome distraction from her recent heartbreak. She decided to fly to Paris for a secret rendezvous with him just days after their vacation aboard the *Jonikal*. She had visited Milan for the funeral of her friend designer Gianni Versace, but the rest of the summer was to be one long vacation in the Mediterranean sunshine. After cruising around the Greek islands with her close friend Rosa Monckton,

Diana returned to London on 20 August to collect a suitcase before flying to Nice, where she was reunited with Dodi for another cruise aboard the *Jonikal*. The world's paparazzi decamped to Sardinia, where the couple were photographed kissing on deck, and not a day passed without the princess and her new lover appearing on the front pages of the daily press. There was speculation that they had become engaged and rumours that the princess, who appeared to have a swollen belly beneath her leopard-print swimsuit, was pregnant. Speculation reached fever pitch when the couple flew to Paris on Saturday 30 August. It was to be a fatal detour. Diana had been due to fly to London to be reunited with her sons, but Dodi decided that a romantic night in Paris would be the perfect end to their holiday. Diana spoke to William that morning from the Imperial Suite of the Ritz. She was regaled with news of her sons' wonderful holiday in Balmoral, and William told her that he and Harry could not wait to see her. As the receiver clicked, William went to inform Harry that Mummy would be coming home tomorrow. It was the last time he ever spoke to his mother.

Dickie Arbiter was about to climb into bed when the phone rang at his Kensington home. It was just after 11.30 on Saturday night, and CNN was on the line wanting to know if the press secretary had any update on the princess following the crash in the Pont de l'Alma tunnel. As Arbiter turned on his television, images of the twisted black Mercedes that Diana, Dodi, their driver Henri Paul and bodyguard Trevor Rees Jones had been travelling in flashed across his screen. At Balmoral, the Queen, Prince Philip and Prince Charles were watching the same pictures and being kept abreast of developments via the Queen's private secretary Robin Janvrin, who was liaising with the French authorities.

Charles was informed his ex-wife had been involved in a crash minutes after it happened late on Saturday night and padded along the corridor to wake his parents. He was told that Dodi was dead while Diana was in a critical condition. Suffering from shock, he paused for several moments outside William and Harry's bedrooms not knowing whether to wake them. The Queen, who was by now fully awake and in her dressing gown, advised her son to let them sleep. At this stage there was no confirmation from Paris as to how seriously the princess had been injured. Some reports claimed she had walked away from the wreckage unscathed, while others said she was in a coma.

Shortly after 3 a.m. on Sunday morning the family was informed by the British embassy in Paris that Diana was dead. It was the duty of Robin Janvrin to inform the Prince of Wales, and it was a wonder that Charles's wails did not wake the entire household. Thankfully William and Harry continued sleeping in their beds. As Charles walked across the moors alone, dawn broke, and it would only be a matter of hours before his sons would awake to the terrible tragedy.

Back at Buckingham Palace Dickie Arbiter was at his desk, telephoning the news through to the necessary advisers, including Charles's private secretary Sir Michael Peat. 'I got a phone call at 3.10 that morning to say that the princess was dead,' recalled Arbiter.

I got into the shower, dressed in a suit and I was in the palace at 3.50 a.m. I phoned Peat, who was somewhere in Wales fast asleep, but he woke up fast enough. He was staggered and had to do some fast thinking. Buckingham Palace was open to the public, and Peat had to decide whether to keep it open or close it. I then called the superintendent at Windsor Castle and Holyrood House to get the flag at half-mast. Later in the day I was in constant touch with the Lord Chamberlain, who was in London coordinating everything. We knew by 8.30 that morning that the Queen's Flight was going out to fetch her. I was shocked but there was no time for emotion, there was a job to do and there was going to be a funeral. At that point we were unsure what shape the funeral would take because it had to be a Spencer family decision. Charles Spencer was in South Africa, and we couldn't make a decision without him so we went ahead with planning the homecoming.

William was immediately aware that something was wrong when he woke up to find his father sitting at the end of his bed. It was 7.15 on Sunday morning, and as he got up and drew the curtains, he could see that his father's eyes were red from crying. The young prince's heart skipped a beat and then Charles delivered the news that would change his life for ever. Diana had been in an accident in Paris, Charles explained. As tears rolled down his cheeks he held his elder son tightly to his chest. She had been chased by the paparazzi and there had been a terrible collision in an underpass. The French medics had not been able to save her.

Too shocked to even cry at first, William told his papa he wanted to be with him when he told Harry. As the sun came up the princes' cries echoed through the corridors. Downstairs the Queen and Philip were dressing for church while people around the world woke up to the news that would trigger an outpouring of grief never before seen in Britain.

Determined that the boys would draw comfort from their faith, the family were driven to mass at Craithie church in the nearby village. Crowds had already gathered to offer their condolences, but there were no statements and no tears. Behind the palace walls the boys were encouraged to cry, but in public they had to be strong. It is the royal way and they duly obliged. Their former nanny Tiggy had flown to Balmoral immediately, and for hours Harry, stunned into silence, would not leave her side. Princess Anne's son Peter had also flown to Scotland to be with his cousins. While they were out Charles arranged for the television in the nursery, which was now a den for the youngsters, to be removed. He wanted them to be spared the pain of the rolling news and the awful images of the twisted wreckage from which their mother had been pulled.

Racked with grief, Charles locked himself away in his study, and made arrangements over the telephone with Diana's sisters Sarah and Jane, who would accompany him on the plane to Paris to bring the princess home that night. He was to be driven from Balmoral to Aberdeen before boarding the flight to the French capital. From his window he could see the boys racing their quad bikes. Later that afternoon and during the awful days that followed, Philip would take the boys fishing and they would wade through the River Dee. These seemed like the most normal things in the world and the boys appreciated the distraction. Sometimes they talked, but often they stood in silence, gathering their thoughts and desperately searching for answers that never came.

In London crowds gathered outside Kensington Palace. A sea of flowers already stretched from the wrought-iron gates to the grassy banks of Kensington Gardens. Many of the mourners had witnessed the wedding sixteen years before and had come to pay their respects to the woman who had captured their hearts.

Back at Buckingham Palace the phone had not stopped ringing. Dickie Arbiter, in charge of coordinating Diana's homecoming, was with the country's new prime minister Tony Blair and the world's press at RAF Northolt awaiting the arrival of a BAe 146 from the Queen's Flight. At 7 p.m. on 31 August 1997 Diana's coffin, which had been draped in the yellow and deep maroon of the royal standard, was carried by eight officers from the Queen's Colour Squadron of the RAF Regiment in the fading light across the tarmac. As the hearse made its way back to London accompanied by a police escort, traffic on the westbound carriage of the A40 stopped all the way back into London. People stood on bridges, walkways and in the roads, their heads bowed as they bid farewell. Candlelit vigils took place outside Kensington Palace as the British public remembered their princess. Charles returned immediately to Balmoral, where he was reunited with his sons.

As the days passed in soft focus, the public mood changed from grief to intrigue and then anger. Where was their monarch and where were the princes? The Queen was in regular contact with Tony Blair in London, where a state funeral was being planned, but had decided it would be best for her family to remain at Balmoral, where the boys were calm and sheltered. It was the first time in her reign that she put her family before duty and it cost her dearly. Not since the abdication had the monarchy been in such crisis. Overcome with grief and shock, the public demanded an explanation, and when the flag at Buckingham Palace was not flown at half-mast there was nearly a revolt. YOUR PEOPLE ARE

SUFFERING, declared the front page of the *Daily Mirror*. WHY CAN'T THE ROYAL FAMILY SHOW THEIR GRIEF? queried the *Daily Mail*. WHERE IS THE QUEEN WHEN THE COUNTRY NEEDS HER? asked the *Sun*. Those close to the Queen insisted that she *was* with her people, two little people who needed her more than anyone else could possibly imagine. But it was not the answer the British public wanted to hear. Opinion polls at the time showed that 70 per cent of the country believed that the Queen's decision not to come back to London had damaged the monarchy, while a quarter said the institution should go. It was the new fresh-faced prime minister, not the sovereign, who was hailed the nation's hero, crowning Diana 'the people's princess' in his public address shortly after her death. For once the political leader of the time was more in touch with the British public than the head of state. The crisis was immortalised in a film called *The Queen* starring Helen Mirren. The movie sensationalised events and its suggestion that the Queen considered abdicating was fictitious, but it captured brilliantly the mood of the British public and the crisis of the monarchy.

By the end of the week the Queen had no choice but to bow to public pressure and returned to Buckingham Palace on Friday 5 September when she made a television broadcast to the nation. In a breach of royal protocol – usually they are not allowed to fly together – William, Harry and Charles boarded the Queen's Flight from Balmoral to London that morning. They had been due to visit the Chapel Royal at St James's Palace to pay their last respects to their mother, but instead they decided to visit Kensington Palace one last time. As they carried out a walkabout in front of the palace's black and gold gates, William looked to his father for strength. Never more than a foot away, Charles gave a nod of encouragement without the need to exchange a word. He would later tell his sons how proud he was of their composure. They knew not to wear private grief in public and showed great strength in the face of the wailing and often hysterical public. As the British people watched William and Harry, who clasped his father's hand tightly as he bravely knelt down to read the hand-written tributes, the tide turned again. In place of anger was pity for the two princes who had tragically lost their mother.

The Queen organised a dinner at Buckingham Palace that night in an attempt to lift the princes' mood. In truth it was her final attempt to persuade the reluctant William to walk behind his mother's gun carriage. The fifteen-year-old prince was resolute that he could not face the walk from Kensington Palace to Westminster Abbey. He was not strong enough; there were too many people; he feared he would break down and embarrass his grandmother. 'It was the duke who persuaded William to walk at the very last minute,' said Lady Elizabeth Anson. 'Philip knew that if William didn't walk he would regret it for the rest of his life. He said to William, "If I walk will you walk?" I think William was overcome with gratitude. He would have done anything for his grandfather, who had been a pillar of strength for him.'

Lieutenant Colonel Sir Malcolm Ross, the master of the household at Clarence House, was informed of the eleventh-hour change of plan and instructed Barnard & Westwood, the Chelsea-based printers who hold the royal warrant, to alter the order of service. They worked through the night, and on the morning of Saturday 6 September William and Harry's names were there in print, and they were there in person to carry out their first and most tragic joint royal duty.

Chapter 6

Coming off the rails at Club H

Harry's the naughty one, just like me.

Diana, Princess of Wales

The best thing for William and Harry, it was decided, was normality. Both boys were back in the classroom four days after they buried their mother at Althorp. There was something comforting about the routine of school, and while William had Dr Gailey to keep a paternal eye on him at Manor House, Gerald Barber was on hand to offer some much-needed support to Harry. 'Harry had a very tough final year,' one of his close friends remembered. 'He was a completely different person when he came back after the summer. He was quieter and far less boisterous. On top of the trauma of losing his mother, he also had the added pressure of having to pass his Common Entrance. He used to have quite a laissez-faire attitude to his studies, but he spent his final year working really hard. His work took his mind off every-thing else and for once we'd spot Harry in the library. He was lucky he had some real friends there.' Among them were Thomas van Straubenzee, Charlie Henderson and Ed Birrell.

During those first weeks of term, Diana's sister Sarah also stepped in to look after the boys. She visited Harry on his thirteenth birthday and took him the PlayStation his mother had bought for him in Paris. Her frequent visits to see the boys were appreciated as much by Charles as they were by William and Harry. The prince cleared his diary where he could and set aside the weekends for his sons at the expense of spending time with Camilla, who had stopped coming to Highgrove for the time being. Charles had recruited Mark Bolland, a vibrant and radical spin doctor, the year before Diana's death, and together with Sir Stephen Lamport, Charles's private secretary, they put in place a plan to resuscitate Charles's battered public image, doubling his official engagements in the months after Diana's death. Polls conducted in national newspapers at the time showed that his popularity was at an all-time low and the majority believed he was not fit to be king. Camilla was also vilified for her part in the breakdown of the Waleses' marriage and cut a desperately lonely figure as she returned to Ray Mill House, the home she had bought in 1995, the same year Camilla's divorce from her husband had been finalised. Conveniently it was just a thirty-minute drive from Highgrove.

The boys had yet to meet their father's mistress, and although William had become curious about his father's female companion, having overheard fragments of his mother's conversations, Harry had no idea who Camilla was, according to Simone Simmons, who watched a televised debate about the future of the monarchy at Kensington Palace with Diana, William and Harry before the princess's death. 'When Camilla's name was mentioned, Harry piped up and said, "Who's Camilla?"' recalled Simone. 'Diana whisked him up the stairs before he had time to ask any more questions.'

For the time being Charles had no choice but to sideline Camilla, who understood that his number-one priority was his sons. In November he decided to take Harry on a trip to South Africa with Tiggy and his son's schoolfriend Charlie Henderson. It was exactly what Harry needed, and he couldn't stop grinning when he got to meet the Spice Girls at a charity concert with Nelson Mandela. He also accompanied his father on an official visit to Rorke's Drift. One day, he promised his father, he would also fight for his country. Charles, who had watched his son grow up playing soldiers, had no doubts. When he got back to Ludgrove, Harry was determined to pass his exams. He was young for his class, and had been kept down a year to help him prepare for his Common Entrance. More than anything he wanted to make his mother proud, and he knew how much Diana had wanted him to join William at Eton.

As Harry swotted away ahead of his exams, William was settling into the Michaelmas Half at Eton. He had received hundreds of letters from fellow pupils offering their condolences. 'When William came back after the summer it was a bit like treading on eggshells,' said a friend. 'Of course we wanted to offer our condolences, but it felt strange walking up to him after chapel and saying something. You also sensed William just wanted to forget the awfulness of what had happened. Many of us wrote letters and William was genuinely touched. After a few weeks everything went back to normal and people stopped talking about what was in the papers. William certainly didn't want to talk about it and we respected that.'

It was a crucial time for the teenage prince, who was studying for his GCSEs. He had a flair for history and enjoyed art, much to his father's delight. He threw himself into his work and became even more competitive in sports. He swam for the school team and represented Eton at football and rugby. His hard work paid off and William passed each of his twelve GCSEs with A grades in English, history and languages.

When he turned sixteen, his first birthday without his mother, he agreed to give his first interview. Given his previously tense relationship with the media, which had worsened almost irrevocably since his mother's death, there was to be no face-to-face meeting. William agreed to answer questions submitted by the Press Association to his father's aides at St James's Palace, but he gave little away. He had learned from his mother how dangerous it could be to say too much and was guarded in his responses. He was enjoying Eton, he said, but he did not much like being in the spotlight. Asked what he planned to study at A level, he revealed that he had a keen interest in art and would be taking biology, geography and the history of art, a subject he would fall out of love with years later. For now, however, it remained a passion, and during his A levels Dr Gailey arranged for William to spend a week doing work experience at Christie's auction house just a stone's throw from St James's Palace. William already knew some of the staff, having helped his mother coordinate the sale of her most famous dresses, which had raised £2 million for charity the June before she died. He had come up with the idea to raise money for the homeless, and Diana had thought it a wonderful idea.

On 2 September 1998, thirteen days ahead of his thirteenth birthday, Harry joined his brother at Eton. William, who had become increasingly camera shy, stayed away from the official photocall, leaving his brother and father, who had driven in his Vauxhall estate to Windsor, to greet the waiting media. Once Harry had taken tea with Dr Gailey and his wife Shauna in the ground-floor dining room of Manor House, where he would have breakfast, lunch and dinner for the next five years, William showed him around the games room and common room, a corridor away in the boys' living quarters. As one of Eton's more relaxed housemasters, Dr Gailey had set up a pool table, and allowed the boys to hang posters of their favourite film stars and models on the walls. In the common room, which was adorned with two oversized and rather scruffy sofas and a collection of plastic chairs positioned around a large TV, hung photographs of their peers in school plays and musicals together with trophies and medals they had won. William showed Harry around the locker room, where the F-tits kept their school books and outdoor boots. It was, noted Harry, very exposed and looked straight on to the street.

William was by now well established and popular at the school. He had a close set of friends who he trusted implicitly and who had become something of a second family to him. According to one former pupil William would often walk around the school with plaited hair. 'His friends would often plait his fringe, which had grown rather long, as a joke. When Robin Janvrin turned up to collect William in the blacked out Range Rover and take him home for the weekend he couldn't believe the state of him. It wasn't uncommon for William to be wearing someone else's pullover. He usually looked a bit of a mess.' As had become a pattern throughout their school days, Harry depended on his brother to help him make friends. Fortunately there were some familiar faces from Ludgrove, but it was William who helped his brother learn the drill at Manor House and get to grips with his ever-changing timetable. They were allowed to sign out on

Sundays after chapel, when they would walk across the bridge to McDonald's and catch the latest action movie at the cinema on Windsor High Street. 'None of us had much money and there wasn't much to do,' one of their housemates recalled. 'We would sometimes sneak to Windsor races, and when we were old enough go to the pub or meet up with some girls from St Mary's Ascot at a local coffee shop. There was no going out clubbing. We had to be back in our house by 8.15 p.m. on Sunday night otherwise there would be big trouble.'

It was not long before Harry was getting himself into just that. He was known as the classroom clown and during Latin would hide behind the floor-to-ceiling curtains giggling as his teacher repeatedly called out his name on the register. At the end of the class the mischievous prince would jump out just as his exasperated teacher Mr Andrew Maynard was preparing to report him absent. But Harry always had an excuse. 'You can't report me. I was here for the whole lesson, sir.' Another favourite trick involved balancing a book on the top of a door so that it fell on the beak's head when he entered the classroom. 'It was never a big enough book to do any damage, but it gave the beak a hell of a fright,' one of Harry's classmates recalled. 'Harry would be the one snorting with laughter, but he never got caught and no one ever ratted on him as we all liked him too much. The more invincible he realised he was, the more he played up.' But Harry's tomfoolery came with a price, and by the end of his second year he had slipped into the bottom group for nearly every subject.

It was Diana who had once remarked, 'Harry's the naughty one, just like me,' but by the summer of 2001 Harry's schoolboy pranks had escalated into something far more serious than class-room jinks. With Charles frequently away on business trips or tucked away at Birkhall, the Queen Mother's cottage on the edge of the Balmoral estate, with Camilla, Harry was left to his own devices. William had left Eton and was on his gap year, leaving Harry with the run of Highgrove. At the boys' request, Charles had agreed for the downstairs cellar to be transformed into a den for them. The cavernous hideaway, which the boys named Club H, consisted of two adjoining rooms with arched ceilings, a state-of-the-art sound system which piped music through the entire cellar, and two large cream sofas. In keeping with William and Harry's sense of humour, a portrait of their ancestor the Duke of Windsor, King Edward VIII, who abdicated from the throne in 1936, was hung in the loo.

The boys, who had asked for the walls to be painted black in one of the rooms so they could throw their own discos, would spend hours entertaining their friends, who were known as the Glosse Posse. This group comprised the young and privileged sons and daughters of wealthy landowners and aristocrats who lived close to Highgrove. Among the regulars were Tiggy's younger brother Harry Legge-Bourke and Luke, Mark and Emma Tomlinson, the children of Charles's close friends Simon and Claire, who ran the Beaufort Polo club. Harry Meade, son of Olympic gold medallist horseman Richard Meade, was also one of the gang.

William knew more girls than Harry, and his friend Davina Duckworth-Chad, whose mother Elizabeth was Diana's cousin, was part of the gang along with Natalie Hicks-Lobbecke, a former Warminster schoolgirl and the daughter of an army officer. While Natalie was linked in the press with William, it was actually a girl called Rose Farquhar who stole his heart during the summer after he left Eton. Part of the hunting and polo fraternity, Rose was the beautiful daughter of Captain Ian Farquhar, master of the Beaufort Hunt, and she and William had known each other since they were children. Rose was a pupil at the nearby Westonbirt School in Gloucestershire and was friends with Victoria Inskip, sister of one of William's best friends, Tom. When it came to girls, the notoriously shy prince was quite the romantic and uncharacteristically confident. He had abandoned his rather crass chat-up line, 'I'm a prince, wanna pull?' and instead spent the summer of the Millennium courting Rose with romantic afternoon strolls and picnics in the Gloucestershire countryside. Rumour has it that on one occasion the couple were stealing a private moment in a field when they were rudely interrupted by a farmer who stumbled across the young lovers.

'William and Rose had a summer romance and she still refers to him as her first true love,' recalled one of the 'Glosse Posse'. 'It was a long hot summer and William spent a lot of time at Highgrove and Rose was always around. She is a country girl at heart and they shared the same interests and the same friends. That summer they realised that they both actually rather liked each other and it was William who made the first move. It was a very sweet and innocent love affair and Rose still laughs about the time they got caught by a farmer in a field. They are still good friends and speak all the time.'

As a teenager Charles had had little interaction with his busy parents and he was determined to have a frank and open relationship with his sons. As they had no mother, he was expected to fulfil both roles and was determined to do his best. He knew his sons needed space but insisted on a no-smoking rule at Club H and alcohol was banned. It was, however, only a matter of time before Harry was discovering all sorts of illicit pleasures in the privacy of his very own underground club. He had his first puff of a cigarette on the sports fields at Eton, but the occasional smoke then become quite a habit and Harry was smoking Marlboro reds on a regular basis by the time he was sixteen. It was an aide who discovered his secret during the weekly clean-out at Club H, but an occasional cigarette was deemed normal enough, even though Charles abhorred the habit. More worryingly, Harry was also underage drinking, and had become a regular customer at the nearby Rattlebone Inn, a sixteenth-century pub in the village of Sherston six miles from Highgrove. While Harry would not be served – he was still only sixteen – his friends would buy him pints and chasers. At closing time they would return to Club H and continue the party. When the unmistakable smell of marijuana wafted from beneath the closed door, however, Charles was alerted.

Harry had no choice but to confess to his papa that he had spent much of the summer drinking and smoking pot. When Charles was fourteen he had got drunk on cherry brandy during a sailing trip to Stornoway with four friends, but he had never tried drugs. Both he and Diana had been staunchly against them and Charles could not believe that Harry was smoking marijuana. He questioned Harry's circle of friends and asked him, 'Are these really the right people to be hanging around with? Are these really the right things for you to be doing at sixteen in your position?' The truth was Harry had been taken to the Rattlebone by William, who was a regular, before he left for his gap-year trip to Africa. Unlike Harry he was old enough to drink the pub's potent Pheasant Plucker cider, and he had spent an afternoon with his friend Tom 'Skippy' Inskip and Emma Tomlinson drinking pints of snakebite, a mixture of cider and beer, which they downed while enjoying a rather un-regal burping competition.

It was only a matter of time before rumours of the illicit goings-on at the Rattlebone and Club H reached Fleet Street. Although every national newspaper had agreed shortly after Diana's death to protect William and Harry from unnecessary media intrusion, this was a story that warranted exposure. On 13 January 2002 the *News of the World* had gathered enough evidence to run the story and splashed HARRY'S DRUG SHAME across the front page. According to the report Harry had spent the previous summer drinking at the pub under the 'watchful' eye of his protection officers, who had been present at the all-night lock-ins. Marijuana had reportedly been smoked in the pub's run-down outhouse and in the backroom bar, which was known as the 'magic room'. On one occasion Harry was asked to leave after drunkenly calling the French bar manager Franck Ortet a 'fucking frog', which led to him being barred. 'Sometimes Harry would get drunk and say "Hey Froggie, get me a pint" and "Come here, Froggie",' Mr Ortet told the *Mail on Sunday*. 'When he was drinking in the pub some of our regulars would call him a little brat under their breaths. They thought it was wrong that there was a prince sitting in their pub drinking underage and raising his voice.'

According to aides working for Charles at the time, there were several damage-limitation meetings between St James's Palace and executive editors from the *News of the World* before the story ran. Mark Dyer, Charles's former equerry and a former Welsh Guards officer who had become close to the boys, was present together with Charles's private secretary Sir Stephen Lamport, his press adviser Colleen Harris and Mark Bolland. Together they convinced the newspaper to run 'the least damaging story possible', and after issuing an apology it was decided that Harry would spend a day visiting Featherstone Lodge, a drugs rehabilitation centre in Peckham, south London.

The Palace tried its hardest to bury the story but inevitably Charles's parenting was called into question. Diana's death was still fresh in people's minds, and if anyone was to blame it was Charles, who, the newspapers pointed out, had been away from Highgrove for most of the summer. Harry was behaving like any other teenager, and given the tragedy of his childhood it was quite remarkable that he had not come unhinged earlier. It was not just the newspapers who were critical; according to one aide the Queen and Prince Philip were 'in despair' when they were informed of the story.

Fortunately Harry escaped an official police warning but the incident sent shock waves through the royal family. It was also the catalyst for the first serious rift between William and Harry, who resented the fact that he had been blamed for everything while William had got away scot-free. It had after all been William who first introduced him to the Rattlebone, and he had hardly been a model of decorum during some of the locks-ins. William, as usual, had come out smelling of roses. The suggestion that the second-in-line to the throne should be caught up in such a scandal was unthinkable; instead it was Harry who took the flak and had to suffer the indignity of being front-page news, together with William's best friend Guy Pelly, the son of a landowning family in Kent and a student at the nearby Royal Agricultural College in Cirencester, who was unfairly blamed by the newspapers for introducing Harry to cannabis. According to one former aide, 'The Palace had to be seen to protect Charles and William, so it was Harry who took the stick. It was decided that Guy Pelly would shoulder the blame and Harry would be named but not William.' No one reported the fact that the weekend the story broke, William, Harry and Guy Pelly were all together at Highgrove – although the princes were barely on speaking terms.

It was left to William to smooth the situation over, and several weeks later he went to see Harry at Eton with his protection officer and Mark Bolland. 'William felt guilty that his brother had taken all the blame while he had come out as Mr Goody Two Shoes. For the first time their relationship really suffered and they barely spoke,' recalled a former aide. 'Harry resented the fact that William had got away so lightly. In the end he forgave William because it wasn't really William's fault, but it took some time. Harry was reeling for a while.'

It was once again the ever-faithful Tiggy and the Van Cutsem family who came to Charles's rescue. From now on when Charles was away, it was agreed that Harry would stay at Anmer Hall, the Van Cutsems' ten-bedroom home in Norfolk. Or sometimes Harry would go to his father's friend Helen Asprey, who now works in the princes' private office at St James's Palace. Most of all he loved staying with Tiggy at the Legge-Bourkes' eighteenth-century family home, Penmyarth House in south Wales. Charles adored Tiggy and her parents – Shan, a former lady-in-waiting to the Princess Royal and her merchant banker husband William. With the Legge-Bourkes there was no time for trouble; they were too busy fishing in the River Usk and exploring the 4,000-acre estate. 'Tiggy was an inspired choice,' recalled Lady Elizabeth Anson, who knows the Legge-Bourke family well. 'She was fantastic with William and Harry. She comes from an outstanding home and a really wonderful family. The boys would have huge amounts of fun when they stayed at her family house in Wales and they were always welcome.' Indeed Harry and Tiggy were so fond of each other that years later when she married former army officer Charles Pettifer she asked him to be godfather to her son Fred.

It was not just to Tiggy that Charles turned to for guidance. Camilla Parker Bowles also had first-hand experience in such matters: her son Tom had been caught in possession of cannabis while reading English at Oxford and was trapped into offering cocaine to an undercover reporter in 1999 while working as a publicist at the Cannes Film Festival. Camilla was in an excellent position to offer Charles sound advice, according to Mark Bolland, who helped coordinate Harry's trip to Featherstone Lodge. 'Of course Camilla recognised the need for the boys to have a strong father figure in their life especially in the years after Diana's death and she encouraged him to spend as much time on his own with them as he could. She was aware of the difficulties of raising teenagers and she was a big support for Charles during this period.' By now Camilla had met William and Harry, which despite everyone's nerves, had gone smoothly. It was Friday 12 June 1998 and just nine days before his sixteenth birthday when William first met his father's mistress. He had returned to St James's Palace after his final GCSE exam and was on his way to the cinema to meet some friends.

Camilla, who was by now a permanent fixture at the prince's London residence, was also at the palace, and Charles, aware that a meeting had to happen at some point, asked William if he wanted to meet Camilla. It had not yet been a year since Diana's death, and while he was still deeply protective of his mother's memory, curiosity got the better of him. Camilla was so nervous that she needed a stiff vodka and tonic afterwards, according to the *Daily Mail*'s royal correspondent Richard Kay, but the thirty-minute meeting was so successful that William suggested that he and Camilla should meet again by themselves for afternoon tea.

While his mother had blamed Camilla for the breakdown of her marriage, William got along well with his father's mistress. They kept to small talk but William discovered he had rather a lot in common with Camilla. She was down-to-earth, and her sense of humour appeared to have rubbed off on his father, who seemed happier than he had been in years. William and Camilla both loved the countryside and shared a passion for riding and fox-hunting – which they agreed should not be banned. William had also become friendly with Camilla's children, who were several years older than him and Harry. Tom was a former Etonian and Oxford graduate while Laura had finished school and taken a gap year. William had been fascinated by her tales of travelling around South America when they were all at Birkhall that Easter. They had not always got along well, and William and Laura used to have terrible fights over who was to blame for their broken homes. According to one family friend of the Parker Bowleses, when Charles telephoned Camilla at the family home in Wiltshire, Laura would pick up an extension and shout down the receiver, 'Why don't you stop calling Mummy and leave our family alone.' She couldn't care less that it was the Prince of Wales; she blamed him for breaking up her parents' marriage and was not afraid to tell William so. 'William would blame Camilla for all the hurt she had caused his mother, which would send Laura into a rage,' revealed a family friend. 'Laura was not having any of it. She would take a hard line and fire back at William, "Your father has ruined my life."' According to school-friends, Laura – like her brother Tom – was teased mercilessly when intimate conversations between Charles and Camilla ended up in the British press. But if anyone could relate to this it was William. He had suffered a similar humiliation, and when they stopped blaming one another's parents and let go of their painful pasts, Laura and William got along well.

A few weeks later it was Harry's turn to meet Camilla, this time at Highgrove, with his father and brother on hand to break the ice. Camilla would later say that she thought Harry had looked at her 'suspiciously', which was probably true. Tiggy Legge-Bourke could not bear Camilla, and picked up where Diana had left off in the war with Charles's mistress. Camilla, who reportedly infuriated Tiggy by referring to her as 'hired help', resented the time she spent with Charles and the boys. It was Tiggy who took the boys rock climbing; Tiggy who accompanied them to Klosters, where she was famously photographed kissing Charles after a demanding ski run; and Tiggy who was the only other person the Prince of Wales allowed to smoke in his company. Eventually it would be Camilla who emerged victorious, when the boys' former nanny was snubbed from Charles's fiftieth birthday party, which William and Harry helped organise. The following summer Camilla and her children were invited on their first 'family holiday' with the Waleses to Greece, where they spent a week aboard the *Alexander*. It had been William's idea and was a major breakthrough. Finally the path had been paved for Charles to be with the woman he loved, but it would be many years before he would make her his wife.

Back at Eton, Harry was working hard to live up to his big brother's reputation: he was still in William's shadow even though he had left the school. Unlike William he had not made it into Pop, the school's prestigious society for sixth formers. William had been one of the society's most popular members, and while he had had the authority to hand out punishments to fellow pupils he rarely did. One of his jobs involved keeping watch on Windsor Bridge for any boys leaving pubs. Drinking was forbidden unless you were in the top year, when you were allowed to drink at Eton's 'tap bar', but more often than not William turned a blind eye and told the boarders to hurry on home and avoid the housemaster. Although he didn't smoke he rarely punished boys he caught illicitly smoking on the sports pitches. 'William was pretty cool and he wouldn't hand out detentions and punishments even though he could,' a friend recalled. 'He was very easy-going and very humble; he didn't go around using his title to get him anywhere, if anything he downplayed it. If people made a deal about who he was he would colour up and move the conversation away from him. He just wanted to be William and like everyone else.'

Harry was the same, and the one place he could be himself was in the Combined Cadet Force, the CCF. Both he and William signed up for the army section. The Duke of Wellington once said, 'The Battle of Waterloo was won on the playing fields of Eton', and the school has produced generations of first-class cadets. Unlike William, Harry missed out on the prestigious sword of honour, but he was promoted to lance corporal in October 2002 and led a detachment of forty-eight cadets in Eton's respected Tattoo. Instead of spending weekends alone at Club H getting up to no good, Harry now preferred to be leading his platoon on training exercises. According to one of the cadets under Harry Wales's charge, the prince took the training more seriously than most:

Harry knew what he was talking about and he didn't take any rubbish. He was very good about motivating us and he cared about his men and wanted us to do well in drill test. He told us to sleep with our guns in our sleeping bags so we were always ready for action. He was known for jumping out of bushes when we were on night watches to keep us on our toes. I remember being on watch and hearing a rustle in the bushes. We all thought it was Harry mucking around, but when ten squaddies jumped out and wrestled us to the ground, we got the shock of our lives. From the other bush we could just hear snorting, which was Harry having a laugh.

Harry also let off steam playing the Eton wall game, a sport exclusive to Eton that is both lawless and dangerous and involves two scrums of ten and a leather ball. A goal has not been recorded since before the First World War, but Harry gave it his best shot. 'You had to be prepared for a beating especially when you were playing against Harry,' one of his teammates told me. 'He was totally fearless and very aggressive when he played. It earned him a lot of respect at Eton because he was able to show he could look after himself. He turned up at Eton a slightly scrawny boy of about five feet and he left having shot up to about six feet with a lot more muscle.' Harry did not escape unscathed: he broke his nose playing rugby when he was sixteen and spent several weeks on crutches a year later after damaging his ankle.

While his concerned teachers had warned that Harry was on his way to failing academically, he managed to pass his GCSEs with respectable grades but struggled with his A levels. After failing his mocks, he eventually dropped a subject, but Harry didn't care. He had ruled out going to university and set his heart on attending Sandhurst, the prestigious Royal Military Academy, but he still needed two A-level passes to get in.

Chapter 7

A gap-year prince but a reluctant king

I loved my gap year and wish I could have another one.
Prince William

Charles sighed in exasperation and noted how determined and extremely stubborn his elder son could be. Not for the first time the two were at loggerheads, and the topic dividing father and son as they stood in the drawing room of St James's Palace was that of William's gap year. It was the summer of the Millennium, and William could not contain his excitement about the twelve months of freedom ahead of him. He and Harry had just had the best summer of their lives, part of which they had spent in Rock, a pretty seaside town in Cornwall. The princes and a group of friends had spent an idyllic fortnight swimming and surfing off the Cornish coast, meeting girls and sampling the beer on tap at the Oystercatcher pub. Now the issue of what William planned to do for the next year could be postponed no longer.

The eighteen-year-old prince had spoken to his friends Luke and Mark Tomlinson about travelling to Argentina to play polo for a season. By now he was an accomplished player like his father, and he wanted to improve his game. From there he intended to join a group of schoolfriends who were backpacking in South America. He had gone to his father to talk about his master plan, and to his anger Charles had vetoed the suggestion. 'It's not fair,'

William complained. 'Everyone else is allowed to go backpacking, why can't I?' He knew full well that he was not like everyone else but the disappointment still weighed heavily on him. He had told his father he had no plans to do work experience in London. 'I didn't want to sit around and get a job back in London,' William later admitted. 'I wanted to get out and see a bit of the world.' On that issue Charles was in full agreement, but the trip had to be vocational, educational and safe. The very idea of the second-in-line to the throne backpacking around a foreign continent was unthinkable. As was often the case in such situations Charles, who has always hated any sort of confrontation with either of his sons, decided to seek advice, and he assured William that a solution would be found.

Charles empathised with his son's frustration. He was desperate for William to have more fun than he had had at that age. When Charles left Gordonstoun, he went straight to Cambridge and then into the armed forces. For him a gap year had been totally out of the question, and Charles had hated the limitations of a life dictated solely by duty. 'You can't understand what it is like to have your whole life mapped out for you,' he had said. 'It's so awful to be programmed.' He was far more relaxed with William than his own parents were with him. He had surprised William when he presented him with a motorbike on his eighteenth birthday that June. 'My father is concerned about the fact that I'm into motorbikes but he doesn't want to keep me all wrapped up in cotton wool,' said William. 'You might as well live if you're going to live. It's just something I'm passionate about.' The fact that William can ride around London without being recognised is still one of his greatest thrills. But although

Charles was lenient in some areas, he was adamant that his son's gap year had to be carefully organised. He enlisted a group of dignitaries to help him plan a suitable year for his son. The group comprised the Bishop of London the Right Reverend Richard Chartres, who has been a part of Charles's advisory panel since their days at Cambridge, former cabinet minister and governor of Hong Kong Chris Patten, William's housemaster at Eton Dr Andrew Gailey and Dr Eric Anderson, who had been Charles's tutor at Gordonstoun and was provost at Eton.

It was agreed that William should get his wish of going to South America, but the trip would have to entail voluntary work, not polo. He would also visit Rodrigues, a paradise island in the Indian Ocean, and revisit Kenya, where he had been three years earlier for a three-and-a-half-month safari. In addition he would do some work experience in the UK, including on a farm near Highgrove. But before all that, it was decided that William would travel to the Belize jungle to join the Welsh Guards on exercise. As the future head of the armed services, he would be expected to have had a career in the military, and a week of training in the jungles of Central America would be an excellent, albeit harsh, introduction.

William took part in an operation code-named Native Trail, which was the toughest expedition of his life to date and made the CCF look easy. Sandwiched between Guatemala and the Caribbean Sea, Belize is hot, humid and dangerous. Temperatures in the jungle rarely dip below thirty degrees Celsius and it is almost permanently wet. William had little time to acclimatise before he was driven deep into the jungle by Winston Harris, a Belizean who had been made an MBE for his work training the SAS in jungle tactics. It was like nothing William had ever experienced before. The jungle was lush, wet and full of snakes, crocodiles and infection-transmitting insects.

His uncle Prince Edward had spent a week there with 40 Commando in 1985 and had found it a daunting experience. William was no different. He struggled with the heat and there was the constant danger of malaria. The young prince's first survival skills were learning how to treat a snake bite and kill a chicken for food. William didn't flinch when he was told to wring the bird's neck – his grandmother had shown him exactly how to do it – although it was the first time he had had to cut a bird's feet off using a machete. Corporal Claud Martinez of the Belizean Defence Force, who took part in the exercises with William, said, 'The prince would make a good soldier. He has the physical structure and mental strength. He was surrounded by men firing machine guns and he still looked at ease. I never saw a moment of panic on his face.' It was training that would serve William in good stead and made him realise just how much he loved army life. The only reminder of home was when Charles emailed William his A-level results. He had got an A in geography, a B in history of art and a C in biology. William breathed a deep sigh of relief. He had the grades he needed to enrol at St Andrews University in Scotland, where he had applied to study the history of art.

Now he could really enjoy his gap year, and after the discomfort of the mosquito-infested rainforest of Belize he was delighted to be heading to Rodrigues, a stunning island off the coast of Mauritius. William flew to the island on a chartered aircraft with Mark Dyer, a former member of the Welsh Guards and former equerry to the Prince of Wales who had become a ubiquitous presence on the prince's gap year, as he would on Harry's. William had enjoyed geography at school, and the trip, which was partly organised by the Royal Geographical Society, had been billed as an opportunity to learn how to protect the area's endangered coral reefs. In truth it was more of a holiday, and William travelled around the nine-mile-long island on a rusty Honda 125cc motorbike meeting the locals and teaching them how to play rugby as well as fish more safely. William, in shorts, T-shirt and flip-flops, loved the anonymity of the trip and checked in as 'Brian Woods' at Le Domaine de Decide, a small and basic resort where he stayed for a month. He had no need to worry about being recognised; there were no photographers on the island. William was left in peace to enjoy the simplicity of living in a spartan hut with a corrugated-iron roof and two single beds for twenty-six pounds a night. Years later he would return to the paradise island with a young lady called Kate Middleton.

On his return from Rodrigues, William came back to reality with a thud. It was the end of September, and before he left for Chile he had to give his first-ever solo press conference. As part of the deal with the media, who had promised to leave William alone during his gap year, the prince had agreed to speak to a cross section of print and broadcasting press from around the world to update them on his trip. It was not something the eighteen-year-old prince was looking forward to, but fortunately his debut press conference, on a warm afternoon on 29 September 2000 in the gardens of Highgrove, went smoothly. While Charles appeared in a suit, William chose to dress down in jeans, his favourite Burberry sweater and North Face trainers. He was understandably nervous and uncomfortable.

William had become increasingly wary of the press following his mother's death and rarely gave interviews. His last official photocall had been when he agreed to give royal photographer Ian Jones unprecedented access during his final months at Eton. Jones recalled William's interest in his occupation and said, 'William had always had photographers in his life and he was curious about our methods. He learned a lot when we worked together.' William had indeed learned a lot and had become adept at spotting the paparazzi, who often lurked in bushes. He had picked up a few tricks from his grandfather, who was known to stalk the grounds of Sandringham at Christmas in search of prying photographers. When Philip eventually found them he would rap on the steamed-up windows of their cars with his walking stick and enquire, 'Having a good snoop, are we?'

While William reluctantly accepted that being in the limelight would always be an integral part of his life he disliked being the centre of attention and said, 'I feel uncomfortable with it.' He was also, he announced, unhappy that his late mother had not been allowed to rest in peace. Since her death there had been a deluge of books, many penned by Diana's trusted former aides, which had upset the princes. At the time their mother's former private secretary Patrick Jephson's memoirs were the subject of a sensational serialisation in a Sunday newspaper. Even in Rodrigues William had been kept abreast of Jephson's revelations, and when asked about them during the press conference he said, 'Harry and I are both quite upset about it – that our mother's trust has been betrayed and that, even now, she is still being exploited.'

He was, however, delighted to be setting off for Patagonia, where he would be taking part in environmental and community projects organised by Raleigh International. He had wanted to go somewhere hot, and while it was not the polo-playing adventure he had dreamed of, those ten weeks in Chile would be one of the most incredible experiences of William's life so far. His fellow volunteers were from all walks of life and a world away from William's sheltered upbringing at the palace. Some were reformed drug addicts while others had served time in prison. Whatever their backgrounds, their tasks were the same, and everyone was expected to get stuck in. There was to be no special treatment for William, and he raised £5,500 in sponsorship. 'I organised a water polo match and got sponsors. I also raised money for a disadvantaged person to come on the expedition with me.'

On 1 October 2000 William boarded a British Airways plane from Gatwick to Santiago. Knowing there would be few luxuries in Patagonia, he happily accepted the offer of an upgrade to first class. He had deliberately chosen to fly out separately from his fellow volunteers to avoid the inevitable send-off by the world's media, who had gathered at Heathrow hoping to wave the prince off. It was only when he was safely on the ground in Santiago that William met a handful of the hundred volunteers with whom he would be spending the next ten weeks. While William was sensibly dressed in the navy-blue Raleigh International fleece which was to become his second skin, Mark Dyer stood out like a sore thumb in a Savile Row suit. William was nervous as he chatted with the small group who had been selected to meet him in the VIP room, but having Ali G, his favourite comedian, on the television broke the ice.

William was immediately popular as for safety reasons the uncomfortable and dangerous two-day road trip to Coyhaique, Raleigh International's headquarters, had been abandoned in favour of a flight to Balmaceda in a plane chartered by the Prince of Wales. Sandwiched between his protection officer and Dyer in the emergency exit seats, William fidgeted nervously during the three-hour flight over the Andes. Inside the terminal at Balmaceda, as he waited to collect his bags, which were covered in 'Priority VIP' labels, he pulled his baseball cap over his face. He was worried there would be press waiting for him outside but as he walked through the sliding doors, there was not a photographer in sight. The prince removed his cap and smiled at Dyer. It was his first moment of gap-year freedom.

When the group arrived at Coyhaique they were exhausted, but there was no time to rest; they had to acclimatise at Field Base, a tented camp surrounded by mountains and miles of barren countryside. The only clue that there was a VIP among the group was the four open-top military jeeps parked at the camp's entrance. Up the hill there was a wooden shelter where foodstuffs and equipment were stored and another smaller outhouse where the group would eat. There was also a small kiosk that opened once a day, where William would buy packets of chocolate-chip cookies. They would be sleeping under canvas, and William, who had elected to share his tent with two girls, gallantly ran to bag the best pitch. The main house was not open to the volunteers, although William was allowed to make urgent calls home to England. For everyone else the solitary telephone box outside the main house sufficed. There was an outside wash-house with communal showers, but they would only have the luxury of a hot shower once a month. The prince insisted on showering alone, even though this meant waiting until the end when most of the hot water had run out. On one occasion he left his Cartier watch in the shower cubicle and was inconsolable until it was found. It was not just that the watch was expensive; it had been given to him by his mother who had engraved William's name on it and he was never without it.

Like everyone else William was expected to get involved in the ice-breaking games, although the name-learning exercise, which entailed every volunteer being carried without being dropped, was farcical. 'Wills! Wills! Wills!' the group shouted as they manhandled the future king to the end of the line. Then there were tests of physical endurance. William was told he had to carry his chosen partner from one end of the field to the other. As he watched his new friends struggle to carry each other across the camp, he invited his female companion to stand on his steel-capped boots, hold on tight and allow him to walk them both across the field. The idea caught on, and by the end of the exercise everyone was copying the resourceful royal.

Proving that he could swim ahead of the fortnight of sea kayaking was never going to be a problem. What William hadn't counted on, however, was the group of photographers that suddenly appeared out of nowhere as he made his way to the lake where they were to be assessed. He had only known his fellow volunteers for a matter of days, but they immediately surrounded him so that not even the longest lens could catch a glimpse. That single action immediately earned the prince's trust. They may not have had much in common, but if these boys and girls could demonstrate such loyalty before the end of the first week, William was more than happy to give everyone a chance. Eventually the photographers gave up and the prince was free to strip off and dive into the lake, where he effortlessly completed the required 500-metre swimming test. William had been looking forward to the kayaking, the first part of the expedition, and had read up on the dramatic Patagonian coastline.

The group would be living in total isolation and camping in the wild. They had come well prepared and carried all the equipment they would need. The first week tested everyone's resolve, and at one point William, like the others, just wanted to come home. The weather had closed in and it rained for days. They tried their hardest to entertain themselves, but their spirits flagged and William spent most of his time in his tent. 'The wind whipped up into a storm. The tents were flapping so violently that we thought they were going to blow away,' he said afterwards. 'Everything was soaked through. I had never seen rain like it. It was so heavy and it just did not stop. It was quite demoralising even though we managed to keep ourselves going by singing and stuff like that. I don't think I have ever been as low as that. Everyone was thinking, why did I choose to come here?'

During those rain-soaked days he lay in his tent reading the best-seller *Bravo Two Zero*, about an SAS mission in Iraq during the First Gulf War, and listening to his portable CD player. His cousin Zara had recorded him a compilation which kicked off with Manu Chao's 'Bongo Bong', which always made him smile. He became a diligent letter writer and would spend hours writing to his family, especially the Queen, whose letters would always begin, 'Dearest Grandmama'. When William came across a fisherman at one of the deep ocean fjords, he would use his best

GCSE Spanish to ask if they could post the letters for him. He would provide enough money for a postage stamp and the fisherman's trouble, and with every faith in the locals handed over his most private correspondence. He could only hope that the letters would make it back home, and miraculously they all did.

William, who was meticulous about making sure his rucksack was always carefully packed and knew where everything was stored, even in the middle of the night, discovered the best way to keep dry and warm was to wear a pair of socks with his sandals. It looked ridiculous, but everyone followed suit. His supply of chocolate-chip cookies also lifted everyone's mood even if it meant piling on a few extra pounds. 'We felt very fat,' he recalled. For the prince, who starts every morning with a short exercise routine, it was a relief when the clouds cleared and made way for blue skies. With the weather much improved, he began his routine with a brief yoga session. William knew some positions from his mother, who practised yoga regularly at Kensington Palace, and his father, who used to train with yoga guru Dr Masaraf Ali. William believes yoga is excellent for the mind and body and still practises today when he has time. Before breakfast, which was always the same lumpy grey porridge cooked over the camp stove, William would teach some of the group how to hold certain positions.

'William would be on his ground mat in his thermal longjohns every morning,' one of the group recalled.

We all felt a bit lazy from sitting around doing nothing because of the weather so we joined in. He would show us how to get into different poses. He knew a lot about yoga and said he practised at home. He was incredibly good at it and was able to hold some of the most advanced positions for minutes on end. He was also an excellent masseur and would often give some of the girls a back rub at the end of the day. He said he and his father benefited from regular massage.

Having their muscles manipulated by the future king proved too much for some of the girls, who descended into fits of giggles.

At the end of the first month it was time for William and his group to spend three weeks tracking and monitoring huemul, an indigenous species of deer that roam the plains of Patagonia. One of their jobs was to shoot the deer with tranquiliser darts and tag them to monitor the population. Trained by the best guns at Balmoral, William was an excellent shot and the best tagger in the group. The rolling hills and expansive scenery, he observed, were not dissimilar to the Scottish Highlands. He was at peace in the beautiful countryside, truly happy and relaxed. For the first and only time in his life he removed the electronic tag around his neck. Surrounded by the snow-capped mountains and with only the huemul for company, there was simply no need for it. William took great delight in ripping it off.

That same night it was bitterly cold, and as the group sat together on the side of a mountain, huddled around the camp-fire, arms linked for extra warmth, the conversation turned to William. The others had spent the past hour discussing what they planned to do when they returned home. Some had places at universities, others had further adventures to look forward to. William quietly listened to their excited chatter. 'You're all so lucky,' he said as the flames flickered across his face. 'I don't have much choice about my future. One day I will be king, and to be honest I'm not much interested in that at all at the moment.'

Silence enveloped the group and the only sound to fill the chilly air was the crackling of the fire. No one quite knew what to say. They all knew who he was, but to them he was just William. In the breathtakingly beautiful mountains of Chile he had had many hours to contemplate his fate and future, and it had dawned on him that this was as normal as his life would ever be. He was on a gap year with a group of people he would never ordinarily have met, in the middle of nowhere, with no sense of commitment or responsibility. 'William just came out with it. There were only a few of us there, and we were all quite shocked,' recalled a fellow volunteer. 'I remember feeling desperately sorry for him. He was a big strapping boy, but he suddenly seemed so vulnerable. We had all formed a very close bond and he obviously felt as though he could open up. I think he saw his future as a huge burden. He knows what his life will be one day and that his freedom would be short-lived.'

For his whole life William had done everything in his power to be ordinary, and was not yet ready for the spotlight. He had had a taste of it in Canada the March after Diana's death, when Charles had taken him and Harry away for a holiday which had also included a few public engagements. The young prince had been met by screaming teenage girls, and while Harry had laughed at his brother's newfound status as a royal heart-throb, William had flown into a rage and vowed never to go on a walkabout again. Of course, he was young and at a difficult age, but 'Wills mania', as it was referred to in the press, had terrified him, and when he turned eighteen he announced he had no intention of taking on public engagements. 'My father wants me to finish full-time education before doing royal duties and so do I. It will be a few years before I do royal engagements, although I expect, as in the past, I will sometimes accompany my father.'

Right now he wanted to be known simply as William, and like his mother he had his own ideas when it came to protocol. Those who know him well say fear of the future is why William lives for the present. He himself admits that he prefers to take one day at a time rather than worry about what the future holds. 'The biggest things he has to deal with are his past and his future,' one of his closest friends explained. 'That's why he enjoys the present so much. He makes an effort to enjoy every day to the full.' Years later, when he turned twenty-one, William acknowledged for the first time in his life the responsibility of his birthright. 'It's not a question of wanting to be; it's something I was born into, and it's my duty . . . Sometimes I do get anxious about it, but I don't really worry a lot.'

William sat on the steps outside the only supermarket in Coyhaique basking in the late-morning sunshine, enjoying the treat which he had promised himself once he had finished his back-breaking task building wooden walkways in the small unspoilt coastal town of Tortel in the heart of Patagonia. The rotisserie chicken smelled delicious, and William tore off chunks of flesh and ate them hungrily – it had been weeks since he had eaten meat, he had been surviving on biscuits, tinned tuna, beans and rice. The hard work was finally out of the way and William was looking forward to going home. He had spent the past month sleeping on the floor of a disused nursery which the volunteers had nicknamed the Hotel Tortel. It was basic, but far more comfortable than a cold and damp ground-mat.

It was the penultimate day of the expedition and everyone was in a good mood. William had made a trip to the store to stock up on some snacks for the party being held at the camp that night. The Raleigh International team leaders had planned a fancy-dress bash, and always the first to dive into the dressing-up cupboard, William had already planned his outfit. Before he left he wanted to sample a local bar and had arranged for his protection officer, SAS-trained Dominic Ryan, to drive him and six of his friends to the outskirts of the town later that day. They settled for a run-down bar, where they ordered litres of cheap red wine and lager on tap.

William, who prefers red wine to beer, had not had a drink for months, and although the wine was rather sharp it went down well. As they sat drinking a noise at the window startled them. Outside three local and rather short photographers were jumping up and down trying to get a picture of William. Suddenly the door swung open and they rushed inside only to be promptly ejected by Dominic, who removed each by the scruff of his neck. The curtains were drawn and the group was left to enjoy themselves in peace. As the drink flowed, the antics became more outrageous, and it was William's idea to incorporate a basket of fresh eggs on the bar into their drinking games. Carefully he placed the eggs in the pockets of his trousers and the others took turns to hurl missiles at him. Several hours and too many drinks later they returned to camp worse for wear and covered in egg yolk. William, who had decided to go to the party as Superman, changed into his thermals and used his poncho for a cape. After borrowing a pair of pants from one of the girls, which he wore over his longjohns, he headed for the party.

According to several of the volunteers he spent the evening 'dancing like a lunatic' before launching himself onto the row of tents at the end of the night. The following morning he left as he had arrived, quietly and separately. Mark Dyer had flown back to Santiago to collect his charge, who was feeling particularly wretched thanks to the cheap Chilean wine that William had nicknamed 'cat's piss'. As he was fast-tracked into the VIP lounge at Santiago, he readily accepted the upgrade to first class and slept solidly on the flight back home.

Chapter 8

School's out for Harry

I want to carry on the things that she [Diana] didn't quite finish. I have always wanted to, but was too young.
Prince Harry on his eighteenth birthday

While William was enjoying his gap year, Harry was counting down the days until the end of school. He had been in regular contact with his brother and longed to share William's adventure but he had A levels to pass first. Unsurprisingly the teenage prince was more interested in having fun than knuckling down, and it was no great surprise when he failed two of his AS levels at the start of his final year. Harry had planned to take geography, art and the history of art, but eventually dropped the latter. Although he had always been in the lowest stream, he was teased over his poor grades and further humiliated when his tutors insisted he joined the year below to catch up. But even that didn't prove sufficient motivation for Harry to start working.

It was May 2003 and just weeks ahead of his crucial A-level exams when Harry and his friend Guy Pelly, who was still a regular guest at Highgrove, sneaked off to the Royal Berkshire Polo Club in Windsor. Guy, who had a reputation for mooning, something Harry had also taken up in an attempt to put off the tourists who congregated on the street outside Manor House, decided to climb to the top of a forty-foot-high VIP marquee and strip naked. With Harry in tow it sparked a major security alert, and when he returned to Manor House there were stern words from Dr Gailey. None of the boys were allowed out after hours during exam time and Harry had flouted the rules. Charles called his son to voice his concern and the following morning Harry's illicit excursion was front-page news under the headline SO HARRY, HOW'S YOUR A-LEVEL REVISION GOING? The answer was it wasn't going well at all, and the prince was on his way to failing his two remaining subjects. It seemed that no matter how many times he had his wrists slapped, Harry would not learn.

I witnessed Harry's partying first hand that spring. I was a young show business reporter at the time for the *Mail on Sunday* and happened to be covering an event at the Kensington Roof Gardens, which is conveniently located just opposite the newspaper's Derry Street offices in west London. I had gone outside onto the terrace for a breath of fresh air and to admire the restaurant's famous flamingos when Harry suddenly emerged from the VIP room. Although it was April it was cool, and as I stood shivering in the night air, Harry waved me in. 'You look freezing,' he said as he tried to light his cigarette in the wind. 'Do come and join my party.' His protection officers were seated at a coffee table at the far end of the room while Harry sat on the floor surrounded by eight pretty girls all clinging to his every word. One of his friends fetched me a glass of champagne while Harry held court. The subject of exams was only mentioned in passing; instead it was plans for the summer that were being excitedly discussed. As he smoked one cigarette down to the filter before lighting another, Harry announced that it was going to be a summer of fun. The fact that it was well after midnight on a Thursday didn't seem to matter to anyone.

He was only eighteen, but his confidence was impressive. He was clearly very sociable, and as he sipped his vodka and cranberry it was obvious that he was relaxed and self-assured among girls. He had recently been voted Britain's most eligible bachelor by society magazine *Harper's Bazaar*, which cemented his standing among the social elite, not that he needed a poll to prove he was popular. Harry was never short of female admirers and had started dating Laura Gerard-Leigh, the pretty eighteen-year-old daughter of a wealthy stockbroker who lived in Wiltshire.

The couple had been introduced through Guy Pelly, and Laura quickly became part of the princes' Gloucestershire set. She was a good match for Harry: she loved the outdoors and in May the couple allowed themselves to be photographed at the Badminton Horse Trials. As they sat chatting on the lawn, it was clear from their body language that they were an item. The story, which ran on page 7 of the *Mail on Sunday*, was a great exclusive. Although she didn't have aristocratic links like most members of the Glosse Posse, Laura came from 'good stock' and lived in a sprawling mill house in the village of Calne, which was a two-hour drive from Eton. 'They have an awful lot in common and share a boisterous sense of humour,' remarked one of their mutual friends. 'He seems to be quite serious at this point.'

A pupil at St Mary's school in Calne, Laura would drive to Eton to watch Harry play the wall game at weekends and afterwards they would go for Sunday lunch in Windsor. Harry was barred from bringing girls back to Manor House, so every few weekends, accompanied by a protection officer, they would stay at

Laura's parents' London town house in Parsons Green. Although the relationship fizzled out after just four months the pair remained close, and the following July (2004) they were seen kissing at the Cartier International Day at the Guards Polo Club, the social event of the summer.

Harry was conscious that he was known as 'hooray Harry' in the press and used his eighteenth birthday in September 2002 to attempt to dispel what he perceived to be the myth of his playboy antics. 'The attention-seeker going too far, too soon, too often' warned the royal commentators of the day. Harry disagreed and used his first official press interview to argue that his critics were wrong. He was not, he insisted, just a party animal. He had seen his Uncle Andrew labelled a playboy and his Aunt Margaret a bon vivant in her heyday, and he was determined not to be stereotyped as the royal rebel. There was far more to him than just partying, and to prove his point he spent the days leading up to his birthday visiting sick children at Great Ormond Street Hospital in London. While it may have been a carefully orchestrated PR exercise, there was no mistaking Harry's natural ease in the role. He was tactile and down-to-earth and able to make the sickest children laugh. While William tended to be nervous in front of the cameras, Harry managed to joke with the photographers while making sure the importance of his visit was relayed. He hoped to continue his late mother's charity work. 'I want to carry on the things that she didn't quite finish. I have always wanted to, but was too young.' These were powerful words. After all, the public had seen remarkably little of Harry since he walked in his mother's cortège when he was just thirteen. By his eighteenth birthday he had grown into an articulate, confident and handsome young man. On the advice of his father's advisers at Clarence House, he also apologised for his drug-taking and underage drinking. 'That was a mistake and I learned my lesson.' It would not be long before Harry was apologising again.

The day had finally arrived. Harry carefully placed the black and white portrait of his mother taken by Mario Testino for *Vanity Fair* in his trunk. It was 12 June 2003, his final day at Eton, and Harry had almost finished packing up the debris of the last five years. The sun streamed through his window as he peeled his favourite poster of the Whistler ski resort in Canada with the slogan 'Great skiing with you' from the wall. He placed it carefully in his ottoman along with his Indian wall hanging and his St George's flag. Polo stick in hand, he said a fond farewell to the room that had been his home and made his way down the stairs to say his goodbyes.

The boy who had walked through Eton's famous entrance holding his father's hand was now a young man. Casually dressed in a blazer, shirt and baggy chinos with a St George's cross on the belt buckle, Harry strode out of Manor House. Carrying his clothes in a black bin bag he walked across Windsor Bridge for the last time. 'Yes!' he shouted, punching the air. He was finally free.

The Palace wasted no time announcing that he would be applying to the Royal Military Academy at Sandhurst, thus becoming the first senior royal to join the British army in forty years. Harry had always wanted to join the army, and he had spent hours excitedly discussing Sandhurst with Mark Dyer, who had attended the military school before joining the Welsh Guards.

Like his brother, Harry had been promised a summer of fun before his gap year officially started. Just to wind up his father he had mooted the idea of spending a year in Argentina playing polo knowing full well that the suggestion, which was only half-intended as a joke, would send his father into a panic. He had also wanted to do a ski season in Klosters, the picturesque Swiss ski resort where Charles skied for years until he had to give it up because of back problems. Having become friendly with Mr and Mrs Bolliger, the owners of the family-run five-star Walserhof Hotel where the royal family often stayed, Harry had reportedly been offered a job working in the hotel's kitchen and cellars, where he would learn about fine wine and cooking.

Concerned that his younger son already had more than sufficient knowledge when it came to alcohol, Charles dismissed the suggestion immediately; once again taking the advice of his trusted aides, he decided that Harry would begin his gap year in Australia working as a cowboy on a cattle station in the outback. Charles had spent several months in Australia as a schoolboy when he went on a brief attachment to Timbertop, an outback offshoot of the Geelong Church of England Grammar School. He had loved the chance to escape Gordonstoun, which he believed was the worst experience of his life, and loved Australia, where he learned to 'conquer my shyness'. He was adamant that Harry's trip was to be educational as well as enjoyable. The fact that it coincided with the Rugby World Cup in Sydney meant there were no arguments. As far as Harry was concerned, Australia was a brilliant suggestion.

The summer came and went in a drink-fuelled haze as Harry celebrated his A-level results – B in art and D in geography. Charles insisted he was delighted: 'I am very proud of Harry.

He has worked hard for these examinations and I am very pleased with today's results.' He was especially pleased with his son's B in art. It was Harry's best grade, and he had showed some of his aboriginal-inspired canvases as part of his final submission, but his pride was dented when his art teacher Sarah Forsyth alleged that he had cheated. Miss Forsyth, who claimed she had been unfairly sacked from Eton the year that Harry left, submitted the claim in 2004 as part of her employment tribunal case. She claimed that she had taped Harry admitting that he had written just a 'tiny tiny bit, about a sentence' of a piece of coursework that counted towards his final grade. Eton refuted the thirty-year-old teacher's claims and Harry issued a statement denying categorically that he had cheated, but it was an accusation that privately devastated him. He had never claimed to be the brightest member of his family, but he was a gifted artist.

Despite the setback, Harry moved on. He had the grades he needed for Sandhurst and a summer to enjoy. He didn't stray far from St James's Palace and was such a regular at the nearby Chelsea watering hole Crazy Larry's on the King's Road that it became known as 'Crazy Harry's'. He also enjoyed drinking at the Collection, a sophisticated two-tiered bar on the Fulham Road, and at Nam Long-Le Shaker, a discreet bar on the Old Brompton Road, Harry held the record for being able to drink three of their White Panther cocktails in a row. The delicious but potent mix of rum, vodka and coconut milk is served in a giant glass and usually requires two people to drink it. When he wanted VIP treatment Harry would head to Mark Dyer's gastropub the So Bar, where lock-ins became a frequent occurrence, much to the annoyance of the prince's protection officers, who would sit in their cars outside the venue waiting for Harry into the early hours. It was common for Harry to be out most nights and very soon he was the subject of more lurid headlines. HARRY IS OUT OF CONTROL the front pages announced amid reports that the prince's team of personal protection officers needed more back-up.

September 22 2003 could not have come sooner for the beleaguered press officers at Clarence House, who had spent the summer fielding suggestions that Harry's gap year was descending into a drunken farce. Suitably there was an alcohol-fuelled farewell party at the Purple nightclub in Chelsea, hosted by William's friend nightclub promoter Nick House. But as Harry left one media row behind him in England, he faced another as soon as he landed on the tarmac in Sydney. In Australia, where the republican movement was growing, there was outrage over the cost of the prince's trip. TV and radio stations were inundated with calls from angry members of the public demanding to know why they were footing the £250,000 bill for Harry's round-the-clock security. The Palace insisted that twelve full-time protection officers together with state police were necessary to protect the prince. It was just months since the unscheduled appearance of Aaron Barschak, the self-styled 'comedy terrorist' who managed to gatecrash Prince William's twenty-first birthday party at Windsor Castle, and in Australia nine years before a deranged student had fired two shots from a starting pistol at Prince Charles, who was on an official visit. The Palace were not prepared to take any risks.

It was a miserable start for Harry, and things would get worse before they improved. While William had enjoyed a peaceful and private gap year, the Australian press would not leave Harry alone. He flew by private jet to Tooloombilla, 370 miles west of Brisbane, where he was to be based for a month at a simple weatherboard cottage on a farm owned by Noel and Annie Hill, son and daughter-in-law of the millionaire polo player Sinclair Hill, who had coached Prince Charles when he visited Australia. A competent horseman, Harry couldn't wait to get into the saddle, but he spent the first days of his trip hiding from the swarm of photographers that plagued the estate. Harry was furious. He had posed for a photocall in Sydney in return for being left alone to get on with his £100-a-week job on the farm. It was worse than anything he had experienced in England and he threatened to go home. The situation was so serious that St James's Palace was forced to issue a statement urging the media to leave the prince alone. 'He wants to learn about outback trades, not dodge the cameras,' one Palace official complained.

As always, it was down to Charles to convince his son to stick it out. As he'd been promised, Harry was allowed to return to Sydney before Christmas to watch the Rugby World Cup. At Eton he had played scrum half and whenever he could went to Twickenham to watch England play. His cousin Zara Phillips was in Sydney with her boyfriend Mike Tindall, who was in the England squad, and together they worked their way through Sydney's finest bars and clubs. The fact that Harry was busy celebrating with an England player and coach Clive Woodward did not escape the Australian media. 'This [trip] is a waste of money,' Professor John Warhurst, chairman of the Australian Republic Movement, told the *Daily Telegraph*.

When he returned home to England it had already been

announced that Harry would be extending his gap year. With his father's approval, he postponed Sandhurst for a year so that he could follow in his brother's footsteps and explore Africa. Having become quickly reacquainted with his favourite London nightclubs he packed his bags in February and flew to Lesotho before he had the chance to read the salacious story of his night with Lauren Pope, a twenty-year-old topless model who he had partied with at Chinawhite. The glitzy London nightclub could not be more of a contrast to Lesotho, a tiny, mountainous land-locked country in southern Africa with one of the highest rates of Aids in the world. Lesotho, which translates as 'forgotten kingdom', has a population of less than two million, more than half of whom live below the poverty line. It is so tiny it often falls off maps of the continent, which is why Harry called the charity which he launched two years after his first visit Sentebale, which means 'forget me not'. While Australia had been intended as a bit of fun, Harry's two-month trip to Africa was all about his pledge to continue his mother's humanitarian work.

Just to make sure Harry stayed focused, his father's head of press Paddy Harverson accompanied him to Africa. 'He is showing a real and genuine interest in the welfare of young people in Lesotho,' said Mr Harverson. 'By coming here he is bringing attention to the problem.' Harry had struck up a warm rapport with Prince Seeiso, the younger brother of Lesotho's King Letsie III. The two filmed a documentary called *The Forgotten Kingdom* about their work at the Mants'ase Orphanage in Mophatoo, a small town two hours from the capital, Maseru.

As soon as Harry arrived, he adapted to life in the blistering African heat. He visited the local barber and had his head shaved to keep him cool during the day and immediately set to work with eight volunteers building fences and planting trees at the orphanage to provide shade for the children, most of whom had lost their parents to Aids. It was hard physical work, but there was plenty of time for fun, and whenever he had a spare hour in the day Harry would gather the children for an impromptu game of rugby. He had packed a football and a rugby ball and patiently explained the rules of the game before splitting the children into teams. They ran around screaming and shouting and kicking up red dust, and Harry was in his element. Like his mother he adored children, and like Diana he was not afraid to get involved with children infected with the HIV virus. 'This is a country that needs help,' said Harry as he appealed to charities in England. He was not afraid of taboo subjects and was close to tears when he held a ten-month-old girl who had been raped by her stepfather. Harry was so moved by the little girl, called Liketsu, that he handwrote messages of support to her carers and secretly returned to Lesotho the following September to see how she was progressing.

The prince was genuinely at home in his new role, and the trip was judged a huge success in the media. While his work in Lesotho had the desired effect of distancing Harry from his wild-child reputation, there was nothing engineered or fake about his enthusiasm. But, being Harry, it wasn't all work, and in April 2004 he made his first of many trips to Cape Town, where he met up with the girl he had been hoping to bump into. Harry had first met Zimbabwe-born Chelsy Davy when she was in her final year at Stowe School. Chelsy had been living in England since she was thirteen when her parents Charles and Beverley, who had moved from Zimbabwe to Durban in South Africa, enrolled her at Cheltenham College where she was a model student. She met Harry through a mutual friend called Simon Diss who was a member of the Glosse Posse and a regular visitor to Club H. According to one friend; 'Simon and Harry were great friends. On one occasion Simon introduced Harry to Chelsy thinking that they would make a good match, but nothing happened at that stage because Chelsy was about to finish at Stowe and go back home to South Africa.' Bright, blond and pretty, Chelsy had notions of becoming a model, but she had a brain and planned to use it. After finishing her A levels she took up a place at the University of Cape Town to study politics, philosophy and economics.

When he met her Harry had been immediately smitten. He had listened raptly as Chelsy enthralled him with tales of riding bareback and how she could strangle a snake with her bare hands. When he travelled to Cape Town that April he had every intention of reconnecting with her. He contacted Simon and asked him for Chelsy's address. 'Harry was desperate to meet up with Chelsy,' recalled a friend. 'He called Simon in the UK and said he wanted Chelsy's details and he got straight on the phone to her. Chelsy wasn't impressed that he was a prince, she just thought he was cute so they met up.' When they did, the chemistry was immediate. They had gone out with mutual friends to a fashionable nightclub called Rhodes House and by the end of the evening were locked in a passionate embrace on the dance floor. Harry made several trips to see Chelsy again before he returned home to England. Sometimes he would fly to Durban with his protection officer and stay at the Davys' family home. On other occasions he stayed with Chelsy and her brother Shaun at their beachfront apartment in Camps Bay. They were wonderful weekends away made all the more exciting by their secrecy. Chelsy wanted to show Harry as much of Cape Town as possible and they spent hours exploring the coast in her Mercedes convertible. When he kissed her goodbye that summer he promised it would not be long before they would see each other again.

Back in England Harry was counting the days until he would see Chelsy again when he got into a fight with a paparazzo outside a London nightclub called Pangea. He had been enjoying a night out with friends and as he left the club a scuffle broke out when the press pack tried to get pictures of the bleary-eyed prince. Fuelled by drink and startled by the flashbulbs, Harry lashed out at photographer Chris Uncle. As his protection officer pulled Harry away, Uncle was left nursing a cut lip. Fortunately he chose not to press charges, but this would not be the last unedifying episode between Harry and the paparazzi. As was becoming a pattern, Harry again left England under a cloud.

The sound of cicadas filled the night air as Chelsy and Harry stared at the stars and raised their glasses to propose a toast. They had travelled by private plane to Entre Rios province in the Mesopotamia region in north-east Argentina for a romantic weekend, and it had been perfect. They had dined by candlelight on fresh barbecued fish after an energetic day of hunting and slept in a king-size bed in a private lodge. As the moonlight caught her beach-blond hair, Harry marvelled at his catch. Chelsy was everything he wanted in a girl. For the first time and to his absolute amazement and delight, he was in love.

Even more astonishing, he privately marvelled as he finished a glass of wine, was the fact that he had managed to keep Chelsy a secret. While some of her friends in Cape Town knew about their romance, Harry had only confided to his brother. Mark and Luke Tomlinson, who were staying with him at the El Remanso polo farm in Buenos Aires, also knew about Chelsy, but no one else. But by the end of Harry's trip in November the story of their romance was out. The staff at the lodge had been aware of Harry's new girlfriend and told the *Mail on Sunday*, which broke the story: 'Harry and Chelsy were like any young couple in love, kissing and holding hands and he seemed quite besotted. They looked madly in love and at one point Harry admitted that she was his first true love.' Unlike his father, it seemed Harry knew exactly what being in love meant. In the past there had been flings and infatuations, including a crush on his friend Natalie Pinkham, but as she would later confide to me, Harry was a drinking pal and nothing more. Chelsy was Harry's first true love and he was head over heels.

After their reunion in Buenos Aires, which only strengthened their feelings for each other, it was apparent that the relationship was serious. By December Harry was back in South Africa, holidaying with Chelsy's parents. The fact that the prince was holidaying with a multimillionaire Zimbabwean businessman and landowner, whose company had been reported to have close links with the country's president Robert Mugabe, was said to be something of a concern to the royal family as were other press claims that Mr Davy's company HHK Safaris offered those prepared to pay the opportunity to shoot elephants and lions. Mr Davy, however, robustly denied any such links stating that he had 'never even shaken' Mugabe's hand, while Chelsy in her first and only public statement made clear that her father's company had nothing to do with poaching. Harry joined his girlfriend and her family on the island of Bazaruto off the coast of Mozambique and spent the pre-Christmas break snorkelling. They saw moray eels and giant grouper and fished for sand sharks in the sparkling Indian Ocean. At the end of the day, Harry, who had become close to Chelsy's brother Shaun, would join the family for 'jolling', drinking games on the beach, when they would knock back 'volcanoes' – vodka shots with chilli sauce. It was the sort of family holiday Harry had never experienced, and he was happier than he had been in a long time. But soon after he arrived home for Christmas, his dream holiday quickly became a distant memory as he became engulfed in the biggest political storm of his life, an episode which threatened to ruin his military career before it had even started.

It was January 2005 and William and Harry had been looking forward to their friend Harry Meade's twenty-second birthday party ever since the stiff card invitation had arrived at Highgrove. Harry's father, a former Olympic showjumper, had organised a grand marquee in the grounds of the family's sprawling estate in West Littleton, Gloucestershire, and guests had been promised dinner, champagne and a night of fun and frivolity. All they had to do was dress up in accordance with the 'native and colonial' theme. William had opted for the fun take and went as a lion with tight black leggings and furry paws. The princes' close friend Guy Pelly went as the Queen. Harry, however, had other ideas, and as he trawled through the rails of Maud's Cotswold Costumes in Gloucestershire around the corner from Highgrove it was a Second World War Nazi outfit that caught his eye. He had, he later confided, chosen the sand-coloured uniform because he thought it complemented his colouring. Of course, he was to have no idea of the devastating repercussions of his ill-starred choice. While the Afrika Korps costume was in poor taste, what is more surprising is that none of the coterie of aides or the protection officers who accompanied Harry to the store thought to tell the prince that his outfit was offensive and potentially inflammatory.

According to guests at the party, who were dressed in safari suits, cowboy outfits and as Red Indians, the chatter dimmed to an awkward silence when the prince arrived, leading one of the 250 guests to remark, 'That's going to land him in trouble.' The off-the-cuff comment couldn't have been a bigger understatement. When one of the guests sold a picture of the prince in his uniform to the *Sun*, Harry found himself at the centre of the biggest storm of his life. There he was on the front page smoking, drinking and sporting the German flag on the arm of his jacket and a red armband emblazoned with the swastika on his left sleeve. The timing of the pictures could not have been worse. It was just days before the sixtieth anniversary of the liberation of Auschwitz and Harry's uncle Prince Edward was due to represent the Queen at the extermination camp in Poland as a mark of respect.

Horrified and stunned by the reaction, Harry immediately issued an apology admitting that his choice of outfit had been 'poor'. While a public apology had sufficed several years ago, this time sorry wasn't enough. There were angry calls for the prince to make a personal apology by the Tory leader Michael Howard, while the former armed forces minister and Labour MP Doug Henderson insisted that the prince be excluded from Sandhurst, where he was to enrol in May. 'If it was anyone else, the application wouldn't be considered,' Mr Henderson remarked. 'It should be withdrawn immediately.' The Board of Deputies of British Jews denounced Harry's outfit as 'clearly in bad taste' while the British press pointed the finger once again at Charles, wanting to know why Harry had been allowed to step out in such an offensive costume. Where was Charles to offer his son the advice he obviously needed and why was he not keeping a closer eye on the wayward prince? The answer was that Charles was in Scotland enjoying a New Year break with Camilla and was refusing to return to London. For the first time William, who had escaped from Harry's drugs scandal unscathed, was also implicated. Hadn't he the foresight to warn his younger brother that wearing a Nazi outfit would only land him in yet another scandal?

According to aides at Buckingham Palace, the Queen was furious and deeply embarrassed. As a future ambassador for the UK and the Commonwealth, Harry ought to have known better, and it was the job of his minders to keep him on the straight and narrow. While her husband was often accused of public gaffes, this sorry episode was unprecedented and potentially very damaging. To the Queen it seemed that Harry lacked both judgement and common sense and was in desperate need of some fatherly attention. Her views seemed to be reflected by the public, 53 per cent of whom in one national newspaper poll thought that Prince William should succeed the Queen as the next monarch in place of Charles. Rattled by the criticism, which had reached as far as Germany and France, Charles insisted that he would not allow Harry to be hung out to dry. His son had apologised, and as far as Charles was concerned that was good enough. With Sandhurst just weeks away, Harry just needed to keep a low profile. There would be no nightclubbing or parties with his friends. Instead Harry was sent to Home Farm to muck out pigs for the rest of the month. The irony of Harry being knee-deep in manure was wasted on nobody.

Chapter 9

The St Andrews years

I just want to go to university and have fun. I want to go there and be an ordinary student. I mean I'm only going to university. It's not like I'm getting married – though that's what it feels like sometimes.

Prince William

While the royal family have traditionally gone to Oxford or Cambridge, Prince William was set on breaking 150 years of tradition by going to St Andrews, Scotland's oldest university. His father, his Uncle Edward and his great-grandfather King George VI had all attended Cambridge but the four-year history of art course at St Andrews, which is considered one of the best in the country, appealed to the prince, who was keen to postpone royal engagements for as long as possible. The Queen was delighted that her grandson had enrolled at the elite college where the Scottish King James V studied in the early sixteenth century. The Queen Mother, who William visited at Balmoral for tea before he arrived for his first day, also shared a connection with the university, from which she had received an honorary degree in 1929.

William arrived at St Salvator's Hall, his home for the next year, on a crisp morning on 23 September 2001. Dressed in what was to become his staple university outfit – jeans, a casual shirt and a warm fleece – he had an unconventional arrival for an undergraduate. More than 3,000 residents, students and well-wishers turned up to welcome him to his new hall of residence situated next to St Salvator's quadrangle and facing the cold grey sea and the cathedral ruins. William greeted the crowds with a cheerful smile and told them how excited he was to be embarking on student life. He settled in quickly, and although the town's 18,000 residents were initially inquisitive, they soon left him in peace. William wanted to be treated the same as everyone else, and at St Andrews he was. He could walk down the street without being bothered and shop at the local Tesco. 'I've had lots of kids come up to me and ask for my autograph [and] I've had a grandmother stop me and ask me if I know a good place to buy underwear,' he later joked.

The centre of the town, which is eighty miles north of Edinburgh, comprises just three roadways, North Street, Market Street and South Street. Peppered with fashionable cafés, lively bars and well-stocked charity- and bookshops, attractive halls of residences and beautiful historic quads, the busy town centre is dominated by undergraduates. When the Palace confirmed Prince William would be starting in the autumn of 2001, the university's registrars recorded a 44 per cent rise in applications, the majority wealthy American heiresses desperate to meet the prince. They were to be disappointed, however, as William missed freshers' week. Even though there were no paparazzi lurking outside nightclubs, William was wary and didn't want to be caught in any compromising situations.

According to one former lecturer at the university, his arrival sent the administration, especially the press office, at St Andrews into a state of panic. They knew the kudos that William would bring to the small university, and while they were keen to capitalise on royal patronage, they were also aware that William would need to be well protected. His room, B31, was situated on the second floor of St Salvator's Hall and overlooked the Scores, which runs the length of the town and boasts incredible views of the thirteenth-century castle and the famous golf course. To the left William could just see the history of art block on North Street, a grey stone townhouse with original fireplaces and chandeliers, where he would attend eight hours of tutorials a week. To his right he had a view of the castle museum, which is set in green parkland overlooking the sea. Like every other undergraduate, William's bedroom was painted cream and had a burgundy-flecked carpet. The room contained a single bed, a mahogany-coloured double wardrobe with a full-length mirror, an armchair and a desk and chair in front of the window. Unlike every other room, however, its window had been reinforced with shatter-proof glass and a bomb-proof door was fitted ahead of his arrival. A small en suite with reinforced walls was built into the room with its own loo, washbasin and walk-in shower, which could be used as a shelter in an emergency. Should there be any need, William's protection officers were just twenty yards down the blue-carpeted and fluorescent-lit corridor, their rooms separated by a small bathroom.

It had already been decided that a small team of Scottish police officers would assist the prince's close protection officers, while the university's principal, Dr Brian Lang, insisted that every student sign a confidentiality agreement when they enrolled promising not to speak to the press about the VIP undergraduate. 'When it was first mooted that Prince William might be coming, the university executives tried to keep a lid on it,' recalled Dr Declan Quigley, who lectured William in his first year.

> They were very nervous about the inevitable hordes of journalists and photographers. The university came to an agreement with the press that they would be allowed access on very limited occasions and would agree to leave William alone for the rest of the time. For the most part they respected that, so in fact his stay there was relatively calm from the point of view of press intrusion. Academically William was also protected. In our department only one person, Dr Mark Harris, was allowed to have any contact with him. That was set up by the deputy principal, who was terrified that William's essays might end up in the *Daily Mail*.

It was a great irony that it would not be the newspapers that ruined William's first week at university. While the vast majority of the press pack which had gathered in the small town ahead of William's arrival had left in compliance with the media embargo, the prince noticed that one crew remained. He alerted the university's press office as it had only been days since the PCC issued a reminder that he was to be left alone. After further investigations it was discovered that the camera crew, who had interviewed several under-graduates, belonged to a production company called Ardent. While it was not entirely surprising that someone had broken the embargo, it was incredible that the cameras belonged to this particular company – Prince Edward's – which was making a TV show called *The A–Z of Royalty* for an American TV network. After all the fuss that had been made about protecting William from the media, it was a member of the royal family, his uncle, who had broken the rules. The British press could barely contain their glee. While the Palace would only say that it was 'disappointed' by the unfortunate episode, Prince Charles was said to be apoplectic. His angry call to his youngest brother at Bagshot Park could apparently be heard in the room adjacent to his study at St James's Palace.

'The Prince of Wales was very unhappy about what had happened,' Mark Bolland, who was in charge of handling William's media relations at St Andrews, recalled. 'A lot of effort had gone into creating an embargo to protect William. No one expected it to be a family member who would breach it.' According to Andrew Neil, lord Rector at St Andrews 1999–2002,

The university authorities, myself on behalf of the students, and the Palace had put a lot of effort into getting the media to agree to leave William alone. We agreed to one photo shoot when he arrived and when that was over, to our amazement everyone left. A few days into term I got a call to say a TV crew was still filming at St Andrews. When we found out it was from Prince Edward's film company, all hell let loose. It was unbelievable, and we were furious as well as bemused. We had squared the paparazzi and every newspaper, and it was the idiot uncle who broke the embargo. He had been taking students out for curries and trying to get information out of them. When Charles heard he went ballistic. I was told from an excellent source that he picked up the phone to his brother and called him a 'f***ing idiot' and told him in no uncertain terms to get out of the town.

As far as Charles was concerned, the incident, for which Edward publicly apologised, only served to highlight his argument that members of the royal family could not pursue independent careers and also carry out royal duties. It was his opinion that if Edward ever represented the royal family he could not have commercial interests, and this sorry episode perfectly illustrated why.

Reluctant to be drawn into family politics, William soon forgot about the embarrassing debacle and set about making friends. Nicknamed 'Sally's', St Salvator's is one of the university's eleven halls of residences and split into male and female living quarters. As he bounded down the stairwell with his folders in his hands, William would often bump into the same brunette, who also happened to be on his course. He had noticed her as soon as he had arrived. It was hard not to. Kate Middleton had been crowned the prettiest girl at Sally's by the end of freshers' week. She was shy and quieter than the other girls, which William liked, and he looked forward to their meetings. Often Kate would go running before breakfast and arrived at the canteen just before breakfast was over. Within weeks William had been bold enough to invite her to join him. Every morning he and his friends sat in the same place next to the head table, where a crimson throne and eighteen seats were reserved for the wardens and deans. The impressive ground-floor canteen was decorated with heavy oil paintings of philosophers from the Scottish Enlightenment and beautiful stained-glass windows, and there was always a cooked breakfast on offer. Being health-conscious, a trait he inherited from his father, William would choose muesli and fruit, as did Kate.

They quickly discovered they had plenty in common. Kate was

The Princess of Wales smiles at Prince Charles as he walks down the steps of St Mary's Hospital in Paddington cradling their firstborn. Prince William Arthur Philip Louis of Wales was born at 9.03 p.m. on 21 June 1982. Not yet a day old, the future king was facing his first press conference.

Diana made a point of keeping her diary free so she could take William and Harry to school every morning. After Mrs Mynors' nursery the princes were enrolled at Wetherby Prep School in Notting Hill Gate, a stone's throw from Kensington Palace.

Diana embraces William and Harry aboard the *Britannia* in Toronto, October 1991. This was one of the family's final holidays before the prince and princess were separated the following December.

William arrives for his first day at Eton in Windsor on 6 September 1995. Hundreds of press gathered outside the gates of Manor House, amid mounting speculation about the breakdown of the Wales' marriage.

Dressed in her green and white checked summer dress Catherine Middleton was one of the brightest pupils at St Andrew's preparatory school in Pangbourne, where she was educated from the age of seven. She was top of the class at sport and represented the school in netball, tennis and swimming. A tall and gangly teenager, she was outstanding at the high jump. William, who was a boarder at nearby Ludgrove, would sometimes visit St Andrew's for away games and pupils recall Catherine eagerly watching from the sidelines.

Diana in the south of France in July 1997 on her last holiday with her sons. They were guests of Mohamed Al Fayed and his children Dodi, Camilla, Jasmine and Omar. Aboard the yacht *Jonikal* the press interest was so relentless that William complained he wanted to go home.

Charles, William, Harry and Widgeon, William's pet Labrador, take a walk by the River Dee in August 1997. Two weeks later Diana was killed in Paris and the boys stayed at Balmoral where they could grieve privately.

Flanked by their father and their uncle, Earl Spencer, William and Harry carry out their first and most tragic public duty, walking behind their mother's gun carriage to Westminster Abbey.

After much discussion William got his wish of taking a gap year, although Prince Charles insisted it be vocational. The prince enrolled on a Raleigh International expedition to Chile in October 2000. In his spare time he read, wrote letters home, practised yoga and made some friends for life.

On the final night of his voluntary expedition to Chile, Prince William threw caution to the wind and let his hair down at a fancy dress farewell party. He donned his thermals, a makeshift cape and a pair of girl's knickers and dressed up as Superman. He drank red wine throughout the evening and thoroughly the worse for wear launched himself onto a row of tents at the end of the night. He joked that he had 'one hell of hangover' on the flight home to London the next day.

Beautiful Rose was William's first love. Part of the Gloucestershire fraternity known as the 'Glosse Posse' William romanced Rose, the daughter of Captain Ian Farquhar, master of the Beaufort Hunt, the summer he left Eton. He was just eighteen but very much a romantic. He would take Rose for afternoon picnics and on one occasion the couple were left red-faced when a farmer stumbled upon the young lovers in a field.

Harry visits children at an orphanage in Lesotho during his gap year in April 2006. He was so moved that he launched a charity called Sentebale, which means 'forget me not', in memory of his mother.

During his gap year Harry went to Cape Town in search of Chelsy Davy, daughter of a Zimbabwean landowner, whom he first met when he was at Eton. Chelsy was to be Harry's first true love

Kate Middleton gazes at William's best friend Fergus Boyd during the 'Don't Walk' fashion show at St Andrews in March 2002. William remarked that Kate was 'hot' and later that night at a party in Hope Street in the centre of town he made his move.

William enrolled at St Andrews in September 2001. During his first term he fell for Carley Massy-Birch. While Kate Middleton had been voted the prettiest undergraduate, Carley's derrière was considered the best at St Andrews, something which may well have irked her rival for William's affections.

Although he had a wobble during his first term William soon settled into St Andrews University. As well as joining the amateur dramatics society he also enjoyed swimming, cycling and surfing during his four years there.

Clutching their work files, William and Kate stroll through the university town of St Andrews in Scotland. The couple, who were both studying History of Art were also in the same halls of residence St Salvator's Hall, known as Sally's. William had noticed the shy but unassuming brunette who had been voted the prettiest girl at Sally's and plucked up the courage to ask her to join him for breakfast. When William had a wobble after his first semester it was Kate who convinced him to come back and change his course.

a country girl who loved playing sports and a keen swimmer like William. She was also a good skier and just like William had enjoyed a gap year travelling around the world before coming to St Andrews. By coincidence, she too had spent part of her gap year in Chile, as well as several months in Florence soaking up the culture and art in the city's famous galleries, and chatted with William about the Renaissance artists they would soon be studying and the modules they planned to take. She got along well with William's friends Olli Chadwick-Healey and Fergus Boyd, the son of a country solicitor from Wiltshire who was with him at Eton. They were part of a group known as the Sally's boys, which also included Ali Coutts-Wood, a former pupil at Uppingham School, Graham Booth, Charlie Nelson and Oli Baker, who would later share a house with William and Kate. If William had a timetable clash, Kate would take notes for him, and at the end of the day they would catch up over a drink in the common room where the floor-to-ceiling Georgian windows looked onto the tidy gardens.

When it came to socialising, William kept a low profile. Although St Andrews boasts more pubs per square mile than any other Scottish town, he preferred keeping company with the Sally's group, who enjoyed dinner parties rather than nights out at the clubs in St Andrews. William is naturally cautious about the company he keeps. He is known to privately vet friends and often plants red herrings to catch out anyone he suspects is selling stories on him. 'People who try to take advantage of me, and get a piece of me, I spot it quickly and soon go off them. I'm not stupid,' he once remarked.

While many of the student organisations were keen to get William on board, including the gentlemen-only Kate Kennedy

Club, which aims to maintain the traditions of St Andrews and 'improve town and gown relations', William kept his distance. He joined the water polo team and would swim most mornings at the luxury Old Course Hotel with Kate. He also enjoyed cycling along the Scores and in the evenings occasionally dropped into the student union for a game of pool. Sometimes he would pay three pounds for a ticket to the Bop, the weekly disco on Market Street, where he could drink 'the cheapest G&T in town', but the truth was that William was developing a reputation for being aloof and even a touch boring. The glamorous undergraduates who spent thousands on new wardrobes and drinking in St Andrews's fashionable bars hoping to chance upon the prince were disappointed.

Having enjoyed performing in school plays, William was keen to join the drama society and in his first semester auditioned for a role in an adaptation of the J D Salinger play *Franny and Zooey* put on by a small independent company called A&E Productions. Accompanied at a distance by his protection officer, William cycled to the Byer Theatre, a recently refurbished glass-fronted venue off South Street, where auditions were being held in one of the second-floor rehearsals rooms. William auditioned for the lead role of Zooey and read straight from the script. Under the dimmed house lights and in front of a small group of students he delivered a convincing and commendable audition. It was not an easy part and the passage of the play selected for the auditions was a conversation Zooey has with his mother while taking a bath.

'William was actually very good,' recalled one of the production team.

It was quite an emotional passage, and we deliberately chose it because it was a way of immediately separating the really good from the average. William fell into the really good category. He wasn't nervous and he gave an excellent recital. He used the script as did everyone else, but he had memorised parts of it. Zooey is a bit of a fragile existential type and William got it immediately. We thought long and hard about giving him the part. In the end we decided to cast someone else. The play was only running for four nights and if William was in it the whole house would be filled to the rafters with press.

Despite being turned down, William went to see the play that November and also went to support Fergus, who would often appear in productions at the Castle, an open-air theatre set in the castle ruins on the seafront close to Castle Sands, the beach where students traditionally strip off and dive into the sea every 1 May. 'William was very loyal and would always go and watch Fergus on the first and last nights. Fergus was very much a budding actor and he starred in several plays, all of which William went to see several times no matter how cold it was,' recalled a former student.

William enjoyed mingling with members of the drama society and during his first semester started dating a pretty English language and creative writing student called Carley Massy-Birch. Tall, dark and stunningly pretty, Carley made quite an impression on the prince, who would cycle to her house in Crail Lane, a cobbled mews off South Street, where they enjoyed reading the papers over a cappuccino at Cherry's café at the end of the street. Often William was invited to supper at Carley's home, where he would fall over her muddy Hunter wellington boots in the hallway. Carley was a country girl and the couple had plenty in common. 'I'm a real country bumpkin,' Carley told me. 'I think that was why we had a connection. William was in the year below and we just happened to meet through the general St Andrews melee. It's such a small place that it was impossible not to bump into William, and after a while there was nothing weird about seeing him around. We got on well but I think we would have got on well even if nothing had been going on romantically. It was very much a university thing, just a regular university romance.' Over supper they would discuss plays and literature and Carley would tell William all about her home life in Devon. Other evenings they would enjoy pints of cider at the Castle pub on North Street and play board games or enjoy dinner parties with their friends. 'There wasn't really a club at St Andrews, so we tended to go to pubs and bars and there was always a good dinner party going on,' recalled Carley. What struck William about Carley was how down-to-earth and normal she was; she had been brought up on a farm in Axminster by her parents Mary and Hugh. On top of that she was gorgeous, and although Kate had been voted the prettiest girl at St Salvator's, Carley's derrière was voted the best at St Andrews.

'We would joke that Carley's bottom had been sculpted by the gods,' recalled one of her friends. 'William was very taken with her, which was completely understandable. She had beautiful long hair and a voluptuous body, which she loved to show off in perfectly fitted jeans and tight corduroy trousers. She was quite a catch and every girl at St Andrews was envious of her because she was with William.' Unlike the hordes of made-up pashmina-clad undergraduates who devoted their time to stalking William, Carley was happy to stay in and cook for him and their romance was so beneath the radar, it was only reported years after they had both graduated. Their affair was to be short-lived, however, and ended somewhat stickily when Carley told William he had to make a decision between her and a young woman hundreds of miles away who seemed to be proving something of a distraction.

It was the summer of 2001, William's final holiday before he started St Andrews, when Arabella Musgrave first caught his eye. She was the eighteen-year-old daughter of Major Nicholas Musgrave, who managed the Cirencester Park Polo Club, and they had known each other since they were little. Although not titled aristocracy, Arabella was a close friend of Guy Pelly's and Hugh Van Cutsem and part of the Glosse Posse. As she walked through the house party at the Van Cutsems' family home, William did a double-take. Arabella had blossomed into a gorgeous-looking girl, and as she sashayed past him, her perfume lingering in the air, he wondered why he hadn't noticed her properly until now. William knew he would make a move on her by the end of the night. They danced and drank into the early hours, and when Arabella said her goodnights, the prince quietly slipped out the room to follow her upstairs. It was the beginning of a passionate romance and the two spent as much time together that summer as possible.

They would dine at the Tunnel House Inn in Coates close to Highgrove, where collages of the regulars cover the old brick walls. With its famous brass fox door knocker and bright-pink-painted entrance hall, it was one of their favourite haunts. Charles was aware of the relationship and had given it his blessing. While she was not the debutante Charles had hoped William would romance, he suspected the relationship would soon fizzle out and instructed William's protection officers to give the couple plenty of leeway. Major Nicholas, however, took a firmer stance, and when he caught Arabella sitting on William's knee while the prince kissed her neck at a party at the polo club, he had a quiet word. Although he was fond of William such displays of affection, he insisted, were not for public consumption

By the time William left for St Andrews in September he and Arabella had already made the mutual decision to end their relationship. William would be meeting new people at university and Arabella could not expect him to wait for her. The problem was that William became bored in Scotland. He missed his friends in Gloucestershire and going to his favourite nightclubs in London. The advantage of St Andrews being so small was that he was well protected, but the town could be claustrophobic. He also missed Arabella, and on Friday nights when he began his journey home to Highgrove he was comforted by the fact that she would be waiting for him.

Charles knew he had a crisis on his hands when William returned home at Christmas and announced he did not want to go back to university for his second semester. He complained he was not enjoying the course and St Andrews was too far away. Charles listened patiently. He knew William could be temperamental and the situation was delicate. Of course William could leave if he was thoroughly miserable, but give it another term, he suggested. As he often did in a crisis, Charles consulted his private secretary Sir Stephen Lamport and press adviser Mark Bolland as well as William's former housemaster at Eton Dr Andrew Gailey who agreed that they would do everything to persuade the prince to stay. The main problem appeared to be that, apart from being homesick, William had no interest in his course and was finding the workload challenging. Despite growing up in palaces where Rembrandts, Vermeers, Canalettos and Van Dycks lined the walls, he had not enjoyed studying baroque and rococo art during his first term. 'It was really no different from what many first-year students go through,' Mark Bolland recalled. 'We approached the whole thing as a wobble which was entirely normal.'

The Queen and the Duke of Edinburgh were kept abreast of the situation. 'He needs to knuckle down and not wimp out,' was Philip's typically blunt response. It could have been disastrous for the monarchy if William had pulled out. The Royal Family enjoyed close ties with Scotland and did not want to alienate the Scots. They were also reminded of the criticism that Prince Edward had faced when he had left the Royal Marines in the spring of 1987. After some frank discussions with William's deans, a deal was struck.

'It would have been a PR disaster for St Andrews if he had left after one term, and we worked very hard to keep him,' said Andrew Neil.

We gave him pastoral care, and when he suggested majoring in geography we made sure there were no roadblocks. The course structure at St Andrews is such that you can actually change the focus of your degree in your first year, and by the time William came back for the second semester he had settled in. He made a lot of friends and, having met him quite a few times, I think he was happy in the town. William was protected by the students who formed a circle around him and looked out for him. He got the blues, which happens. We have a lot of public-school boys and girls who get up here, and by November, when the weather gets grey and cold, wish they were back home. William was a long way from home and he wasn't happy.

'I don't think I was homesick; I was more daunted,' William later admitted. 'My father was very understanding about it and realised I had the same problem as he probably had. We chatted a lot and in the end we both realised – I definitely realised – that I had to come back.' Returning to St Andrews, he was much happier with his switch to geography.

However, the following Easter his beloved great-grandmother passed away at the age of 101. William, Harry and Charles were two days into a holiday in Klosters when they received the sad news, and they immediately flew to RAF Northolt in west London. Charles was inconsolable, and this time it was William and Harry who needed to be strong. The Queen, whose sister Margaret had died seven weeks earlier, was also said to be greatly saddened. It was the year of her golden jubilee, but it seemed she had little to celebrate. The sight of William and Harry walking behind their great-grandmother's coffin from Westminster Abbey brought other tragic memories flooding back.

*　　*　　*

William wasn't always a model student. Dr Declan Quigley recalled the prince once fell asleep during one of his anthropology lectures.

> I remember William was asleep or possibly recovering from a hangover when I was giving what I thought was my most interesting lecture on kingship. There were 250-odd students in the lecture so he probably thought I hadn't noticed. Maybe he just had his head in his hands because he was thinking, Oh God, is that what I have to go through? Perhaps he just didn't want to hear what his destiny had in store for him? My lectures were on ritual. Of course some of the students perfectly understood the comedy of a lecturer talking about the fundamental principles of kingship with the future king present, and some of them thought it quite funny. One mature student came up to me and said, a little shocked, 'You do realise that Prince William attends these lectures.' Of course I knew. I didn't change anything because William was there. I found it quite amusing myself, and if anything tended to play up the comic elements more. I sometimes wish William had had the wit to come up and ask me questions since I was really passionate about the subject in those days, and what I was saying really did have relevance for him.

It was ironic that William was attending lectures on the very subject he struggled to come to terms with. As a very modern royal, his views about the monarchy were at odds with Dr Quigley's, who believed that the king must not be ordinary but extraordinary. 'The really crucial thing about kingship is that a king or queen must be initiated through a ritual to transform him or her from their ordinary status into something quite extraordinary,' explained Quigley, who has written a book called *The Character of Kingship*. 'All these would-be modernisers of the royal family have got it completely wrong. The more like one of us the king becomes, the less there is any reason for having a king. A king is a symbol, not a person.' Perhaps it was exactly what William didn't want to hear, or maybe he was just so bored he switched off. Either way he wanted to enjoy St Andrews and revel in four years of being ordinary, not extraordinary.

It was the night of the annual Don't Walk charity fashion show on 27 March 2002 during William's second semester, when the moment of realisation suddenly hit him. As Kate shimmied down the catwalk at the five-star St Andrews Bay Hotel William turned to Fergus. 'Wow, Fergus,' he whispered. 'Kate's hot!' He had paid £200 for his front-row ticket, and when Kate appeared in black underwear and a see-through dress William barely knew where to look. 'Kate looked amazing,' recalled one of the models. 'Her hair was slightly frizzy and with her wasp-like waist and washboard stomach she stole the show. She always had a complex about her legs, which she complained were too short, but she was great on the catwalk, and everyone including William knew it.'

At a party at 14 Hope Street after the fashion show William decided to make his move. As the music throbbed and beautiful young things sat sipping home-made cocktails on the winding staircase of the student house, William and Kate were huddled in a quiet corner deep in conversation. As they clinked their glasses to toast Kate's success, William leaned in to kiss her. It was Kate who pulled away, momentarily stunned that he had been so bold in a room full of strangers. At the time she was dating Rupert Finch, a fourth-year student, but William didn't seem to care. 'It was clear to us that William was smitten with Kate,' remembered one of their friends who was at the party and witnessed the moment. 'He actually told her she was a knockout that night, which caused her to blush. There was definitely chemistry between them and Kate had really made an impression on William. She played it very cool and at one point when William seemed to lean in to kiss her, she pulled away. She didn't want to give off the wrong impression or make it too easy for Will.'

It was a rebuff, but Kate had wavered. The attraction was evidently mutual. Kate had been hugely relieved when William returned to St Andrews for the second semester of his first year. They had kept in touch over the Christmas break and she had encouraged him to give St Andrews a second chance. She had been homesick too and had become, quite unexpectedly, dependent on William's friendship. She was completely unaffected by the fact that he was a prince; to her he was just William, which was one of the reasons he was always so comfortable with her.

Chapter 10

Kate Middleton, princess-in-waiting

He's lucky to be going out with me.
Kate Middleton on dating Prince William

After her impressive debut on the catwalk, things would never be quite the same between William and Kate. William had insisted in an interview on his twenty-first birthday that he was single, but the truth was he had fallen for his pretty friend. One problem was Kate's relationship with Rupert Finch. It wasn't terribly serious, but Kate, as she would show many times over in the following years, was nothing if not loyal, and William's title was not going to change that. But William was giving off mixed signals, including the romance with Carley, who Kate could not stand. In later years Kate would be nicknamed 'Waity Katie' by the British press as she waited patiently for her prince to propose, but back then in the beginning it was William who had to do the waiting, and the irony of the role reversal has never been lost on Kate.

By the start of his second year, in September 2002, William was living in a flat at 13a Hope Street, a smart house in the centre of the town. One of his conditions for staying was that he would be allowed to move out of halls after his first year, and share an apartment with his friends. It was a luxury no prince before him had enjoyed and exactly the normality that William craved. Of course there were the necessary security issues to consider: the property was fitted with bulletproof windows, a bomb-proof front door and a state-of-the art laser security system that came with a thick instruction manual. The floor-to-ceiling windows were also protected with reinforced full-length pine shutters in keeping with the rest of the street. William's room, which was situated between the galley kitchen and the open-plan living and dining room on the first floor, was the biggest and looked onto an overgrown private garden and the back of the student union building on Market Street.

He had decided to move in with Kate, Fergus and Olivia Bleasdale, a former pupil at Westonbirt School in Gloucestershire who William knew through one of his best friends, Natasha Rufus Isaacs, daughter of the Marquess of Reading. They each paid £100 a week rent for the two storey top-floor flat and shared the cleaning. With its high ceilings and open-plan living area it was perfect for entertaining. 'They did throw dinner parties and took it in turns to go shopping for groceries,' one of their friends recalled. 'William was part of the dinner-party brigade and being seen in Tesco was all part of it. It was a bit of a meeting place for the great and the good. Fergus would get dressed up to the nines and only ever wore different shades of white. He was always immaculately turned out and William was always with him, so it was not uncommon for girls to stake out Tesco in the hope of seeing the pair of them.' Indeed it was while searching for an exotic fruit for dessert that William bumped into his friend, fellow geography student Bryony Daniels. When they were photographed walking in the town together they were immediately linked, but there was nothing going on between them. By now William had decided the only St Andrews girl he wanted was Kate.

William and Kate were determined to keep their fledgling romance quiet, and behind the closed doors of 13a Hope Street they could. Their bedrooms were on separate landings, but by this stage it was nothing more than pretence. William was enjoying a freedom no royal before him had ever had and it signalled how much the royal family had modernised. William and Kate had fallen in love and were enjoying a conventional university romance, albeit one involving elaborate cover-ups and decoys. In a bid to keep their relationship below the radar for as long as possible, they would leave the house at different times, arrive at dinner parties separately and made a pact never to hold hands in public.

In their own apartment they were like any other couple in love. During the cold winter months they would spend their evenings watching DVDs and ordering in pizzas or Indian take-aways from the Balaka, a Bangladeshi restaurant at the end of their road. Sometimes they would venture to the West Port bar on South Street, where Kate loved the decor – whitewashed walls with modern chrome fireplaces and extravagant vintage chandeliers. The bar sponsored a local rugby team called the Rat Pack, which William sometimes played for. The couple were also fans of Ma Belle's, a popular student haunt beneath the Golf Hotel on the Scores, which served a cheap and decent brunch including a salmon teriyaki that Kate claimed was the best cure for a hangover. At night the orange-painted restaurant meta-morphosed into a fashionable drinking venue where cocktails were just five pounds. For dancing the couple would visit the

Lizard, a garish lime-green-and-purple-painted subterranean late-night bar beneath the Oak Rooms on North Street.

Although she had spent much of the first year with the Sally's boys, by the second year Kate had her own social set. She co-founded the Lumsden Club, a women-only rival to the all-male Kate Kennedy Club, and spent much of her spare time planning summer drinks parties to raise money for various charities with her friend Katherine Munsey, who lived several doors away in Hope Street. Her close friend from Marlborough Emilia D'Erlanger was also part of Kate's crowd. The niece of the 10th Viscount Exmouth, Emilia had known William socially for years. She had become close to Kate at Marlborough College and was to prove a loyal and longstanding friend. Ironically, she had been tipped in the press as a girlfriend of the prince's after she accompanied William and the royal family on a cruise of the Greek Islands in 1999 but they never dated and years later William and Kate would attend Emilia's wedding to her long term boyfriend David Jardine-Paterson. She was also friendly with Bryony Gordon and Lady Virginia Fraser, the daughter of Lord Strathalmond, who knew Kate from her former school, Downe House. Leonora Gummer, daughter of Tory MP John Gummer, was also part of their well-heeled clique, along with Sandrine Janet, a pretty French student who was dating William and Kate's flatmate Fergus.

While it was the boys' job to shop at Tesco, the girls prepared the weekly dinner parties. 'Katherine Munsey would go to extreme efforts, and had the silver brought up from London when she was throwing a really big event,' recalled a member of their inner circle. 'She was very stylish and so were her dinner parties, which would consist of courses and courses. They would take it in turn to have parties at each other's houses, which always entailed lots of drinking and lots of fun.' When dinner was over and the claret had switched to port or Jack Daniel's, a bottle of which William would always bring, the friends would enjoy playing drinking games. Their favorite was I've Never, which entails one player admitting to the others something she or he has never done and then asking the others if they have. If anyone has done the deed in question they must take a drink. One member of the group recalled,

William and Kate loved the game, but it went a bit wrong on the one occasion Carley came for dinner. She and William were still friends and Carley lived across the road in Howard Place in her third year. She could literally wave to William from her sitting room, where she would sit knitting by the window, which rather grated on Kate. When it was Carley's turn to play she announced, 'I've never dated two people in this room,' knowing full well that William was the only one who had because Kate was sitting next to him. He shot Carley a thunderous look and said under his breath, 'I can't believe you just said that,' before drinking his shot. Kate didn't speak to Carley much after that but we were in shock. We knew they were together but it was the first time William confirmed his and Kate's relationship in public.

By the end of their second year the relationship was clearly a close one. When William attended Kate's belated twenty-first birthday party in June 2003 at her family home in Bucklebury, Berkshire, the glance she threw him across the room when he walked into the 1920s-themed party was beyond platonic. Such was the speculation about their relationship that Kate's father Michael was approached by a reporter on the doorstep of the Middletons' home. 'We are very amused at the thought of being in-laws to Prince William, but I don't think it is going to happen,' he said when asked about their alleged courtship. But then at William's twenty-first birthday party at Windsor Castle later that month it seemed as though Kate was barely registering on William's radar; he seemed preoccupied with a very pretty girl called Jecca Craig.

William had first met Jecca, daughter of British conservationist Ian Craig and his wife Jane, in 1998 in Kenya during his school holidays. He had fallen in love with Africa, and returned during his gap year to spend several weeks learning about conservation at the Craigs' 55,000-acre game reserve situated in the beautiful Lewa Downs in the foothills of Mount Kenya. William had adored every minute of it and years later would get involve with the Tusk Trust, a conservation charity which finances some of Lewa's activities and of which William is now patron. Mr Craig recalled, 'William just loves Africa, that's clear. He did every-thing from rhino-spotting to anti-poaching patrols to checking fences. He's a great boy.' At the end of the day he and Jecca would eat al fresco and talk of Africa. It was not long before rumours were circulating among their friends that something was going on. William had apparently had a secret crush on Jecca since the first time he met her. She was beautiful, with long blond hair, deep-blue eyes and legs like a gazelle. But when it was reported that the two had staged a mock engagement cere-mony to pledge their love to one another before William returned to England, the prince instructed his aides to deny this had happened.

It was a rare move – usually the Palace never comments on the princes' private lives – but on this occasion William wanted the story refuted. 'There's been a lot of speculation about every single girl I'm with, and it actually does quite irritate me after a while, more so because it's a complete pain for the girls,' he said. The tale had rattled him and embarrassed Jecca, who at the time was dating Edinburgh University undergraduate Henry Ropner, a former Etonian and a friend of William. The denial did little to quash the rumours of a romance however, and as Kate raised her champagne flute to toast the birthday prince at the aptly themed Out of Africa celebration at Windsor Castle, it was Jecca who had pride of place next to William at the head table.

By the end of the summer, however, the relationship seemed back on track and was an open secret at St Andrews, and William and Kate were desperate for some privacy. While Fergus decided to stay on at 13a Hope Street they decided to move out to Balgove House on Strathtyrum, a sprawling private estate a quarter of a mile outside the town centre owned by a wealthy landowner called Henry Cheape, a distant cousin of the prince and close friend of the royals. The impressive four-bedroom cottage was a perfect sanctuary from the hustle and bustle of the town, and with a long gravel drive framed by hedgerows leading from the busy main road up to the house it was far more private than Hope Street. Unmarked police cars patrolled the estate and William's protection officers lived in the assorted outhouses. As with all his residences, the cottage had been made secure for the prince complete with bomb-proof doors and windows. To the right of the hallway was a small lounge with an open fireplace and to the left a large kitchen-diner with a black and white chequered floor where William, Kate and their new housemate Oli Baker spent most of their time. They intended to entertain frequently: William installed a champagne fridge as soon as they moved in, while Kate set about dressing the windows with pretty red and white gingham curtains. As well as the grounds, where they enjoyed long romantic walks, the couple had the privacy of two acres of wild grassland hidden behind a six-foot stone wall. William joked that it was like a miniature Highgrove, and with its crab-apple trees, blooming rhododendrons and patches of wild poppies it was an impressive substitute. When it was warm enough, they would pack a picnic hamper and spend pleasant afternoons stretched out on a blanket sharing a bottle of chilled white wine, an occasional pheasant their only company. They were blissful days, made all the more romantic by the fact that virtually no one knew about their romance. But the secret would soon be out.

Against a backdrop of snow-capped mountains William put his arm around Kate. Wrapped up against the cold mountain air in their salopettes and ski jackets, they waited in line for a ski lift. As the T-bar arrived, William helped Kate on and they glided up the steep mountain, ski poles in their hands. The shot of William gazing lovingly at Kate that was published in the *Sun* newspaper on 1 April 2004 was no April Fool. The rumours, which had been around for months, were confirmed: William and Kate were definitely more than just friends. 'If I fancy a girl and she fancies me back, which is rare, I ask her out. But at the same time I don't want to put them in an awkward situation, because a lot of people don't understand what comes with knowing me, for one – and secondly, if they were my girlfriend, the excitement it would probably cause,' William had remarked in that twenty-first-birthday interview. He was right about the excitement. He had chosen to go to Klosters, where the royal family are photographed every year, and he had made no attempt to disguise his affection for Kate. They were with a group of friends that included Tiggy Legge-Bourke's brother Harry, Guy Pelly and William Van Cutsem and his girlfriend Katie James. The candid shots of them on the slopes had been taken by the world-famous paparrazo Jason Fraser, who had seven years earlier taken photographs of William's mother in the arms of Dodi Al Fayed aboard the *Jonikal*. The Palace was furious and accused the *Sun* of breaching the embargo which protected Prince William while he was at university. But the paper had decided that this was a scoop just too good to turn down. FINALLY . . . WILLS GETS A GIRL was the headline. The truth was he had had this girl for many months. Suddenly the floodgates opened and the world wanted to know everything about this shy, pretty and unassuming girl.

Catherine Elizabeth Middleton was born on 9 January 1982 at the Royal Berkshire Hospital in Reading. The first child of Michael and Carole Middleton, she grew up with her younger sister Philippa, known as Pippa, and their brother James at the family's modest home in Bradfield Southend. In her only ever interview to date Kate recalled how she used to love dressing up as a clown in giant dungarees and play musical statues with her siblings because she has 'always been a keen dancer'. Birthdays were always an occasion in the Middleton household and Kate remembered 'an amazing white rabbit marshmallow cake that Mummy made when I was seven'. Kate's mother Carole Goldsmith came from a working-class background and traced her ancestry back to the coal-mining villages of County Durham, but she was determined to get on and became a stewardess for British Airways in the 1970s. It was while working for the airline that she met Michael Middleton, a flight dispatcher from a distinctly middle-class background, and they were married in 1980, a year before Charles married Diana. While Carole and Michael had been educated at comprehensives, they could afford to send all three of their children to private schools, having set up a lucrative mail order company called Party Pieces. The business, which grew into a successful online company, also enabled them to move into an impressive £1 million home just a few miles away in the village of Chapel Row, near Bucklebury in Berkshire. There was even enough money for a pied-à-terre in London's exclusive Chelsea.

Kate attended St Andrew's Preparatory School in Pangbourne, just four miles from their home. Surrounded by woodland, the private co-educational school is situated in a Victorian mansion and with small classes of between fifteen and twenty it was the perfect environment for seven-year-old Kate to flourish. She was required to wear a green blazer, a white shirt and a kilt and enjoyed school so much that she opted to become a weekly boarder when she turned eleven. It was here at St Andrew's that she showed a natural talent for sport and a flair for acting. Like

William, she appeared in school plays, including a production of *Eliza Doolittle*. She also had a starring role in a production of the Victorian drama *Murder in the Red Barn* in her final term. Aged thirteen she played the heroine who falls in love with the man of her dreams, coincidentally a wealthy young man called William. 'Back then Kate was completely different – shy, skinny. But just look how confident and beautiful she is now,' one of her contemporaries, Kinsgley Glover, recalled when a German television production company managed to track down footage of Kate in the play and it immediately became an internet sensation on YouTube. On a grainy home video Kate, who was known as Catherine at school, acts out a scene from the play in which she speaks to a fortune teller. 'Soon you will meet a handsome man, a rich gentleman,' the soothsayer tells her. 'It's all I ever hoped for. Will he fall in love with me?' asks the teenage Kate. 'Indeed he will,' the fortune teller assures her. 'And marry me?' she enquires clasping her hands to her chest. 'And marry you,' confirms the soothsayer. At the end of the play her beau, William, gets down on a bended knee and proposes. Kate responds 'It's all I've ever longed for. Yes, oh yes, dear William.'

While she managed to get the best roles in school plays, she wasn't always so lucky when it came to boys. Taller than the rest of her year and so thin from all the sports she did, Catherine wore her hair in a bob and was painfully shy about the braces she wore on her top teeth. According to her house mistress, Denise Allford, who was in charge of looking after Kate when she started boarding, she was something of an ugly duckling compared to her younger and more gregarious sister, Pippa, who was also at the school. 'She wasn't particularly pretty as a young girl and she wore braces on her teeth from the age of twelve. She was thin and much taller than the other girls – quite gangly really. Pippa was the more beautiful of the two of them at that age. But Catherine was very determined which seemed to set her apart.'

The sports-mad young Catherine loved snacking on marmite sandwiches and needed constant nutrition to keep her weight up. 'Catherine had a very high metabolic rate and that was always a concern for Carole, particularly when she started boarding,' recalled Mrs Allford. 'She had a tremendous appetite but because she put so much effort into everything she needed a constant supply of calories.' One of the friends in Catherine's class remembers that she was more interested in playing sport than dating. 'Occasionally we would go down to the woods to play spin the bottle but Catherine wouldn't join in,' remembers the friend. 'Instead she would be doing her homework or practising her serves on the tennis court. '

Denise Allford and her husband Kevin, who taught sports, French and German at the school, also recalled how Kate was always awarded top marks for good behaviour. She was outstanding at netball and, like William, she represented her school at swimming. In her final year she was named the best all-round sportswoman. 'She was a 100mph kind of girl and put full concentration into everything she did,' Mr Allford told the *Mail on Sunday*. 'She was a hard worker and would often take herself off to the classrooms to study when everyone else was playing.'

That wasn't to say she was completely disinterested in boys. Her first schoolgirl crush was on Andrew de Perlaky, who now sings with musical group Teatro, using the stage name Andrew Alexander. Kate had first set her sights on her classmate when they starred opposite each other in the school's production of *My Fair Lady* in 1992, when they were just eleven. The following year they got to know each other better through choir practice, and eventually Kate plucked up the courage to ask him out. Unfortunately her friend Fiona Beacroft who was in the same year had also taken a shine to Andrew and got there first. 'Kate fancied Andrew and was trying to work out a subtle way of letting him know,' recalls one of Kate's classmates. 'Eventually she asked him out and she was very upset when he chose Fiona. We were young and these were very innocent first loves, a kiss in the woods and holding hands but they were desperately important moments back then. Kate was really down about it for a while. She had never had a boyfriend, and she really wanted her first kiss to be Andrew. Fiona was blonde and very pretty and a lot more gregarious than Kate.' Years later Andrew recalled 'I remember being flushed all of a sudden and getting tongue-tied. I think I caused myself more embarrassment than I caused her. If she asked me now I wouldn't hesitate to say yes.'

As a shy school girl Kate could only dream of meeting and marrying a prince but fate was to play its hand and William and Kate's paths first crossed when they were just ten years old. Ludgrove was just fourteen miles away from St Andrew's and both William and Harry would visit Kate's school to compete in matches. 'They would come to play hockey, rugby and football,' recalls a former pupil. 'Kate was very sporty. She was the best at the school at tennis and high jump and I remember when Prince William came to play she made sure she was there to watch him from the sidelines. It was a big deal and all of the girls, even the not so sporty ones, would rush to the playing fields to get a glimpse of William. It would be the talk of the school for days and Catherine was very excited by it all.'

Academically, Catherine fared well and although she wasn't always in the top stream she was a good all-rounder. She was a member of the school choir and attended practice in the chapel twice a week, dressed in a white chorister robe. When it came to school concerts, Michael and Carole were always in the audience to cheer her on. 'Her parents were very supportive and would be at every school play to watch the girls,' recalls a parent. 'Carole would do the school run and drop the girls off every morning in the family's Range Rover. She was always well turned out in country casuals and would often stay to chat with the other mothers.' Denise Allford also remembers the Middletons were regularly at the school. 'As parents, Carole and Michael were so supportive and involved, but not pushy in the slightest. They were very proud of their children and rightly so because they all stood out. All three of them were very self-motivated. Mike in particular was affable and always came over to chat.' Carole and Michael were delighted when Kate was made a prefect in her final year at St Andrew's, but according to one of her former classmates she never abused her position: 'Kate was one of the few pupils to be allowed into the senior common room. There were comfy sofas and a television, it was quite a privilege but she never boasted about it. She was always kind to the other pupils, especially the newer ones. She wasn't loud or outgoing. She was demure and very sweet. She stayed in touch with a couple of friends from school but not many. She has changed a lot, she's certainly grown into a beauty and the funny thing is her voice has completely changed. She sounds very posh and she definitely wasn't that well-spoken when we were at school.'

When she was thirteen Kate left the comfortable confines of St Andrew's for secondary school. She had sailed through her Common Entrance and her parents, whose business was thriving, had sufficient funds to enrol her at Downe House, an exclusive Roman Catholic all-girls boarding school in Berkshire. The £22,405 per year school has five hundred and seventy pupils and is considered to be one of the best independent schools in the UK, both academically and in sports, but despite her outstanding track record in the latter Kate struggled to fit in. She was teased for taking her studies too seriously and not being worldly enough. While her peers were interested in fashion and boys, Kate was more interested in studying and sport. Many of the girls were from London and of aristocratic stock – Lady Gabriella Windsor is one of the school's most famous alumni and Kate felt that she simply didn't fit in. According to former pupil Emma Sayle, who was four years above Kate, even her ability on the sports pitch wasn't enough to cement Kate a place in one of the school's cliques. 'It was a very pushy school with incredibly assertive girls and if you were not a straight A student naturally you didn't fit in,' recalls Sayle. 'Kate was lovely and kind but not nearly pushy enough and back then Downe House was very cliquey. There were a lot of girls there who had come from private schools in London, in our year we had a gang called the "London Trendies." It just wasn't Kate's scene. She didn't know anyone and she was very lonely.'

Her parents decided after two miserable terms that their

gifted fourteen-year-old daughter would be better suited to Marlborough College.

The £28,000-a-year private school has an excellent track record for sports, and Kate, who was known as Catherine to her contemporaries, thrived in her new surroundings. The choice of aristocratic parents, the co-educational school was founded in 1843 and consists of red-brick buildings situated in rolling hills on the outskirts of a market town in Wiltshire. Former notable alumni include the poet Sir John Betjeman and singer Chris de Burgh, as well as Princesses Beatrice and Eugenie. Here Kate, who was required to dress in the school's uniform of a long black skirt, was able to integrate with the upper crust of society, but she was shy at first and terribly homesick. She missed her family and her friends and she lacked confidence. After her unhappy experience at Downe House she was worried that she would struggle to find like-minded people but she made friends for life. According to former pupil Clarissa Sebag-Montefiore, Kate was 'ordinary, hard-working, athletic and easy going.' A boarder at Elmhurst House, she was a popular pupil, and when her sister and brother joined the school, she gained even more confidence. She had yet to grow into the beauty who was voted the prettiest girl at St Salvator's, but her easy-going nature ensured she had plenty of friends. 'Kate was nicknamed "Catherine Middlebum", and was always popular because she had no side to her at all,' recalled her classmate Gemma Williamson.

She was serious, studious and shy, and while her dorm-mates illicitly experimented with vodka and cigarettes, Kate sensibly refused, although she would gamely agree to keep watch. Her best friend and room-mate Jessica Hay remembered Kate as a family girl with strong morals: 'She didn't get involved in any drinking or smoking but was very sporty instead and very family-orientated.' She passed eleven GCSEs and three A levels, gaining A grades in maths and art and a B in English. She also captained the tennis team and played netball and hockey for the school. But, unlike her friends, she had no interest in boys. 'We would sit around talking about all the boys at school we fancied, but Catherine would always say, "I don't like any of them. They're all a bit rough,"' said Jessica, who was dating William's friend Nicholas Knatchbull at the time. 'Then she would joke, "There's no one quite like William." She had a picture of him on her wall . . . She always used to say, "I bet he's really kind. You can tell just by looking at him."'

According to Jessica, 'one of Catherine's best assets is that she has always been very sure of herself. She has never allowed herself to be influenced by others. She still doesn't really drink and certainly doesn't smoke. You're much more likely to find her going for a long walk across the moors than going to a night-club. That's why she's so perfect for William. They really are so similar. I really do think she's going to be the one.'

Kate hadn't yet attracted the attention of any boys at Marlborough. Any confidence she had was badly dented when the boys in her class awarded her just ones and twos out of ten for prettiness. Jessica Hay recalled how the boys in their year would hold up paper napkins in the school canteen with the scores written on them. But when she returned to Marlborough after the summer of 1998 Kate had blossomed, according to Gemma Wilkinson. 'It happened quite suddenly. Catherine came back after the long summer break the following year an absolute beauty. Although she was sporty Kate was very feminine too.

She always had a lovely willowy figure, but now she had filled out and the colour was back in her cheeks. She never wore particularly fashionable or revealing clothes – just jeans and jumpers but she had an innate sense of style. With that adorable cheeky little grin of hers, she was a totally different girl – and every boy in the school fancied her rotten.' Kate had gone home and asked her mother, who was always ahead of the trend, to help her update her look. Under Carole's guidance she had returned a ravishing beauty. She had discovered some confidence and breasts – which she was apparently obsessed with. One of her peers recalled in the 2000 Leavers' Yearbook to celebrate the end of their schooling at Marlborough: 'Catherine's perfect looks are renowned but her obsession with her tits are not. She is often found squinting down her top and screaming: "They're growing"'.

After her transformation that summer Kate made it on to the 'fit list' which, according to one former pupil was a list of the prettiest girls in the school. 'There were lists of boys and girls that were hung on the wall next to the canteen, although they were soon taken down by the teachers. Kate was definitely on there and so was her sister, Pippa. They were both pretty and very close. They were in the same house and Kate would always keep an eye out for Pippa. They loved playing sport and were always in the top teams. They were tall and slim, lean and athletic, although Pippa was always slightly skinnier than Kate.'

With her new image and renewed confidence Kate, as she was known at Marlborough, started attracting the attention of her male peers. She was so close to Willem Marx, fellow prefect and one of the school's top rugby players, that rumours abounded that they were an item. Born to a Dutch father Willem was British and had been raised in west London. Classmates remember the pair 'hanging out in the prefects' common room and getting along well.' If there was a romance it was low-key and fizzled out as soon as they left Marlborough. While Kate had set her heart on studying History of Art at St Andrews Willem went to Oxford, but they stayed in touch and when Kate and William split up years later, it was the dashing Willem who was photographed escorting Kate home after a night on the tiles at Boujis. Now a journalist working overseas he has never publicly commented or confirmed the rumours about their friendship. In the yearbook Kate was also linked with her class mate Henry Preston and they were rated one of the year's 'best couples.' According to Gemma Wilkinson these were all innocent romances and Kate was not interested in getting serious. 'I got the distinct impression that Catherine wanted to save herself for someone special,' she told the *Daily Mail*. 'It was quite an old fashioned approach.'

When she finished her A levels, Kate was allowed to take a gap year, part of which she spent in Florence. For three months during the autumn of 2000 she lived with four girlfriends in a top-floor flat above a delicatessen in the city centre, where she coupled her passion for art with learning Italian at the British Institute. She would spend hours wandering around Florence's historic cobbled streets and capturing the beauty of the imposing cathedral on camera. Photography was a hobby she loved and, in later years one she would toy with turning into a profession. During those sunny art-filled days in Florence she soaked up the city and its treasures, and, always something of a wallflower at school, she came out of her shell. While she had never counted herself as pretty, those around her often made a point of commenting on her natural beauty, especially her mother. 'Kate morphed into something of a beauty that holiday, and we all saw it,' remembers a friend. 'Her parents came over to Florence for a long weekend. While her father Michael was quiet, Carole was very gregarious and would not stop telling Kate how beautiful she had become. She had rosebud lips and this amazing mane of hair, and she was gorgeous. When we were at dinner Carole would exclaim to the waiters, "Look at my English rose. Isn't she so beautiful?" Kate would be cringing in the corner, but she knew it was true.'

This was typical of mother and daughter. While Kate could be painfully shy, her mother was confident and proud, and always believed her daughter was destined for great things. She had high hopes for all three of her children. Kate's brother quit Edinburgh University after the first year to get involved with the family business, while Pippa continued her degree in English at the same university. She dated J J Jardine Patterson, a scion of the Hong Kong banking family, and counted Ted Innes-Kerr, son of the Duke of Roxburghe, and George Percy, son of the Duke of Northumberland, as close friends. When Kate became friendly with William, Carole by all accounts was delighted. As far as she was concerned, both her daughters had reached the pinnacle of social success. The press picked up on this and nicknamed Pippa and Kate the 'wisteria sisters' because of their 'ferocious ability to climb the social ladder'. 'Carole has always wanted the best for her children,' recalled a family friend.

She is incredibly close to Kate and largely misinterpreted. It upsets Kate a lot when people say her mother is pushy. Carole is a go-getter who knows what she wants and usually gets it. Yes, she likes the fine things in life, but she and Michael have worked hard to get them. She is a lot of fun, and often sends herself up. When they dine in Mustique and she hears a plane coming in to land, she puts on her best air hostess voice and announces the flight name and landing time – it's very funny. Michael is a man of fewer words, but you can tell he adores his family. He always sits at the head of the table, and you can see his delight as he listens to his children chat about their recent adventures.

While some at the Palace snootily pontificated that Kate was not blue-blooded enough for the prince because of her coal mining ancestry, she is in fact able to trace her heritage back to aristocracy. In the summer of 2010 the *Daily Mail* reported that Kate was in fact a distant cousin of William. Under the headline 'Wills and Kate, the Kissing Cousins!' it emerged that Kate and William were linked – albeit rather tenuously through Sir Thomas Leighton, an Elizabethan soldier and the much-feared Governor of Guernsey who died in 1610. The despot was William's 12th generation great-grandparent and Kate's 11th, thus making them 12th cousins once removed. According to journalist Claudia Joseph, who spent a year tracing the Middleton's family tree, the couple were also linked as distant 17th cousins through Sir Thomas Fairfax, a Parliamentarian general in the English Civil War, who was related to Kate's great-grandmother Olive Lupton, an Edwardian society beauty who died forty-five years before

Kate was born. It was something for Kate's critics who dismissed her as being not good enough for William to think about. Whether she was an aristocrat or not she had other qualities that were far more important to William. She was polite to the photographers who now pursued her and quickly adopted the royal rule of never speaking out. She also insisted that her family never discussed her relationship with William. As Princess Diana's former private secretary Patrick Jephson noted, 'We know very little about her and probably never will, providing they do their job right. Historically a degree of mystery about royalty has been an advantage; we project onto them what we want.' According to one of her friends at St Andrews, she remained level-headed and kept her feet on the ground during the early months of their courtship. 'She never got above her station, and even though she had secured the most sought-after boy at St Andrews she never gloated. She was actually quite insecure about her looks and never considered herself pretty, she was very sweet and very shy.'

Like Diana, Kate quickly had to adapt to being in the spotlight, but her transition into royal life was much smoother. She enjoyed being at Highgrove, Balmoral and Sandringham, where she would accompany William on shoots during the grouse and pheasant seasons. She had practised with William on the Strathtyrum estate, where they were allowed to shoot birds for food as part of their rental agreement. She and William cherished their weekends on the Balmoral estate. Like Charles, who had been given the use of Wood Farm at Sandringham while he was at Cambridge, the Queen allowed William to use a cottage called Tam-na-Ghar at Balmoral as a getaway. Tucked away in the remote countryside, the 120-year-old cottage, which is surrounded by

rolling hills and wild heather as far as the eye can see, underwent a £150,000 renovation complete with a bath tub big enough
for two before William and Harry were each given a set of keys.

After their last class on Friday William and Kate would speed
up to Balmoral from St Andrews in William's black Volkswagon
Golf followed by his protection officers. It was here that he really
got to know the girl who many believe will one day become his
wife and with that, the queen of the United Kingdom. Like
William, Kate loved walking across the moors and strolling by the
River Dee. In the evenings they would cook a meal, share a bottle
of red wine and keep warm in front of a roaring log fire. Sometimes they were joined by friends from St Andrews, and often
Pippa and James, whose trophy stag heads line the walls of the
Middleton family house, would be invited for a weekend's shoot,
when they would compete as to who could bag the most birds.

It was the summer of 2004 when William and Kate's love
affair underwent its first serious test. With one year to complete
before they graduated, the twenty-two-year-old prince needed
some space. Until now they had chosen not to discuss what
would happen after St Andrews, but with their finals looming,
it was an issue that needed addressing.

William decided that a holiday would provide him with some
thinking time and planned a boys-only sailing trip to Greece as
soon as they broke up for the summer holidays. Despite being
an accomplished sailor, Kate was not invited. Instead, William
would go with Guy Pelly and some other friends. Kate had had
a turbulent relationship with Guy and considered him immature
and potentially troublesome. It was Guy who used to buy William
porn magazines when they were teenagers, and she had heard all

about their drink-fuelled weekends at Highgrove. There was also a rumour among their friends that William and Guy had covered one of their girlfriends in chocolate ice cream which they then licked off after a night of heavy drinking at Club H, and the occasion when Guy challenged William to a midnight skinny dip at their friend James Tollemache's twenty-first birthday party at Helmingham Hall in Suffolk. They had both been drinking heavily but that didn't stop them from stripping down to their boxer shorts, diving in and swimming a lap of the murky moat that surrounds the Tollemache's country estate where the Queen is a regular guest. At one point William had relieved himself in a field while Harry, who was seventeen at the time, spent most of the night on the dance floor of the Moulin Rouge themed party with a can of beer in each hand according to one guest.

It seemed wherever there was trouble, Guy was not far behind and Kate was wary of him. She was not surprised when she found out that Guy had arranged the yacht with an all-female crew, but she was annoyed. So she packed her bags and headed home to Berkshire to spend the summer with her family. It wasn't so much the fact that William wanted a break; Kate was beginning to question William's commitment to their relationship, and she also had her own creeping doubts about their future after St Andrews.

A number of things had caused her to question William's commitment, although she had not raised them with him yet. One was William's friendship with an American heiress called Anna Sloan, whom William had met through mutual friends at Edinburgh University, where Anna was studying. Anna had lost her father, businessman George Sloan, in a tragic shooting accident on the family's 360-acre estate in Nashville, and she and William had bonded over the loss of their parents. When Anna invited William and a group of friends to Texas for a holiday before he went to Greece, it hurt Kate deeply. She suspected William might have feelings for the twenty-two-year-old heiress. However, Anna was not in the least romantically interested in William, and the friendship was never anything more than just that.

And then there was William's budding friendship with another stunning heiress, Isabella Anstruther-Gough-Calthorpe. The younger sister of William and Harry's polo-playing friend Jacobi, the impossibly named but exquisite-looking socialite had caught William's attention. While Kate was girl-next-door pretty, Isabella boasted cover-girl looks, a title and a stately pile to boot. That summer William visited the Anstruther-Gough-Calthorpe family home in Chelsea to see her. Isabella, daughter of banking heiress Lady Mary Gaye Curzon, was just twenty-one and single at the time. Sadly for William, she had no aspirations to date a prince and despite his amorous advances declared that she was not interested.

Meanwhile Kate had accepted an invitation to spend a fortnight in France at Fergus Boyd's family holiday home in the Dordogne with some friends from St Andrews. Among the group were Kate's friends Olivia Bleasdale and Ginny Fraser. She had not told them about the trial separation, but from her downcast mood her friends guessed, and one evening she confided to them that she and William were taking a break. 'She was debating whether or not she should text or call him. She got quite drunk on white wine and really let her guard down,' recalled one of the group. 'She said how sad she was and how much she was missing William, but she never mentioned it after that.'

I had reported the news of their separation that summer and tellingly there was no denial from Clarence House. Privately William complained to friends that he was feeling 'claustrophobic' and was already thinking ahead to the summer after graduation, when he was planning to return to Kenya to see Jecca Craig, another fly in the ointment as far as Kate was concerned. 'William has been unhappy in their relationship for a while, but the last thing he wants is a high-profile split in the crucial months leading up to his finals,' I was told at the time. On the advice of her mother, who had been a sounding board that summer, Kate gave William some breathing space.

It was obviously the break that William needed, and by October they were back together again, although Kate had a condition. Word had reached her of William's visits to Isabella and she insisted that William was not to contact her again. With their finals looming in May they agreed to take things slowly. Kate had stayed away from Edward Van Cutsem's wedding to the Duke of Westminster's daughter Lady Tamara Grosvenor that November but she happily accepted an invitation to Prince Charles's fifty-sixth birthday party at Highgrove later that month. Charles already saw Kate as a daughter in-law and the following March he invited her to Klosters for his pre-wedding holiday. Kate was photographed taking a gondola up the slopes with Charles and enjoying lunch with the princes and their friends. It had really been intended as a boys-only trip but this time Kate was not left out.

Charles and Camilla were to be married on 9 April 2005 and

the prince wanted one last skiing holiday with his sons first. Both brothers had given their blessing for Charles to remarry. 'Great,' Harry said on hearing the news. 'Go for it. Why not?' William was to be a witness at the civil ceremony together with Camilla's son Tom, and had the added responsibility of looking after the wedding rings. The British public appeared to have accepted Charles's long-term mistress. In a YouGov poll at the time 65 per cent of respondents said that the couple should be free to marry compared to just 40 per cent in 1998. The Palace had hoped to break the news of the royal engagement, but to their embarrassment the *Evening Standard*, a London newspaper, got the scoop and ran the story on 10 February before the official announcement. Prince Charles's communications secretary Paddy Harverson confirmed the news and explained that there would be no official photocall until the wedding day. The last thing anyone wanted was the newspapers running pictures of Charles and Diana alongside Charles and his new bride. It would cause unnecessary hurt to everyone, especially William and Harry.

The run-up to the wedding was beset with problems. Charles and Camilla wanted a civil wedding at Windsor Castle, but when it was realised that if a licence was granted any other couple could also be married there, the plan was scrapped. Instead it was decided that Charles and Camilla would marry at Windsor Guildhall, followed by a blessing in St George's Chapel in the castle given by the Archbishop of Canterbury for 700 guests, and finally a reception hosted by the Queen. Camilla was dubbed a 'town hall bride' in the papers, and even though over Christmas the Queen had privately given her blessing for Charles to remarry, there was speculation that she would not be attending the nuptials. QUEEN SNUBS CHARLES WEDDING was one of the headlines in the *Daily Telegraph*, while the *New York Post* speculated, QUEEN TO SKIP CHUCK NUPS. Charles was crestfallen that his wedding day was being labelled a 'fiasco', while Camilla was said to be so stressed she had taken up yoga. William and Harry assured their father that he was making the right decision. It was more than seven years since the death of their mother, and although not a day passed when they didn't think about her, they wanted him to be happy. 'We are both very happy for our father and Camilla and we wish them all the luck in the future,' they said in a joint statement. While it had been difficult for them in the early years, the boys realised that their papa was happier with his long-term mistress in his life, and they had warmed to Camilla. 'We love her to bits,' remarked Harry.

Against all the odds the wedding was a success, even though it was delayed for twenty-four hours because of the death of Pope John Paul II. 'Can anything else possibly go wrong?' asked the *Daily Mail*. It was the question on everyone's lips at the Palace too, but when Camilla emerged from the shadows of the Guildhall into the spring sunshine to rapturous applause on Saturday 9 April, it seemed the worst really was finally behind them. Present was a tiny fraction of the number of people that had gathered in the Mall years before to watch Prince Charles kiss the virgin bride Diana, but the crowds that lined the streets of Windsor waved Union Jacks, smiled and wished the couple well. As William gave Camilla a kiss for the cameras, Harry and his cousins Beatrice and Eugenie walked up to St George's Chapel. The impish prince gave a cheeky thumbs up and performed a merry jig for the waving crowds. The most moving tribute that day was from the Queen, who announced at Windsor Castle, 'My son is home and dry with the woman he loves.' For the first time she had given the couple her public blessing.

Camilla was now part of the family, and when William graduated on 23 June 2005 she was there along with Charles, the Duke of Edinburgh and the Queen. William and Kate had dreaded and looked forward to the day in equal measure. They had enjoyed one last party before their finals and in keeping with tradition attended the annual May Ball, organised by the Kate Kennedy Club at Kinkell Farm. Uncharacteristically, Kate drank so much Fergus Boyd had to carry her out before the night ended. Now, as they walked into Younger Hall, which smelled of floor polish and summer, they exchanged a smile and took their seats. Kate looked stunning in a simple short black skirt, white blouse and heels, and sat five rows in front of William, who was dressed in a suit beneath his black gown with cherry-coloured silk lining. He slipped from his seat ten minutes before his name was called, before re-emerging from a side room to join the other graduands. Not only was he anxious about the ceremony, which had attracted numbers of the town's residents and hundreds of press, there had been an embarrassing to-do over the royals' attendance.

The Queen, who had been 'under the weather' according to William, had asked her private secretary to request that the ninety-minute ceremony was moved from the morning to the afternoon to ensure that she had plenty of time to get to St Andrews. While the university was delighted to accommodate the royal party and provided the Queen with a potted history of every student graduating, they had been unprepared to alter the timetable.

According to the university's head of communications, St Andrews has two graduation ceremonies a day, one in the morning and one in the afternoon and it was simply not possible to change them around. 'I'm not surprised the university wouldn't move the ceremony,' remarked Andrew Neil, who left St Andrews in 2002. 'What we did from day one was treat William as normal, so why change it on the final day?' If she was feeling unwell, the Queen did not let it show, and she smiled broadly as William knelt before the chancellor's wooden pulpit to collect his parchment. The Duke of Edinburgh and the recently married Charles and Camilla looked proudly on as a burst of flash photography captured the moment when William Wales was awarded a 2.1 in geography.

Minutes later Kate was called to the stage as Catherine Middleton to receive her 2.1 in the history of art. When it came to the end of the ceremony, the words of vice-chancellor Dr Brian Lang must have seemed particularly poignant. 'You will have made lifelong friends,' he told the graduates. 'You may have met your husband or wife. Our title as the top matchmaking university in Britain signifies so much that is good about St Andrews, so we rely on you to go forth and multiply.'

Chapter 11

Stepping in line at Sandhurst

Nobody's really supposed to love it, it's Sandhurst . . . you get treated like a piece of dirt to be honest.

Prince Harry

Harry had dreamed of joining the army since he was a little boy dressing up in military fatigues and playing toy soldiers. When he was accepted as an officer cadet at Sandhurst his dream came true. Harry would become the first senior royal to join the British army since 1960, when Prince Michael of Kent, the Queen's cousin and grandson of King George V, enrolled at the Royal Military Academy. Traditionally the Windsors have served in the Royal Navy. The Duke of Edinburgh joined in 1939 and commanded the frigate HMS *Magpie*, while Prince Andrew, Duke of York reached the rank of honorary captain in the Royal Navy. Charles also served in the Royal Navy after training as an RAF pilot. Harry had heard all about Sandhurst from Mark Dyer. The college was formed in 1947 by the amalgamation of two previous army training colleges and under its motto 'Serve to Lead' has trained officers from all over the world. At the end of their training Sir Winston Churchill and King Hussein of Jordan both passed out on the famous quadrangle in front of Old College, and now it was Harry's chance to undertake the punishing forty-eight-week training course.

Following his somewhat controversial and unplanned double gap year, the prince was finally ready for some serious work. He had been warned that the first five weeks at the military academy would be the hardest of his life and that 15 per cent of all cadets drop out during this period, but he had already had a taste of what was to come during a four-day assessment in Westbury, Wiltshire. It had been tough, but he had passed the notoriously hard Regular Commissions Board entrance exams with flying colours. Due to enroll in January 2005, he sustained an injury to his left knee while coaching rugby to children in October 2004, and had to delay his entry by four months, but on the morning of 8 May 2005 Harry promised himself he would not fail. As he pulled up at Old College, the grand cream-fronted nineteenth-century building that looks on to the academy's quadrangle, acres of greenery and a man-made lake, Harry took in his new surroundings. His father had driven him to Camberley and now looked proudly on as Harry, still tanned from a two-week safari in Botswana with Chelsy, enrolled as Cadet Wales.

For the first five weeks Harry was allowed to venture no further than the academy's main buildings – Old College and New College – and the exercise fields. While Camberley town has little to offer in terms of nightlife and eating out, it is just thirty-four miles south of London, and the fact that Harry could not leave was a daunting prospect for the young prince. The idea is that by keeping the cadets within the academy, everyone is treated and assessed uniformly and has the chance to bond with their platoon. Harry had been sent a packing list, and after being shown to his room, a cell measuring nine by ten feet containing a sink, a chest of drawers, a cupboard and a desk, he started to unpack. He had brought with him several jars of polish, which he would use daily to buff his army boots, and his own ironing board. For a boy who had never had to press a shirt or shine his shoes, it was a rude awakening.

Harry rose before dawn every morning, when the day started with room inspection by Colour Sergeant Glen Snazle from the Grenadier Guards. His bed, with its single plain blue duvet, was checked, as was his uniform, which had to be pressed in a certain and very particular way. His sink was to be clean, his military kit serviceable and his civilian clothes washed and put away. If his room was not up to standard, he would receive a 'show parade', where he would be inspected again that night. He was not allowed to listen to pop music; instead all radios were to be tuned to BBC Radio 4. Laptops and mobile phones were confiscated on day one, but would be returned after five weeks. Televisions were not allowed in bedrooms, nor were posters, plants or photographs. Harry was expected to report for duty every day, even Sundays, when he would have to attend chapel.

From the moment he was awake he was on his feet, carrying out drill, physical training and domestic chores which included polishing and re-polishing his army-issue black boots until his sergeant could see his reflection in them. Despite being the only cadet with round-the-clock protection, Harry had insisted he wanted to be treated the same as everyone else. It was something the commandant of Sandhurst, Major General Andrew Ritchie, had assured him would be the case. 'I have removed certain cadets from Sandhurst as their behaviour is not up to the standards of an officer, and I would do so again,' said General Ritchie. 'We get used to people here who have worked four hours and slept twenty. Here we reverse that. Some find it a struggle.' The academy's straight-talking Sergeant Major Vince Gaunt was equally direct. 'Prince Harry will call me sir. And I will call him sir. But he will be the one who means it.'

The arrival of such a high-profile cadet inevitably put Sandhurst in the spotlight, and embarrassingly for the academy, which has armed guards at its fortified entrance gates and vehicle checks, there was a major security alert within weeks of Harry's arrival. A British tabloid newspaper claimed one of its journalists had got into the college carrying a fake bomb. It was the latest in a series of security blunders around the royal family, who were still hugely embarrassed that an imposter had crashed William's twenty-first-birthday celebrations while an undercover reporter had spent months working for the Queen at Buckingham Palace.

Unperturbed, Harry immersed himself in the training. 'It's a bit of a struggle but I got through it,' he later said of his five-week induction. 'I do enjoy running down a ditch full of mud, firing bullets; it's the way I am. I love it.' He had discovered a new passion and inner confidence. For Harry the army was a chance to show that despite his past hiccups he could succeed. While he had struggled to keep up at Eton, he was top of the class at Sandhurst. He quickly mastered the basics of general drill and weapons handling but because of his knee he found the physical training a challenge. He was nicknamed 'Sicknote' after he was sent to the private Frimley Park Hospital in Surrey with infected blisters, the result of a five-day exercise in Ashdown Forest in Sussex. Unlike William he was messy, and his sergeant would put him on restricted privileges – confined to the academy

– when his room was not up to scratch. While he was occasionally in trouble with his seniors, he was popular among his peers in Alamein Company, who recalled that Harry would always keep a secret stash of cigarettes under his mattress, having failed to kick the habit.

A world away from Boujis, Sandhurst was the best thing to happen to Harry. He completed a punishing twenty-six-hour race across the Black Mountains in the Brecon Beacons in record time and scored top marks during a training exercise in Cyprus. On his twenty-first birthday, which was a low-key affair celebrated with his platoon in the academy bar, where pints cost £1.20, he made it clear that he had every intention of fighting on the front line. In an interview he gave around the same time he said, 'There's no way I'm going to put myself through Sandhurst and then sit on my arse back at home while my boys are out fighting for their country.' They were fighting words, and Harry meant every one. Showing a new maturity, he also apologised for his past mistakes and for the first time spoke about his ill-advised Nazi outfit: 'It was a very stupid thing to do and I've learned my lesson.'

He could not resist a dig at William, who was set to follow him at Sandhurst. He adored his older brother, but until now he had always lived his life on William's coat-tails. Now Harry was in the driving seat. 'When I have left I'll have to make a special effort to visit him for comedy value just so he can salute me,' he joked. 'Every year we get closer. It's amazing how close we've become. We have even resorted to hugging each other,' he revealed in the same interview. 'Ever since our mother died, obviously we were close, but he is the one person on this earth who I can talk [to] about anything. We understand each other and we give each other support.' He also talked about his father's recent wedding, commenting that Charles was 'much more relaxed' since the marriage. Speaking about Camilla for the first time he said, 'She's a wonderful woman, and she has made our father very happy, which is the most important thing.' He dismissed any idea that she was a 'wicked stepmother' and insisted, 'We are very grateful for her. We're very happy to have her around.'

In the New Year, which William and Kate had seen in together at a cottage on the Sandringham estate, it was William's turn to prove he could rise to the challenge of Sandhurst. The twenty-three-year-old prince arrived in driving rain on 8 January 2006 accompanied by his father and private secretary Jamie Lowther-Pinkerton, a former SAS officer. After being introduced to Major General Ritchie, William signed into Blenheim Company, bade farewell to his father and was shown to his room overlooking Old College, which would be home for the next forty-eight weeks. Not prepared to risk the sort of security fiasco that had marred Harry's arrival, the college worked closely with the prince's team of personal protection officers, who accompanied him on every exercise in their blacked-out cars.

Knowing he would not see Kate for over a month, William had taken Harry's advice and whisked her off on yet another holiday to Klosters after the New Year celebrations. The Swiss resort was one of their favourite places, and Kate had mastered the off-piste runs, occasionally outshining William with her impressive technique. Just two years earlier the couple's romance had been revealed on these slopes as William put his arm around Kate in an unthinking show of intimacy. This time there was no holding back in spite of the cameras. Standing together in the deep powder snow, William pulled Kate towards him and kissed her. It was clear that he had found someone he could love, someone he was completely at ease with, a woman who understood and accepted the huge pressures that came with dating him. Apparently, a number of dates had been pencilled in the royal calendar in anticipation of an engagement announcement.

Such planning might seem a touch premature, but for the royal family this was quite normal. The Palace works months and sometimes years in advance: preparations for the Queen Mother's funeral started in 1969. 'It's being talked about within the Palace very openly,' a well-placed source insisted to me. 'The word is that there might be an announcement in the spring.' It was the sort of predictive story that needed to be taken with a pinch of salt, and Clarence House was quick to deny any concrete plans were in place. But there was definitely something to the story, which was picked up by royal commentators and newspapers around the world. Of course William had yet to pop the question, but as far as insiders at the Palace and his inner circle were concerned it was only a matter of time. There was no escaping the fact that in Kate Middleton Prince William had found a potential bride.

Kate had arranged a farewell drinks party for William at Clarence House and had been dreading the moment they would have to say goodbye. William would miss her twenty-fourth birthday and she wanted to make sure they could at least celebrate before he left for Sandhurst. They had had a wonderful summer after working through their rocky patch. After they graduated William travelled to New Zealand, where he represented the Queen at events commemorating the sixtieth anniversary of the end of the Second World War and spent time with the British Lions, who were there on tour. Then he visited Jecca in Kenya, but this time he took Kate with him. He wanted her to experience the wild beauty of the country he had grown to love and reassure her that she had no cause to worry about Jecca. William had whisked Kate off for a romantic holiday at the Masai Lodge where they stayed at the £1,500-a-night Il Ngwesi Lodge in the Mukogodo Hills of northern Kenya. During the day William worked on the Craig family's Lewa Wildlife Conservancy, which protects the endangered black rhino from poachers. In the evenings he and Kate would sip cocktails and dine al fresco. The post-graduation holiday had been a blissful fortnight, and they had been joined by Jecca and William's friend Thomas van Straubenzee. When they left, William and Kate promised to return again soon.

As William prepared for Sandhurst his girlfriend had moved to London and into the flat her parents had bought for her. As she set about sending her CV to art galleries she had plenty of time to wonder about her future. William, on the other hand, had the next year all planned. He spent a fortnight working at Chatsworth on the Duke and Duchess of Devonshire's 35,000-acre Peak District estate and three weeks doing work experience at HSBC's headquarters in St James Street in London and the Bank of England. He had already decided he wanted to be a pilot like his Uncle Andrew, and had enjoyed the fortnight he had spent working with the RAF Valley Mountain Rescue Team in Anglesey, where he learned about helicopter flying and mountain rescue. Having decided he wanted a career in the military, he joked that he had sent Harry to Sandhurst as his guinea pig.

Joking aside, Sandhurst was unlike anything he had ever known. Echoing his message to Harry, Major General Ritchie told the waiting media that William would be treated exactly the same as every other cadet: 'Everyone is judged on merit. There are no exceptions made.' Occasionally William was afforded special treatment. As the only cadet to be president of the Football Association, he was given leave during his second term to travel to Germany to support England during the World Cup, much to the envy of his fellow cadets. Harry had also been granted leave to compete in the Cartier International polo tournament in the summer of 2005. While the rest of his platoon was in chapel, he had enjoyed a champagne lunch in the July sunshine and mingled with socialites and celebrities in the VIP tent. Such privileges were rare however, and when it came to their training, neither prince was given special treatment.

William was under the command of Sergeant Major Simon Nichols and Colour Sergeants Nathan Allen and Jimmy Parke from the Irish Guards. He took up judo when he started at Sandhurst but found that being left-handed prevented him making much progress. His natural fitness helped him to cope with the punishing training exercises, but his plan to keep up the yoga he had mastered in Chile was abandoned. He was simply too tired to do anything at the end of the day and mornings weren't an option. William made the most of every minute he had to stay in bed and rest his aching body. While he just about coped with the physical exhaustion of the eighteen-hour days, he found the monotony of Sandhurst challenging. On his leaves he complained that he was constantly exhausted and could not get to grips with making his bed 'the Sandhurst way', which included tucking the sheets in with precisely the right number of folds before room inspection at 5.30 a.m.

By spring, with William knee deep in trench training, it was time for Harry to pass out. He had spent weeks preparing for the parade and apart from the occasional blip had proved himself a model soldier. Just days before the passing out ceremony, however, Harry was back on the front pages. He and four other cadets had visited Spearmint Rhino, a lap-dancing club in the nearby town of Colnbrook, and while he had not technically broken any rules (cadets are allowed out as long as they do not socialise within three miles of the academy), the details of their drink-fuelled night out made for rather unsavoury reading. DIRTY HARRY'S NIGHT OUT had included the prince dancing with two strippers and getting drunk. It was embarrassing and very poor timing with Chelsy on her way to the UK from South Africa to celebrate Harry's passing out.

Fortunately 12 April was gloriously sunny and nothing was going to spoil Harry's big day. Immaculate in his pressed cere-monial dress, Harry looked every inch a second lieutenant. He had signed up to join the Blues and Royals, the British army's second oldest regiment and part of the Household Cavalry, and now had the qualifications to do so. Harry was pleased as punch, as was his grandmother, who had come to inspect the parade for the first time in fifteen years. The Duke of Edinburgh, the Prince of Wales and Camilla, Duchess of Cornwall, elegant in a dark purple outfit, were also there to watch Harry pass out, along with William, who saluted his brother as he marched past in front of Old College. Harry had also invited his former nanny Tiggy to the ceremony along with Mark Dyer and Jamie Lowther-Pinkerton.

The Queen, dressed in a beige three-quarter-length coat with fur-trimmed cuffs, addressed the senior cadets, who had spent weeks polishing their boots and equipment ahead of the Sovereign's Parade. As she inspected the 219 officer cadets she paused in front of her grandson to check every button was polished and every hair was in place. Of course it was, and Harry could not resist a grin at his grandmother. The Queen described the day as 'a great occasion' and spoke of the importance of effective leadership. 'This is just the end of the beginning, and many of you will deploy on operations within months or even weeks. I wish you all every success in your chosen career. My congratulations, my prayers and my trust go with you all.' After Major Stephen Segrave rode his horse up the steps of Old College, a tradition which stems from the 1920s when Major William 'Boy' Browning first decided to do the same, Harry and his platoon slow-marched into the building, as the band, in bearskins and red tunics, trumpeted out 'Auld Lang Syne'. Eating his lunch and toasting his friends, Harry could hardly wait until later that night, when he would be reunited with Chelsy. The couple had not seen each other since their New Year holiday.

When she touched down on the tarmac at Heathrow it was clear that she was to be treated like a princess for the duration of her stay. At Harry's insistence she was met by two armed policemen, who whisked her through the terminal and into a waiting chauffeur-driven four-by-four. Harry and Chelsy had agreed that she would not come to the ceremony; instead she would make her entrance at the passing-out ball.

She did not disappoint Harry when she stepped through the doors of the gymnasium, which had been dressed with white flowers and scented candles. He had excitedly told his friends all about his 'knockout' girlfriend and his fellow officers had seen pictures of Chelsy in the newspapers, but in the flesh she was even prettier. She stole the show in a stunning silk turquoise bias-cut silk dress that clung to her curves and dipped daringly at the back to reveal acres of tanned skin. She had had several fittings at home to make sure the evening gown was perfect and had arranged her hair in a loose chignon. Harry kissed her as they danced the night away to the sound of a live jazz band. They shared cigarettes and flutes of champagne under the night sky and wandered hand in hand around the gymnasium, which had been transformed into a labyrinth of different rooms and dance floors. There was a casino, an ice sculpture from which guests could drink shots of vodka, and a chocolate fountain in which to dip marshmallows and strawberries. In another room footage of the afternoon's ceremony was being played on a loop on a giant screen. Any worries Chelsy may have had about her boyfriend's night out the week before were now a distant memory. They were happy, in love and most importantly together again.

But as William downed glass after glass of red wine, Kate Middleton was conspicuous by her absence. Harry had been allowed to bring eight guests to the ball, but this was Harry and Chelsy's night and the two girls had always had a slightly frosty relationship. Although Chelsy gets along well with Kate's sister Pippa who she occasionally goes out with, she and Kate are less friendly. They got off to an ill-fated start when Kate offered to take Chelsy shopping on the King's Road the last time she was in London. When Chelsy, whose sense of style is very different from Kate's, snubbed the invitation, Kate was said to be offended. Feeling slightly isolated, William proceeded to drink his fill before retiring to his room alone. At midnight, as tradition dictates, to the backdrop of an impressive fireworks display that spelt out CONGRATULATIONS in the night sky, Harry finally ripped the velvet strip from the sleeve of his jacket to reveal his officer's pips. He had proved his critics wrong. He was now a cornet in the Household Cavalry and within weeks would be training with his regiment and preparing for war.

Despite hangovers William and Harry continued celebrating the following night, and this time Kate joined the royal clique at Boujis nightclub in Kensington. As the DJ played their favourite tunes, the bar's amiable owner Jake Parkinson-Smith strolled over to check that everything was in place. Kate had ordered a round of the club's signature Crackbaby cocktails, a potent combination of vodka and fresh passion-fruit juice topped up with cham-pagne and served in a test tube, and by three in the morning the group had run up a notional £2,500 bar bill – notional because, as always, the charge was waived. The DJ played his final tune of the night and it was time to leave, but the fun was set to continue for both the boys. William had an Easter break to Mustique with Kate to look forward to, while Harry was heading off to Mozambique with Chelsy. It would be his last holiday for a while. When he returned to the UK he would start an intensive twelve-week training programme at the Household Cavalry's headquarters in Bovington Camp in Dorset. The imposing walls of the military camp could not be a starker contrast to the deserted palm-fringed beaches of the Caribbean, but Harry soon acclimatised. He was a trained officer now and equipped to lead his men into war, which was exactly what he planned to do.

Chapter 12

William's wobble

I'm only twenty-two for God's sake. I am too young to marry at my age. I don't want to get married until I am at least twenty-eight or maybe thirty.

Prince William

As she took her place in the front row Kate Middleton looked every inch the princess-in-waiting. Accompanied by her parents Michael and Carole, she had been given a VIP seat at the passing out ceremony and could not contain her excitement. Dressed in an elegant red dress coat, black leather gloves and a broad-rimmed black hat, she looked smart and sophisticated, if a little older than her twenty-four years. She had wanted to make an effort and had deliberated over her outfit for weeks determined to get it just right. While it was William's big day, it was the second time Kate would be in the official presence of his grandmother, and she wanted to leave an impression. Just seats away from the Queen, Prince Philip, Charles and Camilla, she certainly stood out among the other guests, many of who were in long dark overcoats wrapped up against the December cold.

As William found Kate in the crowd he smiled. He was glad she was there to see him pass out. Over the past months, although they had seen little of one another, she had been a great support. The official inquest into his mother's death had been published that week, concluding the crash in Paris nine years before had been a tragic accident, and relief as well as pride seemed etched on William's face. 'I love the uniform. It's so sexy,' Kate whispered to her mother as they took their seats. Dressed in No.1 dress, a dark blue tunic and trousers, with white tabs on the collar and a red stripe down each leg, William proudly wore the red sash that accompanied carrying the Sovereign's Banner for the best platoon of the year.

As the brass band broke into a cheerful rendition of Abba's 'Dancing Queen', Kate smiled and reflected on the months that had passed since their graduation. Their relationship had withstood post-university teething problems and was going from strength to strength. The very fact that Kate and her parents – who William had grown fond of – were at one of the most important occasions of his life spoke volumes. Bookies William Hill slashed their odds on a royal engagement from 5–1 to 2–1 and eventually stopped taking bets altogether. Kate's position in the 'firm' seemed in no doubt. Two weeks before she had even been invited for a weekend at Sandringham where she looked confident and quite the country girl as she shot under William's watchful eye.

Now that it was clear that theirs was not just a university romance, aides at the Palace suddenly started paying attention to the middle-class girl who had so captured the prince's imagination. Mindful of the mistakes that had been made with Diana, it was unanimously agreed that Kate should be introduced to royal life as quickly as possible. William may not have asked her to marry him, but there was no disputing how important a part of his life she had become. At his request, it was decided that Kate should be advised on how to cope with the intense media interest in her. William was determined that Kate should suffer none of the loneliness or isolation his mother had felt in the early days of her courtship. Kate was given the support of the Prince of Wales's press team and, when she was with William, her own protection officer. At a polo match she was spotted with her own two-way radio in case she required back-up. She received advice on how to handle the photographers who followed her about, which included watching footage of the late Princess of Wales to see how she had coped with the paparazzi. According to friends, Kate found it all fascinating if 'a little creepy'.

With or without a ring on her finger, Kate had become one of the world's most photographed women, and unlike Chelsy who hated the attention, she was surprisingly confident. Always impeccably dressed, she was advised never to talk to the press, but to politely smile at photographers, who she handled with aplomb. During a visit to the horse trials at Gatcombe House with her mother shortly after she graduated in August 2005, Kate had been asked to pose. 'If I do it now I'll have to keep doing it at skiing or every time,' she told them. It was a calculated response that showed how well she had been briefed. By now Kate had the number of Paddy Harverson saved in her mobile phone, and when a German magazine pinpointed the exact location of her Chelsea home, called him. She had panic buttons linked to the local police station installed at the property. Charles was made aware of the situation and instructed his lawyers Harbottle & Lewis to send out letters to Fleet Street editors pointing out that Kate was a private individual and should be left alone. The problem was that Kate, like Diana, had become a story in her own right. When newspapers and magazines published pictures of her, sales rocketed. People wanted to know everything about Kate.

Being William's girlfriend seemed to take up most of her time, but Kate had set up a children's clothing business under the umbrella of her parents' company Party Pieces. Travelling frequently to Milan for materials, she quickly ran into debt and sought the advice of William's friend Jamie Murray Wells, a successful Internet entrepreneur. Although James was just twenty-four, he was making millions through his venture Glasses Direct and William considered him a safe pair of hands. At a summer party at the Kensington Roof Gardens – owned by Sir Richard Branson, whose children Holly and Sam are friends of William and Kate – she asked for his advice. As she queued at the dinner buffet she confided to James, 'The business is running into debt, but I really want to prove to my dad that I can do this without asking him for any money.' It was a fascinating insight into her developing character. Until now Kate had not seemed career driven, but here she was trying to find a solution to her problems without asking her parents to bail her out.

An answer was just around the corner: by November 2006 Kate had been offered a job as an accessories buyer for the high-street chain Jigsaw. The Middletons were good friends of John and Belle Robinson, who own the successful company, and William and Kate had been guests at their luxury holiday home in Mustique that Easter. The Robinsons had waived the £8,000-a-week rent after William complained that he could not afford to holiday on the exclusive Caribbean island. Instead he made a donation to a hospital in St Vincent, and in return the pair had enjoyed the run of the hillside house, which has five double bedrooms, a gazebo and an infinity pool overlooking the sweeping white sands of Macaroni Beach.

At Jigsaw Kate was allowed to work a four-day week, which enabled her to enjoy long weekends with William. It was perfect for her but less ideal for some of her colleagues. 'Kate told me that some of the people she worked with were mean to her and made her sweep the floors after a fashion shoot,' recalled Kate's friend Emma Sayle. 'Kate stuck it out though and she loved the job. She always said she had great fun travelling to fairs across the country, where she would hunt for ideas and inspiration.' While she was keen to be treated the same as everyone else, it was clear that the attractive brunette who drove herself to work in a silver Audi A3 hatchback was no regular employee. The fact that she regularly graced the front pages of newspapers and magazine covers was something of a giveaway.

Earlier that year, in March 2006, she had been photographed with Charles and Camilla in the royal box at the Cheltenham Gold Cup meeting. She had not attended the royal wedding because of protocol, but she had attended the May wedding of Camilla's daughter Laura Parker Bowles to Harry Lopes, grandson of the late Lord Astor of Hever, in the Wiltshire village of Lacock. She seemed to all intents and purposes part of the family, and the question on everyone's lips was when she and William would be walking up the aisle. Woolworths had already started manufacturing wedding memorabilia, including William and Kate china, ahead of an announcement; the press toyed with the will-they-won't-they question; and the couple kept a chart of newspaper speculations on a royal wedding. While Kate was relatively relaxed about the constant conjectures, William was less comfortable.

The fact that wedding memorabilia had already been manufactured had eerie echoes of the past. When Diana had last-minute jitters about her wedding to Prince Charles her sisters Sarah and Jane had told her, 'Bad luck, Duch. Your face is on the tea towels so you're too late to chicken out now.' William had witnessed his parents' marriage crumble under pressure and he didn't want to endure a similar fate. He was also aware that his father had been pressurised into marrying Diana because she was deemed a suitable bride. He was reluctant to bow to similar pressure and vowed not to be hurried to the altar. He had made his feelings clear, even telling a journalist in an off-guard moment that he had no plans of getting married any time soon.

The music was loud in the fashionable Casa Antica nightclub in Klosters, and William had been enjoying an evening with Harry and Kate. It was April 2005, and with just days to go before Charles and Camilla's wedding the subject of matrimony was on the agenda. For once William had agreed to chat with a reporter, who boldly asked him if he and Kate would be next. William blushed before rebutting the question. 'Look, I'm only twenty-two for God's sake. I'm too young to marry at my age. I don't want to get married until I'm at least twenty-eight or maybe thirty.' If it hurt Kate when William hinted that his younger brother Harry was more likely to tie the knot before they would, she didn't show it. She insisted she was in no hurry to settle down, but in truth she longed for security. While William would have the structure of the army and a strict timetable of engagements to keep him occupied, Kate's future was far less certain.

Despite William's protestations, speculation that the pair

were on the verge of announcing an engagement wouldn't go away. In November 2006, just before William graduated from Sandhurst, Kate was invited to Sandringham for the royal family's traditional Christmas lunch, the first time a girlfriend had received such an invitation. The story, published in the *Mail on Sunday*, was not denied by Clarence House, who simply said it would not discuss royal guests. The year before Kate had joined the royals for their traditional Boxing Day shoot, which had given her the perfect opportunity to use the binoculars that William had given her as a Christmas present. But this Christmas she planned to be with her family at a rented manor house in Perthshire and declined the invitation to Sandringham.

William had promised Kate he would join the Middletons to celebrate Hogmanay at Jordonstoun House and Kate was eagerly awaiting his arrival. The eighteenth-century property on the outskirts of Alyth was set in snowy countryside. A Christmas tree twinkled in the grand drawing room, and with open fires burning in every room, the setting could not have been more romantic. But at the last minute William had a change of heart and decided to stay with his own family instead. He informed a tearful Kate during a late-night conversation on Boxing Day of the change of plan. For William it was no big deal, but for Kate the cancellation was a sign of something more sinister to come. She had good reason to be concerned. William had been having second thoughts and sat down with his father and his grandmother to have a frank discussion about his future with Kate. Both advised him not to hurry into anything.

Kate turned twenty-five on 9 January. The day before William had joined the Blues and Royals regiment of the Household

Cavalry at Combermere Barracks in Windsor where he would be stationed until March. They had had a joint celebration at Highgrove before he reported for duty but Kate was still reeling over William's snub in Scotland. In the newspapers, however, the engagement rumour was gathering momentum once more. Kate's birthday was preceded by an article written by Diana's former private secretary Patrick Jephson in which he claimed that Kate was on her way to becoming a royal bride. Under the headline THE NEXT PEOPLE'S PRINCESS, the article was highly speculative, but there was no doubting the thrust of the piece – William was set to make Kate his bride and her twenty-fifth birthday looked like a likely date for an announcement. 'The smart money now says that brand Windsor is about to get a much-needed injection of fresh young glamour to complement its established octogenarian market leader,' he wrote in the venerable *Spectator* magazine. The story snowballed, and by the morning of Kate's birthday hundreds of photographers were camped outside her house waiting for the 'pre-engagement picture'. The rumours could not have been further from the truth – William had no plans to propose. Instead he phoned Kate from the Combermere Barracks in Windsor to apologise. William was furious that Kate's birthday had been spoilt and in an unprecedented statement complained she was being harassed and said he wanted 'more than anything' for her to be left alone. For the first time Kate felt overwhelmed and desperately isolated. Usually she smiled brightly for the photographers, but this time as she made her way to work she looked as though she was about to crack under the pressure. As always in a crisis, she depended heavily on the support of her mother and sister. The Middleton mantra is 'Grin and bear it', which was exactly what Kate did, although her smile was beginning to wear thin.

For the first time those close to the couple began to speak of doubts about their relationship. The plans for a spring wedding were shredded as quickly as they had been drawn up, and the talk now, among their friends at least, was that an engagement was certainly not on the cards. William had started a two-and-a-half-month tank commander's course at Bovington, and although they enjoyed a skiing trip to Zermatt in March he and Kate were spending less time together. He had warned her that his schedule was packed and he would have little time to visit her. She understood but was upset when William came to London and went clubbing instead of seeing her. On one occasion he had spent the night at Boujis flirting with another girl. William was with Harry and a group of friends including Arthur Landon, Hugh Van Cutsem and Jack Mann, the son of ex-SAS officer Simon Mann, when Tess Shepherd walked into the club. The petite blonde knew some of William's friends and before long she and William were dancing, arms entwined, on the dance floor.

As March drew to a close William and Kate's relationship became increasingly strained. As if the embarrassing night at Boujis was not enough, William further humiliated Kate when he was photographed with his arm around Ana Ferreira, an eighteen-year-old Brazilian student, at a nightclub in Poole not far from Bovington. From the picture it looked as though William had his hand on her breast. He had spent much of the night dancing on a podium with a local called Lisa Agar, and this time there were pictures to prove it. It was the final straw for Kate, and she delivered an ultimatum: either she had his full commitment or they were over. She was no longer prepared to be made a fool of. When they attended Cheltenham races at the end of March, their body language spoke volumes. Walking several steps ahead of Kate, William, his head cast down and his hands dug deep in his pockets, was deep in thought. By now both of them knew that their love affair had run its course. Kate's ultimatum backfired and William told her that they should have a break. Over the Easter weekend they agreed to separate for the second time.

While Kate mourned the end of their relationship at home with her family, William celebrated his 'freedom' in London at Mahiki. The two-storey bar in Mayfair had become a popular haunt with the princes. With its kitsch interior of bamboo screens, round wooden tables, retro-style ceiling fans and wicker basket chairs, the club, run by entrepreneurs Piers Adam and Nick House, is modelled on a Polynesian beach bar. A wooden canoe from Fiji hangs over the main bar to complete the look. While Boujis is smart and sophisticated, Mahiki is laid-back and fun, but the wealthy clientele have serious money to spend. The signature drink, the Treasure Chest, which is served in a wooden chest containing brandy, peach liqueur, lime, sugar and a bottle of champagne, costs an eye-watering £100.

It was hard not to draw comparisons between William and his father. Had William also met the right woman at the wrong time? Haunted by the spectre of the past, there were real fears at the Palace that Kate would become the next Camilla. While William partied, Kate received a message of support from the Duke of Edinburgh. So often misinterpreted as aloof and out of touch, he assured her that William would present a ring 'when the time is right'. It was a well-intended reassurance that Kate valued.

While many might have moped, Kate was in no mood to indulge in prolonged self-pity; nor was she going to get depressed about the spiteful comments from some that she was too middle class to be dating a prince. Instead she put on a brave face and a thigh-skimming minidress and partied. Her message to William was clear: 'Look what you're missing!' In the past some of William's friends had been lukewarm to Kate. They greeted her arrival at Boujis with stage whispers of 'Doors to manual', a reference to her mother's career as an air hostess and hitherto the source of much mirth, but now they rallied round. Guy Pelly, once viewed by Kate with suspicion but now a close friend, assured her that she was welcome at his club. They had not always seen eye to eye, and Kate had once complained that Guy was a bad influence on William. Once, when they were on holiday together, Kate had admonished William and Guy for recklessly riding their mopeds on the lawn in front of their villa where anyone could see them. Then there was Kate's habit of checking out restaurants to make sure their table was sufficiently discreet. But despite their differences Guy recognised that Kate was good for William. He knew the prince well and advised Kate to give him some space. From someone best known as the jester of the royal court, it was wise counsel.

Not for the first time Kate bided her time and immersed herself in a project. Her close friend from Marlborough Alicia Fox Pitt had signed up to the Sisterhood, a group of twenty-one girls who planned to row from Dover to Cap Gris Nez near Calais in a dragon boat to raise money for charity. It proved to be exactly what Kate needed. 'Kate was very down and I think the training became her therapy,' Emma Sayle, who was in charge and became close to Kate, recalled.

Kate had always put William first and she said that this was her chance to do something for herself. I told her she was welcome to join but she had to do the same training as the rest of us. That involved a 6.30 a.m. session and two evening sessions a week. On top of that she was also in the gym and she lost a lot of weight. We trained on the river in Chiswick and Kate started off paddling with the others but I decided to put her on the helm because she was an excellent boatman and really well coordinated.

Unknown to anyone outside their inner circle, William and Kate were already heading for a reconciliation, according to Emma.

She was in touch with William the whole time, and by the end of her training she was back together with him and said she had to pull out of the race. William wanted her to do it and planned to meet her on the finishing line, but the whole thing was becoming a media circus. Kate said she was under a lot of pressure to pull out by Clarence House, which was a shame because it was the one chance Kate could prove to the world who she really was.

The problem was once again that Kate had become the story. She had been photographed during a training session and the picture was published on the cover of *Hello!* magazine. Previously Kate had complained about media intrusion and had asked for the Prince of Wales's lawyers to get involved. Now she was gracing a magazine cover. It was an unfortunate turn of events. 'Is it just me who is baffled by this young woman who, having winged, moaned and stamped her feet over the press attention heaped upon her as potential bride-in-waiting to a royal now seems driven by the oxygen of publicity?' enquired the *Daily Mirror*'s columnist Sue Carroll. The *Daily Mail*'s royal commentator Richard Kay noted, 'Clarence House had watched on with growing unease as the Sisterhood's practice sessions had become a magnet for the paparazzi.' Kate pulled out of the race in August, but by then she and William had been secretly dating again for a couple of months.

William had invited Kate to a fancy-dress party at his barracks in Bovington, and it had been clear to everyone there that they were back together. William, in hot pants, a 'wife beater' vest and policeman's helmet, had followed Kate around 'like a lost puppy' all night. Kate, who looked stunning and toned from her training, was dressed in a revealing naughty nurse's outfit. The theme for the night was Freakin' Naughty, and blow-up dolls were hanging from the ceilings while provocatively dressed waitresses handed out potent cocktails. Outside, guests played on a bouncy castle and dived into a paddling pool full of gunge, but William and Kate stuck to the dance floor. 'They couldn't keep their hands off each other,' recalled a guest. 'William didn't care that people were looking. At about midnight he started kissing her. His friends were joking that they should get a room, and it wasn't long before William took Kate back to his quarters.'

On 24 June 2007 I revealed on the front page of the *Mail on Sunday* that William and Kate were together again, having been given the nod by a senior Palace aide that the relationship was back on track. By coincidence I had spent that weekend with Guy Pelly and William's close friend Tom Inskip at the Beaufort Polo Club. William and Kate had been due to attend but instead were holed up at Highgrove alone. They were back together and this time it was for good.

Chapter 13

Boujis nights

Look but don't touch, touch but don't taste, taste but don't swallow – rules are broken – Boujis

It was a Tuesday evening in June and a frisson of excitement rippled through the beautiful crowd at Boujis nightclub in South Kensington. One of its most famous patrons had just been whisked through the club and down the stairs to the exclusive VIP room. The group of long-legged blondes on the small dance floor had flicked their glossy hair and pouted at the young celebrity as he made his way through the throng. The resident DJ played his favourite house track, Shakedown's 'At Night', and Jake Parkinson-Smith, the club's affable manager, had cleared the velvet-upholstered suite ahead of the royal party's arrival. Parkinson-Smith has known both William and Harry for years and has a reputation for looking after his royal friends, who include the princes' cousins Princesses Beatrice and Eugenie. Harry's favourite drinks, Belvedere vodka and cans of Red Bull, along with several bottles of Dom Perignon champagne, were already chilling in stainless-steel ice buckets.

Ahead of his arrival a team of protection officers had swept the room and taken seats at a discreet table, where they sat sipping Coke. The prince, dressed in jeans and an open-necked shirt (like everyone else he had been asked to remove his baseball cap), jumped up onto the sofa, an impish grin on his excited face. 'Let's party,' he shouted above the din, a £180 magnum of vodka held high above his distinctive crop of red hair.

Boujis DJ Sam Young has known the princes for a while. 'The reason the boys come back time and time again is because they feel relaxed and in an environment they trust. Boujis is like a private house party. They even used to have their own barman called Gordon to look after them.' Tables 11, 12 and 13, which are close to the VIP room, had also been cleared that night to ensure that there could be no snooping on the royal party – which was just as well because Harry was out with the one girl guaranteed to rile Chelsy Davy, who was at home in South Africa working hard for her finals.

Natalie Pinkham, a pretty TV presenter, was Harry's date for the night. The twenty-nine-year-old had met the prince in 2001, when her then-boyfriend England rugby captain Matt Dawson introduced them at a match. With her impressive knowledge of sport and her ability to drink most grown men under the table, Natalie immediately hit it off with Harry. Natalie recalled their first meeting: 'Matt introduced us and I looked after Harry with Clive Woodward's wife Jane while we were in the stands, not that he really needed looking after. We just chatted to him and then Matthew and I became friends with him. I realised very quickly what a normal bloke he was. I was in my final year at university at this point and our friendship has continued since then.' They stayed in touch, and Harry would send Natalie emails while she was cooking baked-bean suppers in her student hall at Nottingham University to the disbelief of her housemates. In December 2001 there were reports that Harry had sent her a thong for Christmas and that he 'fancied her rotten' despite the six-year age gap. 'We get on well and have a lot of fun, but that's as far as it went,' Natalie told me.

The daughter of a barrister and property developer, Natalie is ambitious, good-looking, great fun and, much to her credit, fiercely protective of her friendship with Harry. On this particular occasion they were in the mood to party, and the champagne corks continued to pop as they danced and chatted in the dimly lit VIP room. When it came to closing time, Harry suggested continuing the party at Mark Dyer's house. The army officer turned publican often allows his basement flat to be used as a party venue for Harry and his friends – much to the annoyance of the long-suffering protection officers, who have to wait patiently in their cars until their royal charge is ready to call it a night. At Dyer's Harry can be himself, safe in the knowledge that what goes on inside those four walls stays there. The drink always flows freely, and good-looking girls are never in short supply.

By all accounts the evening had been a great deal of fun, but by 5 a.m. Natalie was ready for bed. As the prince escorted her to his waiting Range Rover, Natalie, a little unsteady on her feet after eight hours of drinking, begged Harry for a kiss goodnight. 'Not here,' he said before whisking her back down the steps. They emerged seconds later, blissfully unaware that their late-night encounter had been captured by a long lens. When the story hit the newspapers the next day, there was an awkward long-distance call to Chelsy in South Africa. It wasn't the first time Harry had had to explain himself.

It was May 2006 and Harry was a month into his reconnaissance training with the Household Cavalry at Bovington in

Dorset. Unlike Sandhurst, where he had been expected to adhere to a strict timetable, he had plenty of free time and on Fridays he couldn't wait to get home to London and hit Boujis, where he was afforded VIP treatment – known at the club as the 'royal comp'. Like William, Harry's royal status guaranteed him free drinks as well as the company of an endless supply of gorgeous young women. Sadly for Chelsy, 2006 was a summer of rather tacky confessions.

First was the rather breathless account of Catherine Davies, a thirty-four-year-old mother of two who claimed she was seduced by the soldier prince at a house party in Fulham. 'I was absolutely speechless. I was against the wall and he literally lifted me off the floor and gave me a lovely kiss which I was stunned by,' she told the *Mail on Sunday*. Miss Davies was apparently not the only woman to succumb to the prince's charms. That July he reportedly danced with a well-known page three girl and a masseuse who claimed the prince had kissed her on the lips at Boujis. The flurry of tabloid tales left Chelsy in tears and cast fresh doubts on their relationship. It was her best friend Kirsten Rogers, who Chelsy grew up with in Zimbabwe, who telephoned Harry to admonish him for being insensitive. When term finished, Chelsy flew to London to spend some time with Harry. They had not seen each other since their idyllic fortnight in South Africa that spring, and Chelsy was running up huge bills on her mobile phone talking to Harry. She had told her friends in South Africa that she was in the relationship for the long term but was worried about her boyfriend's roving eye. Harry assured her that she was the one, and for the first time Charles gave his seal of approval, allowing Harry and Chelsy to share a room at

Highgrove. They also rented a four-bedroom house just a fifteen-minute drive from his officers' mess so that they could have some privacy.

If his indiscretions had put pressure on their relationship it didn't show, and the couple were inseparable that summer. They went to London to see friends and partied at their favourite nightclubs. In July they attended the Cartier International Day, where high-profile guests paid £200 for the privilege of watching the young royal play polo for the Prince of Wales's team. Harry did not leave Chelsy's side, a stark contrast to the previous year, when I witnessed Harry and Guy Pelly dancing wildly on the tables in the Chinawhite marquee after the prince had scored the winning goal. Harry was in the mood to celebrate, and cigarette in one hand and vodka and cranberry in the other, he had been surrounded by a gaggle of pretty girls. This time he was with Chelsy, in a stunning off-the-shoulder chiffon dress, and on his best behaviour. At one point they escaped the crowds to share a hot dog in the car park.

Harry was calmer when Chelsy was around, and her positive influence had not escaped the notice of his father. When she flew home in August she was confident they could last the distance. Secretly they had hatched a plan for her to move to Britain, where she would enroll on a postgraduate course. It was not long and she promised she would be worth the wait. This time she had no need to worry about Harry getting up to no good. On the advice of the boys' protection officers, Charles had told William and Harry to stay away from Boujis. There had been one too many headlines along the lines of THE BOOZE BROTHERS and they needed to keep a low profile. The Queen and the Duke of Edinburgh were said to be concerned that the princes were becoming too well known for their late-night antics. While no one was suggesting they should live like monks, they were in the public eye and some decorum needed to be preserved.

With his military training due to end in October, Harry had to knuckle down to some serious work. Although the Household Cavalry is best known for its ceremonial presence at state occasions, one of the key reasons both Harry and later William chose to join the regiment is that it carries out front-line reconnaissance work. At the Royal Armoured Corps centre at Bovington Harry was acquiring the skills that would enable him to lead twelve men into a war zone, where his job would be to scout out enemy positions using Scimitar armoured vehicles.

It was the middle of August; Iraq and Afghanistan were both possible destinations, and there was a real chance that Harry would be flying out the following spring. 'Harry has started preparing himself for war,' I was told. 'He expects to be sent to Afghanistan to join the rest of his regiment.' The Ministry of Defence appeared to confirm the story: 'There is a requirement for reconnaissance troops in Afghanistan and there is a squadron from the Blues and Royals there at the moment. However, the current regime is due to change next spring.' But within weeks the prospects of Harry going to war looked unlikely. Senior sources in Harry's regiment explained that sending the prince off to war was proving a nightmare. Every day there were fresh reports in the press about where Harry and his men would be posted thus endangering not only the prince's safety but that of his men.

Chief of the General Staff Sir Richard Dannatt was in the

unenviable position of deciding Harry's fate. There was a real risk if he sent the prince to war that Harry would be targeted by insurgents, and the Taliban were already baying for his blood. Extremist websites were offering bounties for Harry's head. He was a trophy as far as the enemy was concerned, and for the top brass at home sending Harry to the front line was an enormous worry. The Taliban were stepping up their attacks: forty-one British service personnel had been killed in just five months and there were real fears that Harry could become another casualty. Southern Afghanistan is one of the most dangerous places in the world, and no place, some argued, for the third-in-line to the throne. Even if Harry was to be stationed at headquarters in Kandahar, he would still face daily rocket attacks. A troop of a hundred Household Cavalry had been deployed to Helmand that spring, and one man had been killed and five seriously injured when their Scimitar armoured vehicle hit a landmine during an operation near Musa Qaleh.

General Dannatt's decision would not be made lightly; it carried so many ramifications for the royal family and the country as a whole if the worst happened. But what was the point of spending hundreds of thousands of pounds of taxpayers' money sending William and Harry to Sandhurst if they would never have the opportunity to put their training into practice? As head of the armed forces and Harry's commander-in-chief, the Queen had made it clear to senior officials at the Ministry of Defence that she would support a decision to send Harry to war, and the prince later acknowledged, 'She was very pro my going.' The Queen was proud of her grandson's achievements and did not believe that his hard work should be wasted. As the spare, Harry was in a different position to his older brother and made his feelings clear: if he wasn't going to be sent to war, he might as well hand in his uniform. His Uncle Andrew, the last royal to be sent to a conflict zone, had expressed similar sentiments in a BBC documentary in 1991: 'Had I not gone to the Falklands my position within the navy would have been untenable.'

Harry had spent weeks training for battle at remote army stations around the UK. According to one officer who trained Harry on pre-deployment exercises at Castlemartin, the MoD's 2,400-acre firing range on the south Pembrokeshire coast, he was an exemplary leader.

We did a lot of training just after Christmas, which involved firing with the Scimitars. We also did small-arms firing in Lydd down on the south coast and at Thetford, where we practised what we would be doing on the front line. Harry was very good and came across as a competent commander. He's got a strong and confident personality and he has a very easy manner with the soldiers. Harry was taught about IEDs [improvised explosive devices] and mines. He and his troop had to experience being in the middle of a simulated explosion and Harry did well. He kept his nerve and led his men to safety. He also did cultural training, where he was briefed on the culture and language of the hostile territory he was being prepared for.

Harry's favourite part was training in 'minor aggro'. He was taught how to get himself and his troop out of a hostile situation, and how to fight his way out of an ambush. One of the exercises involved him being petrol-bombed. He was dressed in combat gear, a protective helmet and a riot shield, and had a petrol bomb thrown at his feet. He responded exactly as he should have done and stamped his feet hard on the ground so the petrol ran off him and he could kick the fire out.

On 21 February 2007, after weeks of speculation, Harry finally received the news he had been waiting for. He was to join the Household Cavalry's A Squadron on a six-month tour of duty in Iraq that spring. The Ministry of Defence released a statement approved by Clarence House:

We can confirm today that Prince Harry will deploy to Iraq later this year in command of a troop from A Squadron of the Household Cavalry Regiment. While in Iraq, Cornet Wales will carry out a normal troop commander's role involving leading a group of twelve men in four Scimitar armoured reconnaissance vehicles, each with a crew of three. The decision to deploy him has been a military one . . . The Royal Household has been consulted throughout.

Harry was finally going to war. It was to be the first time a senior member of the royal family had served on the front line since Prince Andrew had fought in the Falklands twenty-five years earlier. Harry was thrilled, and at the end of April Chelsy, who was travelling around South America on her gap year, flew back to London to accompany him at his sending-off party at Mahiki. That night Harry was on his best behaviour. Just a month earlier, having ignored his father's instructions to stay away from his favourite night spot, he had been involved in an embarrassing scuffle outside Boujis. Flushed from drinking the club's signature Crackbaby cocktails, the prince, who once again had been partying with Natalie Pinkham, lunged at a photographer before losing his footing and falling over in the gutter. It was a humiliating end to the evening. At the sending-off party it was clear that his impending deployment had had a sobering effect on the prince, who left the party with Chelsy shortly after midnight. Once again the roles were reversed, and it was William who was last on the dance floor until the early hours with his friend Holly Branson.

Harry was on a high but his elation was to be short-lived. Within weeks of the announcement there was a dramatic U-turn. On the evening of 16 May General Dannatt announced that the twenty-two-year-old prince would not be going to Iraq after all. It was simply too dangerous. Just weeks before, two men from the Queen's Royal Lancers had been killed when their Scimitar vehicle was blown up while out on patrol in the desert. 'There have been a number of specific threats – some reported and some not reported – which relate directly to Prince Harry as an individual,' explained Dannatt, who had just returned from Iraq. 'These threats expose not only him but also those around him to a degree of risk that I now deem unacceptable. I have to add that a contributing factor to this increase in threat to Prince Harry has been the widespread knowledge and discussion of his deployment. It is a fact that this close scrutiny has exacerbated the situation and this is something that I wish to avoid in future.'

It had already been decided that Harry should lead a support troop doing deep desert patrols rather than reconnaissance, where he and his men would have been more exposed, but even being a part of a much larger force was seen as too risky. There had been too much speculation in the press about where Harry and A Squadron would be sent, and the Ministry of Defence had learned of plots to seize the prince and smuggle him across to Iran, where a rescue operation would have been near impossible. Abu Mujtaba, a commander in the Mahdi Army, the Shia militia loyal to the radical cleric Moqtada al-Sadr, told the *Guardian* newspaper, 'One of our aims is to capture Harry; we have people inside the British bases to inform us on when he will arrive.' A royal hostage crisis was something the Ministry of Defence was simply not prepared to risk. It was Jamie Lowther-Pinkerton, the prince's private secretary, who informed Harry of the eleventh-hour decision. Publicly he put on a brave face, but it was enough to make him reassess his career.

Clarence House acknowledged that the prince was 'very disappointed' but insisted that he 'fully understands and accepts General Dannatt's difficult decision'. There is no doubt it was the toughest test of his commitment to his military career to date. Harry knew there was no guarantee this wouldn't happen again. He had no intention of being a toy soldier and was incensed when the pressure group Republic described his training at Sandhurst as a 'scandalous waste of taxpayers' money'. If his military future was twiddling his thumbs in an office, he would rather quit the army now and do something worthwhile with his life. He had set up his own charity Sentebale to help children in Lesotho. If the military could not find a place for him, Harry would find another outlet for his passions and talent. As far as he was concerned, he had spent his whole life defending himself against accusations that he was little more than a playboy. Joining the army had given him the chance to prove his detractors wrong and show that there was much more to him.

Friends of the prince suggested it was no exaggeration to say that Harry slipped into a state of depression upon hearing the news. 'Harry was devastated,' an officer who had trained with him told me.

> His soldiers ended up going to war without him, which was incredibly hard. He had spent months with his team getting them ready to go to war. He was 100 per cent focused and spent a lot of time with his men. To watch them going off would have been one of the hardest things for Harry. He'd done all his training, but he wasn't allowed to go and do the job he'd been trained to do. It was very hard and we all felt sorry for him. He felt as though he was letting his men down by not going to Iraq with them. He saw them as his soldiers and he felt a huge sense of responsibility for them.

'I have never seen Harry so down in the dumps,' one of his best friends told me over a lunch at the Automat restaurant in Dover Street, just up the road from Mahiki. 'His words are that he is absolutely gutted, he feels all his training has been a waste of time.' Harry told his colleagues, 'If I am not allowed to join my unit in a war zone, I will hand in my uniform.' William, as always, was on hand to support his brother, but there was little comfort he could offer and he knew he would face a similar fate. As second-in-line to the throne, he realised that he too would have to watch his fellow officers go to war while he stayed at home. Harry joined his brother in D Squadron of the Blues and Royals until the MoD decided exactly what to do with him. His senior officers assured him they would exhaust every option to get him to war; in the meantime they told him to sit tight.

It was not surprising that Harry's rebellious streak emerged again. If he couldn't be a soldier prince he might as well be a party prince, and he hit his favourite nightclubs hard. PR DISASTER BUT HOPE OF SECRET ROLE FOR HARRY was the *Evening Standard*'s front page. Aware that he was fast losing interest, the MoD decided to send him to Canada. Harry had had several talks with General Dannatt and senior officials, who explained that he was going to be retrained as a battlefield air controller. It was, they explained, the easiest way to get him to the front line, but it needed to be done covertly. In May Harry flew to Alberta, to the British Army Training Unit in Suffield 160 miles south-east of Calgary, to spend three months learning how to carry out live-fire exercises. But within days of his arrival Harry was on the front page of a local newspaper, photographed in a provocative clinch with a waitress. He had gone to a late-night bar, with two of his bodyguards and a group of army colleagues to drink sambuca shots and rum and Coke. The worse for wear, Harry couldn't resist chatting up one of the waitresses, an attractive twenty-two-year-old called Cherie Cymbalisty. 'He was very forward and told me I was stunning,' she recalled. 'He certainly didn't mention anything about having a girlfriend. He sure didn't act like he had one.'

This time it wasn't just Chelsy asking questions. Harry's men were fighting in Iraq, and here was the third-in-line to the throne chatting up girls apparently without a care in the world. While one could forgive him for letting off steam, here was Harry acting the fool when the death toll of British servicemen in Afghanistan had just reached sixty. As his grandmother privately remarked, sometimes Harry just lacked common sense.

Chapter 14

Remembering Mummy

We wanted to have this big concert full of energy, full of the sort of fun and happiness which I know she would have wanted. And on her birthday as well, it's got to be the best birthday present she ever had.

Prince William, 2007

By the start of August Harry was back home from Canada. The speculation about his being posted to Afghanistan had finally subsided, much to the relief of General Sir Richard Dannatt, who had started secret talks with the Queen, Prince Charles and Harry's private secretary about the possibility of deploying Harry to the front line by Christmas. It was therefore the epic concert that William and Harry were planning to commemorate the tenth anniversary of their mother's death that filled the pages of the press.

They had first announced their intention of organising a memorial service and concert in memory of their mother the previous December. On 1 July 2007, after seven months of intensive planning, the concert was actually going to happen. It had always been William and Harry's plan to celebrate what should have been Diana's forty-sixth birthday, as this marked a decade since her death, but the event was not to be a maudlin affair. The brothers decided that the concert should reflect their mother's joie de vivre, and the eclectic line-up of West End show casts, performances from the Royal Ballet and some of the world's biggest rock stars perfectly captured the mood. From the outset William had said that he and Harry wanted to 'put their stamp' on both the memorial service and the concert. 'We want it to represent exactly what our mother would have wanted. So the church service alone isn't enough,' he said. 'We want to have this big concert on her birthday full of energy, full of the sort of fun and happiness which I know she would have wanted. It's got to be the best birthday present she ever had.'

It may have been ten years since her death, but Diana's memory was still vivid – and not just for the princes but also with the public, who still adored her, and the newspapers, which remained infatuated with every detail of Diana's life. The public side, Harry said, was only a very small part of their mother. They liked to remember her without the cameras, when she was 'just Mummy', dancing barefoot to Michael Jackson in the drawing room of Kensington Palace and making them laugh with her naughty jokes.

Until now they had had little opportunity to put their own mark on their mother's memory. There had been calls for a memorial, but the £3 million fountain in Hyde Park opened seven years after her death was at first felt feeble and inadequate. William and Harry had joined their father, the Queen and the Duke of Edinburgh for the opening, but the fountain had been dogged by controversy. It simply didn't seem appropriate or fitting to many, including Diana's friend Vivienne Parry, who was on the committee of the Diana, Princess of Wales Memorial Fund.

I had a falling out with Rosa Monckton, who was also on the committee, over the fountain. She said it was sleek and elegant and I said it looked like a puddle. I heard Diana herself say she didn't want a statue, and she wasn't keen on having a hospital or anything named after her. There was a tension between what the Spencer family wanted and what the nation wanted. The British public wanted a monument they could go and visit and take their children to, but sadly the fountain never was.

As if to advertise its failure, the fountain became clogged with leaves and was fenced off as a health and safety hazard. By the end of that first summer it was more of a sputter than the majestic fountain it was intended to be – and subsequently became closer to being.

Having recently turned twenty-five, William was legally entitled to the income accrued on the £6.5 million left to him in his mother's will. Unusually, Diana's will had been changed by a variation order granted by the High Court three months after her death, to protect her sons. Essentially the changes meant that they could not access the capital of her £12 million estate until they were thirty, but they could access the interest it had earned without consulting the trustees. It was also agreed that William and Harry would take over the princess's intellectual property rights, which had been given to the Diana, Princess of Wales Memorial Fund. While William appreciated the work the fund had done, he was determined to give it a serious shake-up. There was a feeling, particularly within the Palace, that Diana's name, which at one stage had appeared on margarine packets, had been cheapened and over-commercialised.

'The boys were wisely kept out of all the rows that were going on, but there were huge problems with Diana's image,' recalled Vivienne Parry. 'Diana's sister Sarah and Paul Burrell, who was also on the committee, decided to give Flora the rights to use Diana's signature on their margarine packets. Sarah had actually signed it off even though we were all opposed to it, as was Diana's mother Frances, who was still alive at the time. Diana's name was and still is very powerful, and it's understandable that William and Harry are so protective of their mother's legacy.'

The concert and memorial were perfect opportunities for the boys to reinvent their mother's image. It was William and Harry's first joint charity venture and their most ambitious project to date. The concert, which would take place at the new Wembley Stadium, was to feature twenty-three artists and would be broadcast around the world by the BBC. Everyone remembered the young and vibrant Diana dancing to Duran Duran at Live Aid twenty-two years before. Now the very same band, who had lined up to meet the princess and shake her hand, would be singing for her together with, among others, Tom Jones, Rod Stewart, Supertramp, Lily Allen, Joss Stone and Take That.

William and Harry made the decision early on that it was to be a party for the younger members of the royal family, and while some of Diana's family were invited, the old guard, including their father, who according to William didn't know how to pronounce Beyoncé's name, were not. Although the princes did not have their own private office at this stage, they had a team of aides at the Palace to help them plan the event. Sir Malcolm

Ross, who had coordinated the Queen's successful golden jubilee celebrations in 2002, was in charge of the operation together with Geoffrey Matthews, the princes' private secretary, and their personal secretary Helen Asprey. An advisory board of key figures from the music and entertainment industry, including Nicholas Coleridge, managing director of Condé Nast, Andy Cosslett of Intercontinental Hotels Group, Willie Walsh, chief executive of British Airways, Universal Music's chairman Lucian Grainge, the director of the National Theatre Nicholas Hytner and Sir Tom Shebbeare, director of Prince Charles's charities, was also created to work alongside the boys' aunt Lady Sarah McCorquodale. Theatre impresario Andrew Lloyd Webber had also agreed to be involved, and by the New Year plans were well under way. Both William and Harry were kept abreast at every stage of the planning by Jamie Lowther-Pinkerton, who travelled around the country with detailed plans of the ever-changing event for the boys to authorise.

William wanted to oversee every last detail, and was given permission to leave his regiment in Dorset to come up to London for regular meetings at Clarence House. According to one senior royal aide who was present, he chaired every meeting with confidence and authority. 'William was very hands on. He would arrive in meetings totally au fait and up to speed. He had enormous skill, which I was quite taken aback by, and he was incredibly competent. If there was a point he wanted to take further with anyone individually, he would close the meeting, thanking everyone for their time, before asking the person he wanted to speak to if they would stay behind. He got the job done, and we were all very happy with how he handled it.'

With so much hype in the weeks leading up to the concert, it was decided this was the perfect opportunity for the boys to give an international television interview. Given their mother's popularity in the States, it was suggested that they appear on America's biggest breakfast programme, NBC's *Today*, which paid a reported $2.5 million for the exclusive. A year earlier William and Harry had appeared on British television with their father to be interviewed by Ant and Dec for the thirtieth anniversary celebrations of the Prince's Trust. They appeared relaxed as they sat on either side of their father as he spoke about the work of the trust. But this time the spotlight was firmly on them. The footage, as far as NBC was concerned, was worth every dollar.

It was honest and compelling, and William and Harry came across exactly as their mother would have hoped. They were normal; they had girlfriends; they hated the press attention that came with their titles and were uncomfortable with intrusions into their daily lives. If they had not been born princes, William said he would have loved to be 'some sort of heli pilot working for the UN maybe', while Harry said he dreamed of being a safari guide in Africa. Harry claimed only the people who actually knew them really understood them. There were questions about Kate Middleton, and William, who had obviously been well briefed ahead of the interview, gave nothing away. He certainly wasn't prepared to confirm whether she would be coming to the concert.

Sitting on a cream sofa in the drawing room of Clarence House dressed in chinos and open-necked shirts, the brothers took it in turns to answer the questions. In front of the cameras they were relaxed, shared an easy on-screen banter and finished one another's sentences. There were jokes about Harry having done nothing in the run-up to the concert, while William claimed to have had all the bright ideas. Their self-deprecation and warmth won them an army of fans. This after all was the first America and the rest of the world had really seen of the boys since they walked behind their mother's coffin ten years before.

For the first time the boys opened up about Diana's death and how they had coped without her in their lives. Harry spoke with great candour about his mother and how he was haunted by what had happened in the Pont de l'Alma tunnel on 31 August 1997. 'For me personally, whatever happened . . . that night . . . in that tunnel . . . no one will ever know. I'm sure people will always think about that the whole time,' he said. 'I'll never stop wondering about that.'

'Straight after it happened we were always thinking about it,' added William. 'Not a day goes by when I don't think about it once in the day . . . For us it's been very slow . . . It has been a long time.'

Harry talked about the trauma of being continually confronted with images of their mother since her death and his sadness that the tragedy would never be a closed chapter in their lives.

It's weird because I think when she passed away there was never that time, there was never that sort of lull. There was never that sort of peace and quiet for any of us. Her face was always splattered on the paper [sic] the whole time. Over the last ten years I personally feel as though she has been – she's always there. She's always been a constant reminder to both of us and everyone else . . . When you're being reminded about it, [it] does take a lot longer and it's a lot slower.

While time had healed the rawest wounds, it was clear that the pain of losing their mother so suddenly and publicly had left a deep scar.

When asked how they coped with life in the goldfish bowl of royalty it was Harry who answered: 'We know we have certain responsibilities, but within our private life and within certain other parts of our life we want to be as normal as possible. Yes, it's hard because to a certain respect we will never be normal.'

When on 1 July 2007 Sir Elton John took to the stage at the new Wembley Stadium to introduce William and Harry the applause from the crowd of 63,000 people was thunderous. They had both admitted to being nervous, but as they stood in front of a giant screen illuminated with the letter D, Harry found his confidence. 'Hello, Wembley,' he shouted to the crowds. He looked to William and grinned broadly. The day was blessed with fine weather and Elton John opened and closed the concert on a black-lacquered grand piano. There was no rendition of 'Candle in the Wind', which he had sung at her funeral; the mood was of celebration, not sadness. The outpouring of grief ten years earlier was a distant memory. There would be no more tears, this was a time for happiness, but as the black and white images of Diana taken by her favourite photographer Mario Testino flickered across the stage, there was no mistaking the emotions she still elicited.

As the cameras focused on the royal box, William and Harry, surrounded by their friends and relatives – among them Princesses Beatrice and Eugenie, Peter and Zara Phillips and Earl Spencer's daughters Kitty, Eliza and Katya – beamed with pride. At one point William raised his arms in the air and started wiggling his hips only to be chastised by his brother. Kate, dressed in a white Issa trench coat, stood two rows behind William and was careful not to meet his eye, although keen-eyed watchers might have read much into her singing along with every word of Take That's 'Back for Good'. She had in fact spent the days leading up to the concert sitting at the kitchen table in Clarence House going through the final running order with William and helping him with the speech cards he kept in his blazer pocket throughout the day. It was the first time they had appeared in public together since the news that they were dating again, but Kate wanted the day to be about Harry and William and insisted on sitting with her brother James. Chelsy, who had flown in from Cape Town, was seated on Harry's right-hand side in the front row. Pretty in a black dress, her blond hair scraped back into a ponytail, they danced together and were inseparable at the VIP party after the show.

Although Palace aides were concerned that the late-night party could send out the wrong message in the run-up to the anniversary of Diana's death, William and Harry were adamant that they wanted to thank everyone who had been involved with the concert. Event planner and nightclub owner Mark Fuller, who is also a long-serving ambassador of the Prince's Trust, said it was their way of saying thank you. 'People were desperate for an invite to the after party, but the boys wanted to keep it intimate and low key. Everyone agreed to help out for free and the boys were incredibly grateful. They made a point of coming and thanking every waitress and kitchen porter before the party started,' said Fuller, who was in charge of the catering and helped to look after the star guests. The boys were on their best behaviour, although Harry couldn't resist sneaking off with Chelsy for a little time to themselves. It had always been William and Harry's intention that any funds raised from the concert would be split among their charities, and the £1 million that was raised was divided up between eight, which included Sentebale and Centrepoint.

The hour-long memorial service, which was held at the Guards Chapel in the Wellington Barracks on 31 August, was understandably a more sombre affair, and the message was as clear as it was simple: let Diana be celebrated for her life, and let her rest in peace. The candlelit ceremony took place just a stone's throw from Buckingham Palace, where back in July 1981 Diana had kissed her prince charming on the balcony in front of adoring crowds. The Right Reverend Richard Chartres, Bishop of London, echoed William and Harry's pleas for their mother's memory to be finally laid to rest. In Paris a sea of flowers had been laid above the Pont de l'Alma tunnel, while flowers, cards and poems from members of the public were pinned to the gates of Kensington Palace and Althorp, Diana's childhood home and final resting place.

But as had been the case for most of Diana's married life, Camilla unwittingly cast something of a shadow over the memorial service. There was a furore when it was reported that the duchess would be attending. Camilla herself had had misgivings and wanted to stay away, but Charles had insisted she be there. Diana's close friend Rosa Monckton, who had spent ten days holidaying with the princess shortly before her death, voiced her opposition in an article for the *Mail on Sunday*. 'I know such services should be an occasion for forgiveness, but I can't help feeling Camilla's attendance is deeply inappropriate.'

While Camilla was said to be tearful over the criticism levelled at her and the invidious position she found herself in, Charles, who can be stubborn especially when it comes to the subject of his late ex-wife, insisted that Sir Michael Peat, his private adviser, continue to brief his press aides that the duchess would attend. William and Harry had invited their stepmother, but as the day drew nearer Camilla found herself under terrible pressure, and she and Charles argued on a daily basis over whether she should attend. It was only two years since Charles and Camilla had married, and the public had by no means embraced their potential future queen. Camilla was still viewed with suspicion and disliked by many, and her public image remained fragile. William and Harry were upset the service was being overshadowed by the controversy and there were fears of a public backlash if the duchess turned up. Eventually the Queen intervened at the eleventh hour and gave Camilla her blessing to stay away. Camilla issued a personal statement: 'On reflection I believe my attendance could divert attention from the purpose of the occasion, which is to focus on the life and service of Diana.'

At the service William sat in the front pew next to the Queen, who was dressed in vibrant purple. He had chosen to give a reading from St Paul's letter to the Ephesians; Harry would deliver the eulogy. The boys had asked 500 friends and family, including many members of their mother's former staff from Kensington Palace. Diana's chefs Mervyn Wycherly and Chris Barber, who had also attended William's confirmation, as well as her former secretary Victoria Mendham, were invited. Representatives from the plethora of charities of which Diana was patron also filled the chapel along with prime ministers past and present and stars from the world of show business. Twelve of Diana's godchildren, her godparents, and all of her pageboys and bridesmaids were also there. Her former butler Paul Burrell, who had been at the centre of an inquiry into a number of the late princess's missing personal artefacts, was pointedly not invited, nor was Mohamed Al Fayed. His daughter Camilla, who had shared the boys' last summer with their mother in St-Tropez, was the only member of the Fayed family at the memorial. William and Harry had personally written to her and asked her to come.

When I interviewed Camilla Fayed much later she said,

I was very surprised. I was the only one in my family to be asked along. Of course they couldn't ask my father. I still don't know to this day why they invited me. I was very nervous about going. I hadn't seen or spoken to William since the summer Dodi and Diana died. We were desperate to write to them or speak with them, but we were told not to have any contact, which was very hard because we had all grown close that summer. I couldn't believe I was finally going to be able to see William and Harry at the memorial service. I had Elton and his husband David Furnish to look after me – they are very dear friends and they were an amazing support. Without them I don't know if I could have gone. I spoke to William and Harry and they both thanked me for coming. I would have loved to talk to them more but it wasn't really the time or the place. We both lost loved ones that day; our lives were both torn apart. I lost my brother and it has taken me years to be able to talk

Kate, second from left, shares a drink with fellow students Bryony Daniels, who was once erroneously linked with William, Katharine Barton, Libby Hart and William's good friend from Eton, Fergus Boyd. Dinner parties were popular among the young students and William would always arrive armed with a bottle of Jack Daniels.

William and Kate had their first wobble in the summer of 2004 and decided to have a break. It was the end of their third year at St Andrews and William went away on a boys only holiday to Greece. By October they were back at college and had worked things through. When they attended a gala dinner William couldn't keep his hands off Kate. Speaking about the split Kate has said, 'I think at the time I wasn't very happy about it but actually it made me a stronger person.'

After four years William finally graduated from St Andrews on Thursday 23 June 2005 with a 2:1 in Geography. Locals lined the streets to bid farewell to the student prince who in turn thanked the people of the Scottish town for their kindness.

Against all the odds, Prince Charles eventually married his long-term mistress Camilla Parker Bowles on 9 April 2005 at Windsor Guildhall. The Queen, who had refused to acknowledge Camilla in the past, gave her blessing for them to wed, while William and Harry said they were delighted for their father.

Harry – now 'Cornet Wales' – passes out at the Sovereign's Parade at Sandhurst on 12 April 2006. William had to salute his brother.

Bleary-eyed Harry trips up outside Boujis nightclub in South Kensington after one too many Crackbaby cocktails in March 2007. He lunged at the paparazzi who were trying to get a picture of him leaving with his friend Natalie Pinkham.

William embraces Kate on the slopes while skiing in Zermatt in March 2007. Just days later they attended the first day of the Cheltenham Festival race meeting in the UK where their body language speaks volumes. They split that Easter.

William and Harry dance in the Royal box at the concert for Diana on 1 July 2007. While Chelsy Davy sat in the front row Kate sat two rows behind William next to her brother James. It was the first time the couple had been seen in public together since I revealed in June that they were back together following their break-up earlier that year.

William takes to the air for his first solo flight at RAF Cranwell in Lincolnshire in January 2008.

Dressed in uniform and an army-issue helmet Harry goes out on patrol through the deserted town of Garmsir. He is armed with his rifle and a 9mm pistol strapped to his chest. The twenty-three-year-old Household Cavalry officer spent ten weeks secretly fighting the Taliban in the volatile southern province of Helmand in Afghanistan.

William and Harry Wales give a rare joint interview at RAF Shawbury in June 2009. The boys were living together at a rented house close to the airbase and William joked that he did all the housework while Harry kept him awake with his snoring.

Having led his Sentebale team to victory during the annual Veuve Clicquot Manhattan Polo Classic in May 2009, Prince Harry completes his first solo overseas tour to the United States. He raised £100,000 for his charity and charmed the Americans.

Team Wales, princes William and Harry, arrive in Semonkong, Lesotho on horseback in June 2010. They were halfway through a six-day tour which had started in Botswana and was to end in South Africa. Harry had been keen to show his older brother the work his charity Sentebale was doing in one of Africa's poorest countries. The tour, their first together, was deemed a huge success both at the Palace and in the press.

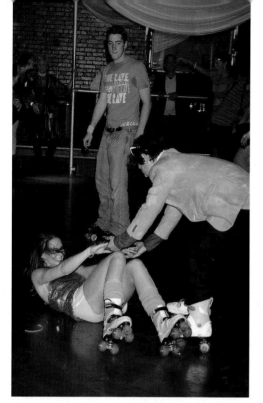

Kate Middleton gets a helping hand after she takes a tumble during a charity roller skating disco in September 2008.

William works his magic on the crowds outside Government House in Melbourne, Australia in January 2010. The prince travelled to Australia after carrying out a three-day state visit to New Zealand in place of the Queen. Wills mania swept across the country and the trip was deemed a huge success.

Chelsy and Harry are closer than ever at the prince's graduation ceremony at RAF Middle Wallop in Hampshire in May 2010. Chelsy greeted Prince Charles and Camilla with a kiss and watched proudly as the Prince of Wales awarded Harry his wings. Harry, who graduated as an Army Air Corps pilot, was delighted – and surprised – to be told that he had qualified to fly the Apache helicopter. Just months later, however, Chelsy announced she was moving back to South Africa throwing their six-year relationship off course once again.

Tanned from their recent holiday to Kenya, William and Kate attended their friend Harry Meade's wedding in November 2010. It was the first time Kate had been seen in public since July and for once the couple arrived together and smiled broadly for the cameras. No wonder Kate, who was dressed in a tailor-made Issa gown, looked elated – William had proposed to her in Kenya, but they were to keep their engagement a secret for nearly a month.

Finally the secret is out and at 11 a.m. on Tuesday 16 November Clarence House issued a statement confirming that William and Kate were engaged to be married. The happy couple faced the world's press at a photo call at St James's Palace and gave their first ever interview to ITV. It was the first day of Kate's new life as a future princess and she proudly showed off her sapphire and diamond engagement ring – once worn by the late Princess of Wales – for the first time in public.

about that summer. It was a tragedy that destroyed both our families. For me it was very important that I was there to represent my father and our family, and it was very honourable of the boys to invite me. I'm so glad I went.

Like many of the congregation, Camilla was moved to tears when Harry delivered his eulogy. Wearing his regimental tie, he spoke of his mother's 'unrivalled love of life, laughter, fun and folly'. She was, he said, 'our guardian, friend and protector. She never once allowed her unfaltering love for us to go unspoken or undemonstrated. She will always be remembered for her amazing public work. But behind the media glare, to us, just two loving children, she was quite simply the best mother in the world.' He added, 'We would say that, wouldn't we? But we miss her. Put simply, she made us and so many other people happy. May this be the way she is remembered.' His lip quivered, but despite the emotion of the moment Harry did not lose his self-control. His heartfelt tribute was as spine-tingling and touching as the solitary card on top of Diana's coffin, which had borne the single word 'Mummy' written in his hand.

When Harry returned to sit down, he walked across the church to the pews where the Spencer family was seated and joined them. It was the first time the two families had been together since Diana's funeral, at which Earl Spencer had given his heartfelt but bitter eulogy in which he claimed Diana 'needed no royal title to continue to generate her particular brand of magic'. His defence of his sister, while applauded by the nation was seen as a thinly veiled attack on the Windsors, and the families had not spoken since. Many wounds were healed that day.

Chapter 15

Off to war

There's no way I'm going to put myself through Sandhurst and then sit on my arse back home while my boys are out fighting for their country. That may sound very patriotic, but it's true.

Prince Harry, September 2005

It was half past eleven on Friday 9 November 2007 when the promoter of the Amika nightclub received a call on his mobile from a rather refreshed-sounding Prince Harry. 'We've just finished dinner. We want to come and party! We're on our way down now.' The newly refurbished nightclub was located on Kensington High Street in west London and had a VIP room that could only be accessed using a special swipe card. Harry, who was stationed just twenty miles away at Windsor, had become a regular at the club, which was popular with the well-heeled Chelsea crowd who could afford the fifteen-pound cocktails.

There was no chance of a repeat of the Boujis episode when Harry had lunged at a photographer: the prince was driven into a private car park beneath the club and whisked into the venue through labyrinthine corridors without the paparazzi even knowing he was there. He always shunned the VIP room, which came complete with its own team of staff, a vintage champagne bar and extravagant velvet wallpaper. Instead he preferred to sit at a booth in the corner of the club's main room, where he had a perfect view of the stage on which half-naked dancers performed in a cage. Anyone else would have to spend a minimum of £1,500 for the privilege of sitting at this, the best table in the club, but the bill was always waived for Harry.

He walked into the club, his baseball cap pulled low over his face, collapsed into the deep black leather seat and reached for the magnum of vodka already on ice. Several jugs of mixers had also been arranged on the table, but Harry was not interested in watering-down his drinks. He called over the waitress and asked for half a dozen shot glasses. It had already been decided who would be waiting on Harry and his group of friends that night, and as the gorgeous Trinidad-born Christiane made her way over to the table, Harry stood up to greet her.

On the last occasion he had dropped in with Chelsy, who had come to London for a break from Leeds University, where she had started a postgraduate course in law in September. Clearly happy to be reunited, the couple celebrated with two magnums of Möet et Chandon and sneaked off to share cigarettes in the corridor leading to the car park, another privilege reserved solely for them. At the end of the night Harry had laughingly tried to pay the £2,000 bill with his army identity card only to be informed that the drinks were on the house. So too were the magnums of vodka slipped into the boot of the protection officers' Range Rover courtesy of the bar manager because the drinks fridge at Clarence House had, according to Harry, run dry.

On this occasion he was not with Chelsy but his friend Arthur Landon, the youngest man on the *Sunday Times* Rich List, and Arthur's make-up artist girlfriend Charlotte Cowen. Harry was uncharacteristically subdued and sat in the corner, uninterested in the elegant girls circling his table hopefully. It was only when Christiane sat down to chat with him that Harry perked up. He had known her from Boujis, where she used to wait on the VIP tables, and they got along well. Having secured her telephone number Harry had spent the past fortnight texting her, and the rumour among his friends was that she had recently accompanied the prince home to Clarence House. News of their friendship had even reached Christiane's home town in Trinidad where her family and friends were devouring every detail of the burgeoning romance, even though Christiane loyally refused to discuss the relationship. 'Trinidad society is abuzz with some girl who has been seeing Prince Harry,' I was informed. It had not taken long for the news to travel halfway across the globe. Chelsy was furious and told Harry the relationship was over. It was not just his wandering eye; she was desperately homesick and miserable in Leeds. Things had got off to an inauspicious start in September, when Harry had kept her waiting at Heathrow airport for close to an hour after she landed. When he eventually arrived looking like he had just rolled out of bed, he swore furiously at the photographers who had gathered en masse in the terminal.

Just ten minutes away, Chelsy was hosting her own party at the trendy members-only Cuckoo Club in London's West End. Dressed in a tight-fitting minidress, she was surrounded by her close group of girlfriends, including her best friend Olivia Perry, known to everyone as 'Bubble'. As Chelsy leaned in and told them the news, the girls, champagne glasses in hand, were on the edge of their seats. 'It's over,' Chelsy told them dramatically before draining her flute. 'He doesn't make enough effort, and

I need to be my own person. I don't even know if I can trust him any more.' As Bubble put a comforting arm around her, the others nodded their agreement that she had made the right decision. Harry was crazy to let her go, but Chelsy had already planned to go back to Africa for the Christmas holidays, where she planned a girls' holiday to Kenya.

As far as she was concerned, she had sacrificed her family and a life that she loved to move to Leeds, which was grey, drizzly and miserable. It was unacceptable, she complained, that Harry had only been to visit her once that term. The town, which boasts a lively nightlife, had been Harry's suggestion, but the glamorous picture he had painted of the northern town was not quite the reality. Chelsy was living in a shabby part of the city, and the terraced house, where her small ground-floor flat looked onto a rubbish-strewn front yard, was a world away from her £350,000 glass-fronted beach house back in Cape Town. Harry's protection officers had voiced concerns about the Leeds property being so exposed, but Chelsy had insisted on 'living like a student'. It meant the pair had had to meet up at a friend's house when Harry did visit.

It was far from ideal, and Harry, she noted, had also changed. He had missed her twenty-second birthday that October. Instead he flew to Paris to watch England play South Africa in the rugby World Cup, which he celebrated with a marathon drinking session. It had been a different story the previous year, when Harry had secretly flown to Cape Town to celebrate Chelsy's twenty-first birthday. The theme for the night had been the Roaring Twenties, and halfway through the evening Harry had taken off his shirt to reveal a white T-shirt bearing the slogan 'Stylin' (on to a good thing) hands off!' It was a clear sign to anyone remotely interested in Chelsy that she was Harry's girl.

Ironically, now they were living in the same country, the relationship was beginning to suffer. Chelsy felt taken for granted and was lonely in Leeds. Although she had never been close to Kate Middleton, she was the only person who could understand the pressures of dating a prince. It was after all only a matter of months since Kate had been in exactly the same position. As with so many things, William and Harry's love lives seemed to mirror one another. Leave him to get it out of his system, Kate counselled. Boys will be boys, and if he's flirting, turn a blind eye. He loves you and will come back to you. Kate may well have been right, but her advice fell on deaf ears. Chelsy was not prepared to be made a fool of. Back in South Africa she had always been the prettiest girl in her glamorous and wealthy clique. She was never short of male attention, and Harry worried particularly about an old friend from Zimbabwe, Bradley Kirkland. Known to his friends as 'Jabu', he was close to Chelsy, and although they had never been romantically linked, Harry, who had heard that Jabu had once referred to him as a 'wet fish', felt threatened by the handsome student who hunted crocodiles as a hobby.

In truth Harry had nothing to worry about. Chelsy adored him. She had been saving herself for someone special, and Harry was her first love. This was just a blip – one of many break-ups – and within weeks they were back together. This time, however, their reunion was more brief and passionate than hitherto. Harry was being posted to Afghanistan.

It was the moment Harry had been waiting for. He had known ever since his failed deployment to Iraq in the spring that General

Sir Richard Dannatt had made it his personal mission to get him to the front line. Now he had found a way. Only Harry's family, a handful of senior Ministry of Defence officials and Prime Minister Gordon Brown knew about it, but there were already whispers in the press that Harry could be heading for Afghanistan. Paddy Harverson wrote to news organisations warning them not to publish speculative stories, but General Dannatt knew that if it was to work Fleet Street had to be in on the secret. When Prince Andrew had fought in the Falklands a D notice had been issued. This was a blanket ban on writing about the prince's mission. It had worked, and there was no reason it shouldn't with Harry. The prince was not a fan of the British media: they photographed him when he fell over outside nightclubs, and deep down he still held them partly responsible for his mother's death. This time he had no choice but to trust them. Together with Paddy Harverson, Dannatt held several off-the-record meet-ings at Clarence House with select members of the press, and it was agreed that there would be a media blackout on the prince's deployment. Every editor promised not to break the embargo until Harry was safely home on British soil. There had to be a pay-off, however. In return for their cooperation, they wanted an interview before he left, and access to Harry when he was in the field and after he was back home. Harry agreed.

Just two journalists, one print and one broadcast, were invited to Clarence House for the secret press conference. Harry revealed his grandmother had informed him that he was finally going to war. The Queen and Charles had had a two-hour meeting with General Dannatt ahead of the decision and both had given the operation their blessing. 'She told me I'm off to Afghanistan, so that was the way it was supposed to be,' said Harry, who was in civilian clothes. He was due to fly to Kandahar the following day and had been briefed on the questions beforehand. He seemed confident and surprisingly relaxed about the task ahead of him.

He had spent one month in the summer training at RAF Leeming near Northallerton in north Yorkshire as a forward air controller. This involved guiding close air support on to enemy targets. He wasn't entirely sure what he would be doing when he arrived in Afghanistan. 'It's still slightly unclear,' he said. 'Anyone who goes out to Afghanistan on operations is multi-tasking. Essentially I'm going to be TACP, which is tactical air control party, which is linked in with the RAF and fast jets and supply drops and all these bits and pieces. I've still yet to find out all the details of what I'll actually be doing.' Put most simply, it was air traffic control: it would be Harry's job to guide aircraft, from fast jets carrying bombs and surveillance planes to regular troop transports and supply drops. He was working to House-hold Cavalry commanding officer Lieutenant Colonel Edward Smyth-Osbourne, who had liaised closely with General Dannatt to get Harry to the front line. It was different to the reconnais-sance work he had been trained to do, but Harry had been well prepared. 'I never thought I would see myself doing [this] in the army. I have been trained for it. I haven't spent a day at Heathrow or anything like that, but to the extent that the army can train you for air traffic controlling, I have been trained for it.'

There was no hiding his delight that he was finally going to war, and he admitted that he felt a huge sense of relief: 'a bit of excitement, a bit of, phew, finally get the chance to actually do the soldiering that I wanted to do ever since I joined'. For the first time he publicly acknowledged his frustration at not being sent to war with his men in April. 'It was very hard and I did think, well, clearly one of the main reasons that I'm not likely to be going was the fact of who I am.' He was candid when he was asked if he wished he wasn't a prince. 'I wish that quite a lot, actually.' He had, he admitted, at one point considered reassessing his future in the army. 'I wouldn't use the word *quitting*. It was a case of I very much feel like if I'm going to cause this much chaos to a lot of people, then maybe I should bow out, and not just for my own sake, for everyone else's sake . . . It was something that I thought about, but at the same time I was very keen to make this happen – or hope for the opportunity to arise and luckily it has.'

Harry knew that Afghanistan would be 'no great holiday resort'. 'I just want to put it into practice and do the job . . . and essentially help everybody else . . . and do my bit,' he insisted. He was also continuing a long line of royal tradition of military service. The last British sovereign to see action was the Queen's father, King George VI, who fought in the Battle of Jutland in May 1916 as a twenty-year-old sub-lieutenant in the Royal Navy. The Queen joined the Women's Auxiliary Territorial Service towards the end of the Second World War and became the first female member of the royal family to be a full-time active member of the forces. Her husband, the Duke of Edinburgh, served in the Royal Navy from 1939 to 1952 and fought in the Second World War in the battle of Matapan aboard HMS *Valiant*, where he directed the battleship's searchlights while under fire. And in 1982 Prince Andrew, who served in the Royal Navy for over twenty years, flew as a second pilot in Sea King helicopters on anti-submarine and transport duties during the Falklands War. Charles had been commander of the minesweeper *Bronnington* and successfully shadowed a Soviet submarine that had strayed into the Channel. In fact of the recent royals only the Earl of Wessex had had a less than succesful military career after failing the Royal Marine Commando training course. Now it was Harry's turn to prove he could fight for Queen and Country.

It was 14 December 2007 and bitterly cold at RAF Brize Norton in Oxfordshire, the very airfield where ten years earlier Harry's mother had arrived on her final journey home. Wrapped up against the bracing wind in his warmest kit, Harry quick-marched up the steps of the C-17 RAF Globemaster III transport aircraft. His Bergen was stuffed to the brim and weighed twenty-five kilos. In it he had supplies for the next four months including a small radio, his all-weather sleeping bag, an inflatable air bed, protective goggles, sun cream, a paintbrush to clean the sand from his weapons and a supply of his favourite Haribo jelly sweets. His pistol and SA80 A2 rifle had been separately packed in a weapons bundle and would be given to him as soon as they landed. Round his wrist he wore a red and blue Help For Heroes band, as did Chelsy, who was one of the few people who knew Harry was going to war.

This was no ordinary flight: the aircraft was big enough to transport tanks and helicopters, and there were no seats. Instead webbing hung from the sides, in which the soldiers could sit during the eleven-hour flight to Kandahar. It was bumpy and uncomfortable, and once they had taken off, Harry spread his sleeping bag on the floor and tried to get some sleep. He had been instructed to wear his helmet and Osprey body armour upon landing. His uniform, which bore the Blues and Royals' eagle badge, also carried his army number WA 4673 A. Once they had safely landed he was given forty-eight hours to acclimatise before he was flown by Chinook to Forward Operating Base (FOB) Dwyer, a dusty outpost in the middle of Helmand Province, considered by many one of the most dangerous places on earth. The base, the size of four football pitches, was uncomfortable and austere. It had been fortified with HESCO bastions, collapsible wire-mesh containers filled with gravel. Harry was just seven miles from Garmsir, a deserted front-line town, and would soon discover that there was little left of the burned-out and looted high street, once the centre of a bustling commercial town.

Cornet Wales had been well briefed. He was now one of the 30,000 British military personnel to have served in Afghanistan since the US-led invasion in 2001. Initially British forces helped secure the capital, Kabul, before moving into Helmand Province in the south of Afghanistan in 2006. It was hoped that the Americans and British could extend government control into this Taliban heartland; instead the coalition has faced stiff resistance and years of bloody fighting. By the time Harry went to war eighty-nine British soldiers had been killed, sixty-three of them in action against the Taliban, while hundreds more had been injured.

It was on the sandy battlefields of Afghanistan that Harry finally got to put his training to the test. To the pilots in the sky he was Widow Six Seven, a radio call sign keeping a close eye on them and an even closer watch on the enemy. Harry was assigned his own restricted operating zone, which was several square kilometres around FOB Dwyer. It was his job to identify Taliban forces on the ground, verify their coordinates and clear them as targets for attack. He would spend hours poring over maps, surveillance images and video footage of enemy positions, and had to log every detail identifying, confirming and pinpointing the Taliban. Crucially, coalition air assets needed his permission to enter his air space, and within weeks he would be coordinating his first-ever air raid.

In the FOB operations room Harry monitored every movement on a sophisticated live airborne video feed linked up to a computer, which was dubbed Taliban TV or Kill TV. 'Terry Taliban and his mates, as soon as they hear air, they go to ground, which makes life a little bit tricky,' Harry explained. 'So having something that gives you a visual feedback from way up means that they can carry on with their normal pattern of life and we can follow them. My job is to get air up, whether I have been tasked it a day before or on the day or when troops are in contact.' He was working alongside Corporal David Baxter, a twenty-eight-year-old former tank driver from Bendooragh near Coleraine in Northern Ireland, who had trained with him in the Household Cavalry. Harry quickly earned the respect of the corporal.

He's a really down-to earth person. To be honest I don't think anyone thinks of him as third-in-line to the throne or anything. You just take him at face value as any other officer . . . He's fitted in really well. The first time he took over the net from his predecessor he was straight in there. He's really confident and sounded like he'd been there for quite a considerable amount of time. He's always got a rapport with the pilots that he's talking to. I'm sure they would be quite shocked as well if they knew who they were talking to.

Harry's easy nature and sense of humour quickly won him the friendship and trust of his comrades. When there was no threat of attack he chatted over the radio with the pilots about their homes and families. 'It's good to be relaxed and have a good chat. When you know things are hairy, then you need to obviously turn your game face on and do the job.' He particularly liked Michelle Tompkins, a Harrier pilot who would describe the breathtaking views from her cockpit. She had a bird's-eye views of the snowcapped mountains and laughed when Harry joked that conditions were perfect for skiing. Of course none of the pilots had the slightest inkling that Widow Six Seven was in fact Prince Harry, even though his clipped English meant he was a hit with all the female pilots. 'We said, "Flirt with her any longer and you have to get a room",' joked Harry's commanding officer, battery commander Major Andy Dimmock. 'He said, "Does that count as the Mile-High Club?"'

Incredibly Harry's troop leader on desert manoeuvres in Helmand turned out to be Captain Dickon Leigh-Wood, a twenty-seven-year-old from Fakenham in Norfolk who had gone to Ludgrove with William and Harry. 'It was a massive surprise,' said the captain of his chance encounter with the prince. 'I think he is loving it. He loves the privacy – there's no paparazzi chasing him. He hasn't got his bodyguard team in the field. He's with the boys, who he gets on with incredibly well. He's always playing rugby or football or sitting around the fire telling stupid stories.'

On Christmas Eve Harry asked to be posted to the Gurkhas at FOB Delhi in the perilous Garmsir area close to the border with Pakistan. Delhi consists of shattered buildings and the remnants of a once respected but now bombed-out agricultural college. The town's high street was the British front line, and between Harry and the enemy was 500 metres of no-man's-land consisting of abandoned trenches and the remains of what used to be working farms. The base was under daily attack and the nearest hospital a thirty-minute helicopter ride away, but despite the basic conditions, Harry could not have been happier. 'What it's all about is being here with the guys rather than being in a room with a bunch of officers . . . It's good fun to be with just a normal bunch of guys, listening to their problems, listening to what they think.'

In the ghost town of Garmsir Harry could not have felt further from home. In his US Stars and Stripes baseball cap with its slogan WE DO BAD THINGS TO BAD PEOPLE, which he had traded with another officer for his fleece scarf, he was barely recognisable. He was sunburned and his red hair matted with sand. He slept in a mortar-proof billet which contained a narrow camp bed with a mosquito net, a locker made from an old mortar shell box and a rug embroidered with pictures of tanks and hand grenades. Like everyone else he was rationed to one bottle of drinking water a day, and once he had drunk that, the vile-tasting chlorinated water had to suffice. Food consisted of boil-in-the-bag chicken tikka masala and corned beef hash. Harry missed his favourite Big Macs, and the only luxuries were his Haribo sweets and a few bags of South African biltong, which would arrive in the post from Chelsy. There were no hot showers, and when the fine dust that collected in every crevice became unbearable, only freezing-cold water was available. Shaving was restricted to once every three days and the rounded ends of missile cases were used as shaving bowls. Harry revelled in the simplicity and anonymity of this life. 'Delhi is fantastic. I asked the commanding officer if I could come down here and spend Christmas with the Gurkhas because I had spent some time with them in England on exercise in Salisbury. Everyone is really looked after here . . . The food is fantastic – goat curries, chicken curries.'

Harry spent Christmas Day patrolling the bombed-out town and enjoying a game of touch rugby with his new friends. 'Not your typical Christmas,' he remarked. 'But Christmas is overrated anyway.' Back at home the press kept their word and little was made of the fact that Harry was absent from the family's traditional lunch at Sandringham. When the Queen delivered her traditional Christmas Day speech, she poignantly prayed for the safe return of every soldier in Afghanistan. Few knew she and the rest of the royals were feeling the same fear and worry as every other family who had a son or daughter on the front line that Christmas. As the royal family raised their glasses to absent friends they were reminded of Harry, who had organised a sweepstake before his departure in which everyone had had to guess the name of Edward and Sophie Wessex's baby boy born on 20 December. The winner was to be presented with the prize, a substantial amount of cash, at Christmas Day lunch. Harry had his money on Albert Archibald. The money, it was decided, would stay in the pot until both boys were home.

As he patrolled the derelict streets in his wraparound shades, an Afghan scarf and his army-issue helmet, a nine-millimetre pistol strapped to his body armour, Prince Harry was unidentifiable. A boy on a donkey trotted past and didn't give Cornet Wales a second glance. Out on patrol, home was a Spartan armoured vehicle containing everything the soldiers would need to survive for days on end. It was unimaginably uncomfortable. The men heated drinking water in a boiler built into the back door powered by the Spartan's engine. Tea and coffee tasted identical, but when the temperatures dropped to minus ten at night they were grateful for a hot drink. At night Harry and his men slept in shell scrapes – make-do shelters made by attaching tarpaulins to the vehicle, which kept the elements out, but there was no padding and his bones dug into the Spartan, leaving him black and blue. 'I can't wait to get back and just sit on a sofa. It's going to be ridiculous after bouncing around in a turret. My hips are bruised, my arse is bruised,' he complained. Nevertheless he loved the routine of army life and seemed more comfortable being a soldier than a prince. 'Just walking around [with] some of the locals or the Afghan National Police – they haven't got a clue who I am. They wouldn't know. It's fantastic,' he told John Bingham, the journalist who accompanied him to the front line for the Press Association. 'I'm still a little bit conscious [not to] show my face too much in and around the area. Luckily there's no civilians around here . . . It's sort of a little no-man's-land.'

He didn't mind not being able to wash, nor did he miss alcohol or nightclubs. He didn't even seem bothered by the 'desert roses', mortar-carrying tubes angled into the ground which served as urinals. Apart from the tasteless boil-in-the-bag meals there was little he disliked about being in a war zone. 'What am I missing the most? Nothing really,' said Harry, sitting on his cot in FOB Delhi. 'I honestly don't know what I miss at all. Music – we've got music. We've got light; we've got food; we've got non-alcoholic drink. No, I don't miss the booze, if that's the next question. It's nice just to be here with all the guys and just mucking in as one of the lads . . . It's bizarre. I'm out here now, haven't really had a shower for four days, haven't washed my clothes for a week, and everything seems completely normal. I think this is about as normal as I'm ever going to get.'

Although it was dangerous, life was also monotonous. In his free time he read magazines, and his well-thumbed collection of lads' magazines ensured he was popular. He also had time to reflect on his life. At times, he admitted, his thoughts turned to his mother, but he never allowed himself to dwell on the past. 'I suppose it's just the way it is. There are other people out here who've lost parents . . . Hopefully she'll be proud. She would be looking down having a giggle about the stupid things that I've been doing, like going left when I should have gone right . . . William sent me a letter saying how proud he reckons that she would be.'

Like everyone he looked forward to receiving mail, which could arrive as infrequently as every two weeks or even longer. He did not receive his father's Christmas card until February. To fill in the hours he often played poker with his fellow officers or had a kickabout with a makeshift ball made from loo rolls and gaffer tape. Every week like everyone else he was allowed thirty minutes on a satellite phone. Harry used these precious moments to call home and speak to his family. From a private corner in the camp, where the service dipped in and out of signal, he also called Chelsy. She would fill him in on her days and make him laugh with tales of the disastrous dinner parties she regularly hosted at her student digs. Cooking, Harry knew, was not her strong point, and a fellow officer told how he burst into laughter as Chelsy relayed how she had burned yet another lasagne. She kept the conversation upbeat, and only afterwards would she allow herself to cry. She was desperately worried for his safety and, according to one of her closest friends, wrote letters to Harry every day. They also managed to communicate intermittently on Facebook, on which Harry used the pseudonym 'Spike Wells'. 'F***ing cold here. Like insanely cold bit weird!! Anyhoo, gotta go, lots of love to you, probably see you soon unfortunately for you, hehe! Laters ginge!' In another he simply told the girl he calls 'Chedda' he was missing her. 'I love you. I mis [*sic*] u gorgeous.' Their troubles were behind them and it was thoughts of being reunited with Chelsy that kept Harry going. He had a picture of her in his pocket, and according to another officer spoke proudly of his 'beautiful' South African girlfriend and how he couldn't wait to be with her again. Unfortunately for Harry, it would be sooner than he expected.

Cornet Wales stared at the screen forcing his eyes to stay open. He had not slept for seventy-two hours, and as he kept his gaze on Taliban TV beads of perspiration collected on his forehead. It was New Year's Eve and this was Widow Six Seven's opportunity to prove his worth. A Desert Hawk drone, a small remote-controlled spy aircraft the size of a large model aeroplane, had spotted what looked like Taliban fighters in his operating zone. Harry had been watching them using its surveillance cameras and thermal imaging devices for three long nights. Everything had gone through his mind. Was it the Taliban or could the figures be civilians? He knew he could not afford to make a mistake. Targets had to be positively identified and present a threat to coalition forces before he was allowed to call in a strike. Instinct told him his hunch was right – it was the Taliban and it was time to strike. Just to be sure he stayed up till midnight watching the area, and at 10 a.m. the next day his suspicions were confirmed when the enemy opened fire on a small British observation post on the front line. Within hours Forward Operating Base Delhi was under heavy attack and Harry needed to call in an air strike. It was what he had been trained to do, and within seconds he had been assigned two F15s. The warplanes, armed with 500-pound bombs, appeared on his radar six miles from the target, and Harry guided them in. The pilots radioed 'in hot', the call sign that they were ready to strike. Sweat dripped from his forehead as Harry calmly issued the authorisation: 'Cleared hot.' Within seconds the planes had dropped their munitions and two ground-shaking explosions rocked the network of Taliban bunkers he had been watching for days. As the firing around him subsided, fifteen Taliban fighters emerged from their shelters. It was ruthless but Harry knew what he had to do next. He called the jets back and verified the co-ordinates. A third bomb exploded moments later and suddenly there was no sign of life.

It was Harry's first strike and a complete success, but it was just the beginning. Only days later he would see action again. On 2 January Harry started a week at a nineteenth-century fort not far from FOB Delhi, one of the only elevated watch points on the front line. His boss, Major Mark Millford, officer commanding B Company of the 1st Battalion the Royal Gurkha Rifles, described the area as 'about as dangerous as it can get'. Harry was just 500 metres from the enemy trenches when twenty Taliban were spotted moving towards his position. The Gurkhas with Harry fired a Javelin missile at the enemy, but they kept advancing. Harry seized a fifty-calibre machine gun and pulled the trigger, the distant plumes of smoke serving as his aim. Wearing earplugs, Harry gritted his teeth, focused on his target and pulled the trigger again. It was the prince's first firefight, and he grinned as a Gurkha recorded the moment on Harry's video camera, which he had been using to make a diary. 'This is the first time I've fired a fifty-cal,' he said, exhilarated by the thirty-minute battle from which he and his men emerged victorious. He was just 500 metres from Line Taunton, the heavily forti-fied trench system which marks the start of the Taliban-controlled area in Helmand. 'The whole place is just deserted. There are no roofs on any of the compounds; there are craters all over the place. It looks like something out of the Battle of the Somme,' he continued as the camera panned around the battle-scarred land.

On the other side of the world the rumour that Prince Harry was fighting on the front line in Afghanistan was beginning to gather momentum. The news had broken in January in an Australian magazine called *New Idea*, which had chosen to ignore the embargo on Harry's deployment. There had been no denial from Clarence House or the Ministry of Defence, but fortunately the story had not been followed up. General Sir Richard Dannatt was still concerned about the prince's security, however, and as a precaution the six SAS soldiers who had taken him out to Afghanistan were flown to FOB Edinburgh, where Harry had been stationed for several weeks.

Edinburgh is only seven kilometres away from the Taliban's heartland around Musa Qala, and the routes to it are heavily mined. The war-torn town had just been retaken in a two-week assault by British and American troops, and the locals were living in fear. The Taliban had wreaked havoc, burning the locals' houses and destroying their crops and animals. Harry was to join a troop of Spartan reconnaissance vehicles in an attempt to capture the remote village of Karis De Baba, where it was suspected the Taliban were regrouping. It was an honour for the prince to be sent, and a personal tragedy that he never made it. He had come so far and much further forward than he ever imagined he would. At times it was dangerous. During one ground patrol of Musa Qala his Scimitar nearly hit a Taliban landmine. The mine was spotted by a drone just in time, and Harry made light of the incident, insisting he was at no more risk than any other soldier, but he had come perilously close. On another occasion Harry was caught in crossfire. He had been bringing Chinooks into FOB Edinburgh to fly casualties out to the nearest medical base, and without warning found himself under rocket fire, missiles exploding just fifty metres away. He was ordered to take cover and escaped unscathed.

Away from the front line, renowned US blogger Matt Drudge

had picked up *New Idea*'s story and run it on his website the Drudge Report, which is read by millions of people around the world. With the story on the Internet it was impossible to contain, and the news spread like wildfire. Harry was on radio duty on the morning of 29 February, when the first reports started to filter through that his cover had been blown. In London Chief of the Defence Staff Sir Jock Stirrup and General Dannatt spent the morning in meetings. They decided to pull Harry out just after midday. Harry's evacuation had already been planned and the SAS troopers had a Chinook waiting to take him to Kandahar. It was too risky to keep him in Afghanistan, especially in the Taliban heartland, where Harry would be a prize trophy. Cornet Wales was given no explanation; he was simply told to pack his bags and informed he was on his way to Camp Bastion, the forward coalition base. He had a few minutes to say goodbye to the men he had served with. 'They were upset, they were pretty depressed for me. They were just like, "It would be nice to keep you here."'

Prince Harry didn't smile as he descended the steps of the RAF TriStar passenger jet at exactly 11.20 a.m. on Saturday 1 March. His ginger beard glistened in the sunlight and he still bore a film of fine desert dust on his weathered skin. His combats were dirty, and he was desperate for a bath and a cooked meal, but he was still gutted to be back so soon. He had flown into RAF Brize Norton in Oxfordshire with 160 troops including two seriously injured soldiers from 40 Commando Royal Marines. His father, who told reporters of his relief that Harry was safely home 'in one piece', and William were both waiting on the ground for him. 'I didn't see it coming – it's a shame,' Harry said when he was asked how he felt about his premature homecoming. 'Angry would be the wrong word to use, but I am slightly disappointed. I thought I could see it through to the end and come back with our guys.'

For a young man who had always had a fractious relationship with the media, he could not help but feel resentful of the press. 'I am very disappointed that foreign websites have decided to run the story without consulting us,' he said. 'This is in stark contrast to the highly responsible attitude of the whole of the UK print and broadcast media.' For once the British press wasn't in the firing line. Prime Minister Gordon Brown described him as an exemplary soldier and said; 'The whole of Britain will be proud of the outstanding service he is giving.' Getting Prince Harry to the front line had been a triumph for the army after the fiasco earlier that year, when the decision to send him to Iraq had been reversed. Two months later on 5 May Lieutenant Wales, dressed in desert camouflage, received a service medal from his aunt Princess Anne, who is colonel-in-chief of the Blues and Royals. Chelsy was seated next to the Prince of Wales, who was wearing the Household Cavalry's burgundy and navy tie, and William at the ceremony at Combermere Barracks. It was the first time Chelsy had been invited to an official engagement and she was delighted to be there. Harry made it clear he had every intention of getting back to the front line as quickly as possible. 'I don't want to sit around in Windsor,' he said. 'I generally don't like England that much, and you know it's nice to be away from the papers and all the general shit they write.'

Chapter 16

Brothers in arms

The last thing I want to do is be mollycoddled or wrapped up in cotton wool because if I was to join the army, I'd want to go where my men went and I'd want to do what they did. I would not want to be kept back for being precious or whatever, that's the last thing I'd want.

Prince William, 2004

From the king-sized canopied bed Kate Middleton could hear the sea lapping on the shore. It was midday and not only too hot to sit out; a plague of sandflies had descended on the paradise island of Desroches in the Seychelles forcing the couple to seek shelter in their luxury bungalow. Neither William nor Kate complained. It was late August 2007 and the first time they had been completely alone since their break-up in the spring. William had hired out the exclusive five-star Desroches Island Resort, which consists of luxury bungalows looking out over the turquoise Indian Ocean. With a population of fifty and just three miles long, the paradise island was the perfect escape, but just to make sure they could not be spied on the pair had checked in under the names Martin and Rosemary Middleton. Tanned and happy, they spent their days kayaking and snorkelling in the shallow waters of the coral reef and had swimming competitions in the pool before breakfast.

At night the staff laid a table for two on the sand complete with silver cutlery, crystal glasses and a crisp linen tablecloth, where they enjoyed fresh fish barbecues and bottles of chilled wine. It was just the two of them, and there was plenty of time for talking and plenty to talk about. After getting back together in June, William and Kate had deliberately kept a low profile. Kate had not sat with William at Diana's memorial concert at Wembley Stadium, nor did she attend the church service at the Guards Chapel. Behind the closed doors of Clarence House, however, William and Kate were seeing each other as often as possible. It had taken just days for the prince to realise that ending their relationship was a mistake, but weeks before Kate agreed to give William a second chance. She had, according to her friend Emma Sayle, been deeply affected by the break-up. 'William was the love of her life, and she admitted that to me, but she said their relationship was hard because they were constantly in the public eye. When they got back together Kate said they had a lot of issues to sort out.' Understandably, Kate wanted assurances from William. They had been together for six years and both of them knew that at some point they had to address the future. For a young man who has an inherent fear of tomorrow this was not easy for William, but the tranquil backdrop of the Seychelles was as good a place as any to discuss it.

Under a moon so bright it cast their shadows across the beach, William assured Kate she was the one. For the first time they discussed quite seriously the subject of marriage. William, who had inherited something of his father's fear of commitment, knew he would lose Kate if he could not give her some form of guarantee. 'They didn't agree to get married there and then; what they made was a pact,' a member of their inner circle explained. 'William told Kate she was the one, but he was not ready to get married. He promised her his commitment and said he would not let her down, and she in turn agreed to wait for him.' The problem was William had his career to think about, and while Kate needed reassurance, he also needed to know that she understood everything that came with marrying him. He would always have to put duty first. She loved him, that he knew, but being a royal meant making sacrifices. William was due to spend six months on attachments with the Royal Air Force and the Royal Navy, but that was all to come. For now they were together.

The pact they made that night in Desroches would stand them in good stead. While Harry's career hung in limbo following his return from Afghanistan, William's had been meticulously planned. In September he graduated to troop commander and was now qualified to be deployed to a war zone. He was stationed with D Squadron of the Household Cavalry at Combermere Barracks in Windsor, where he led a troop of twelve men – himself plus a sergeant, two corporals and eight troopers – and was shaping up as quite the royal soldier – or 'combat wombat', as his father affectionately called him. But regardless of how good a soldier he was, William knew he would never fight like Harry, although he had made his intention to go to war clear before he joined Sandhurst:

The last thing I want to do is be mollycoddled or wrapped up in cotton wool, because if I was to join the army I'd want to go where my men went and I'd want to do what they did. I would not want to be kept back for being precious or whatever, that's the last thing I'd want. It's the most humiliating thing and it would be something I'd find very awkward to live with, being told I couldn't go out there when these guys have got to go out there and do a bad job.

It was a topic he revisited when he was interviewed by NBC presenter Matt Lauer ahead of the Concert for Diana. When asked about his future career in the armed forces he said, 'What's the point of me doing all my training and being there for my guys when I can turn around to somebody and say, "Well I'm far too important, I'm not going"?'

But William had been advised that he would never be sent to the front line, and when his squadron was deployed to Afghanistan for six months, William was left behind. He found it as difficult as Harry had, but Lieutenant Wales put on a brave face. It was, he said 'for good reasons I was not able to deploy to Afghanistan'. He couldn't wait for the New Year, when he would join the Royal Air Force. Ever since he was a little boy, when he and Harry had been allowed to sit in the cockpit of their father's helicopter, William had wanted to fly.

It was freezing cold when he arrived at RAF Cranwell in Lincolnshire on 7 January 2008. William had just returned from a New Year break at Balmoral with Kate, and neither of them knew how long it would be until they were together again. The air force college, which is the oldest in the world, was a bit like Sandhurst – impressive from the outside and practical on the inside. The base comprises its own runway, educational facilities, gym, swimming pool and halls of residence including York House, the Grade II listed building where William was to live. This had been named after his great-grandfather Prince Albert, Duke of York (later King George VI), who was appointed to command a squadron at Cranwell in 1918. His room, which measured fifteen feet square, was sparsely furnished with a single bed, a fitted wardrobe and a small en-suite bathroom. It was five miles to Sleaford, the nearest town, and a short walk to Cranwell village. All around was the green Lincolnshire countryside.

William's working day started at 8 a.m. and finished at 5.30, when he was free to do as he chose. His father, who had learned to fly at the same base, had warned William there would be little time for socialising. Charles had trained on a Mark 3 Provost and graduated as a flight lieutenant on 20 August 1971. William couldn't resist a smile as he walked past his father's portrait, which hung in College Hall to the left of the Rotunda, on his way to class. His father had been right – the lessons were hard – and William spent every free hour studying and getting to grips with the cardboard cut-out flight deck presented to every officer cadet for training purposes. Unlike most cadets, who train for a minimum of three years before becoming an operational pilot, a fast-track course had been specially prepared for the future king. 'We've adapted his course and cut out anything superfluous because we're not teaching him to be an operational pilot; we're teaching him to be a competent pilot,' said Squadron Leader Kevin Marsh, who oversaw William's attachment.

William had been concerned that he would never realise his childhood dream of learning to fly. Flying in the RAF depends on perfect vision, and William is short-sighted. It could have been a problem, but because he was already a serving officer in the Household Cavalry, he was accepted into the RAF. Like everyone else, he attended the Officers and Aircrew Selection Centre and a medical board prior to his attachment, and he was ordered to wear prescription glasses. 'William wasn't allowed to wear his own spectacles,' said a senior officer. 'He had to wear MoD-prescribed glasses, which weren't very attractive.' They did the job, however, and within a fortnight he took to the skies for the first time.

As he took the controls of the Grob 115E William took a deep breath and carried out the final checks. He had been trained by Squadron Leader Roger Bousefield, who had approved his solo flight on the small propeller-driven aircraft, which is used for elementary flying training by the RAF. 'God knows how somebody trusted me with an aircraft and my own life,' he joked when he was safely back on the tarmac. After completing his elementary training in the Grob, William was sent to RAF Linton in Yorkshire, a two-hour drive from Cranwell. Here he learned to fly the Tucano, a more advanced aircraft. As he had expected, there was little time for Kate, who fitted around his working week, and in March they managed to jet off to Klosters for a week's skiing. The intensity of his tailored fast-track course had its advantages: though Kate got to see little of her boyfriend, there was no repeat of his antics at Bovington, where William would go out for late-night drinking sessions with his platoon. Because of the 'bottle to throttle' rule, which means pilots can't drink alcohol for ten hours prior to any flying duties, there was no bad behaviour at Cranwell, and William limited himself to two pints a day and on some days didn't touch alcohol at all. Occasionally on Thursday nights he and his fellow flying officers would allow themselves an early drink at the nearby Duke of Wellington pub followed by a fish-and-chip supper.

Most weekends he would head home to see Kate. She didn't much fancy the long drive from London to Cranwell, and besides William's mess offered little privacy. When he was half an hour from central London William would call her from his mobile to let her know he was almost home. Kate, who was freely waved in and out of the cast-iron gates of Clarence House had already drawn a hot bath and dinner was in the oven. 'She was almost motherly to him,' one of their friends recalls. 'William would be exhausted when he got back, and after dinner they'd watch a movie together and he'd often fall asleep before the end of it.' Sometimes they entertained at Clarence House, where William and Harry have private quarters. Kate had spent several weeks overseeing a minor refurbishment and had selected fashionable designer wallpaper from Osbourne & Little on the King's Road and encouraged the boys to invest in a cycling machine for a makeshift gym, which they set up in one of the spare rooms.

At weekends they enjoyed cooking traditional English suppers like bangers and mash. Kate would grill the sausages while William mashed the potatoes under strict instructions not to use too much butter. If Harry was around, he was usually on drinks duty. It was the closest William and Kate had come to domestic bliss since their university days, and their friends noted how happy and comfortable they were in each other's company. As Kate darted around the kitchen searching for utensils, William would give her a kiss when he thought no one was looking. He had developed the habit of finishing his girlfriend's sentences, while she had learned to read him better than anyone else. She could tell when he wanted their guests to leave and when to get out the Jack Daniel's because William was in the mood to party. When Harry was home from Windsor they would entertain late into the night.

Their father and grandparents had told them to steer clear of the glitzy nightclubs they loved in London. Harry had been the recipient of numerous death threats posted on Al-Qaeda websites following his return from Afghanistan, and William had been warned to stay away from Boujis. When he and Kate went to the club in October 2007 chaos broke out as they tried to leave. It was the first time they had been seen together in public since their split, and as they left a scuffle broke out among the waiting photographers, who had gathered on the corner of Thurloe Street. There must have been fifty paparazzi hovering outside the club and everyone wanted a picture. Kate was nearly hit by a camera as she clambered into the waiting Range Rover, while a scowling and worse-for-wear William, accompanied by his protection officer, battled through the crush. 'Come on, guys. Let us get in the car,' the prince shouted. One photographer, who had grabbed the car's left-hand wing mirror, was still attached to the Range Rover as it sped off, while some of the others followed the royal party on bikes. William was furious. The fact that the inquest into the death of his mother was still taking place made the harassment particularly upsetting.

When photographs of the couple were published on the front page of the *Evening Standard* under the headline BOUJIS NIGHTS ARE BACK AGAIN an aide at Clarence House made a formal complaint. They described the press pack's behaviour as 'incomprehensible' given the coroner was addressing the issue of paparazzi intrusion the night Diana died in Paris that very week. It was a dangerous incident and exposed just how vulnerable the princes were when they went out. The Queen was not impressed. Not for the first time she questioned why her grandsons and their girlfriends were so intent on visiting such high-profile establishments. 'The Queen cannot understand why her grand-children go to places where they will be photographed and attract attention,' I was told by a family friend. 'Philip has told William and Harry to stay away from Boujis for a bit.'

A celebration was definitely in order, however, when William qualified as an RAF pilot on Friday 11 April 2008. He had tele-phoned his grandmother with the good news before calling Harry to announce that he had a plan to get to the Isle of Wight that weekend for their cousin Peter Phillips' stag party. Like his father, grandfather Prince Philip and great-grandfather George VI, William was getting his wings. It had been decided that the ceremony would take place at RAF Cranwell because it could accommodate the press, who were just as interested in Kate, who would be there for the ceremony. As Air Chief Marshall the Prince of Wales pinned the RAF's prestigious flying badge onto his son's pristine uniform, he smiled broadly before shaking his hand. In 1971, when Charles had graduated, the Duke of Edinburgh had done the very same thing. Dressed in a military-style cream coat and her trademark black knee-high boots, Kate sat in the audience with William's private secretary Jamie Lowther-Pinkerton and the Duchess of Cornwall. Two years earlier she had watched William pass out at Sandhurst; now he was Flying Officer Wales, and it was only a matter of hours before he would put his new aviation skills to the test.

After completing security at RAF Cranwell, William took the controls of the Chinook. He was heading for a civilian airfield on the Isle of Wight, and the two-hour sortie had been approved by senior flying officers. The rain that morning had cleared and conditions were perfect for the low-level flight south to London. As he steered to the east of the capital through busy civilian airspace, his first landing spot came into view. It had already been cleared for William to land at Woolwich Barracks in south-east London, where Prince Harry was waiting for him. It took an hour for William to fly Harry across the south of England. Below they could see the rush-hour traffic choking up the motorways. At 4 p.m. precisely they touched down at Bembridge Airport on the Isle of Wight, which meant they had plenty of time at the bar. If they had driven, they would still be north of London.

It was quite a story to tell their twenty-nine-year-old cousin and his friends and quite a story for the press. ROYAL STAG SENSATION was the *Sun*'s front page, while the *Mirror* led on FURY OVER WILLS' STAG PARTY JAUNT. A bitter row was quickly escalating over the cost of the flight. Although the trip had been cleared by the RAF, which described it as a 'legitimate training sortie which tested his new skills', a number of MPs demanded to know why the prince had been allowed to use the £10 million RAF helicopter as his personal transport when there was a shortage in Afghanistan. As far as they were concerned, the flight, which cost £15,000 in fuel, maintenance and manpower, benefited no one other than William and Harry, who had made the journey to the Isle of Wight in record time simply for a party. 'This is serious kit with serious running costs,' said the Liberal

Democrat defence spokesman Nick Harvey. 'The public will not appreciate it being used as a stag-do taxi service.'

Clarence House refused to comment, but when it emerged that William had also flown a Chinook to Sandringham and Highgrove and to his girlfriend's house in Berkshire several weeks earlier, the episode descended into farce. Kate and her parents had apparently watched in delight as William, who had flown from RAF Odiham in Hampshire to the Middletons' family home on 3 April, practised taking off and landing in a nearby field. By now the Chinook flights had blown up into a major row at the RAF, where top brass wanted to know why William's superiors had allowed the sorties, during which two pilots, a navigator and a loadmaster had accompanied the prince. William's requests to 'buzz' his girlfriend and his father and fly to the Isle of Wight had been approved – the flights were part of an authorised intensive training course on the Chinook – but a senior RAF source admitted, 'We recognise how such activities might be perceived at a time of heavy operational commitments in Iraq and Afghanistan.'

It wasn't the first time William had been criticised for using the RAF as a private taxi service. When he was on work experience at RAF Valley in December 2005 he had flown from Anglesey to RAF Lyneham in Wiltshire in a Hawk jet so that he could collect a pair of boots. Now his Chinook flights had cast a shadow over what should have been one of his proudest military milestones.

As the row over the Chinooks rattled on, the RAF decided it would be an opportune time to send William to Afghanistan. On 26 April 2008 Prince William touched down in Kandahar.

The thirty-hour visit was top secret and only reported once

William was safely back in Britain. WILLIAM FLIES TO WAR ZONE (AND NOT A STAG DO IN SIGHT!) was the headline in the *Daily Mail*, which reported the story two days after William had returned to the UK via RAF Lyneham. It was not quite as dramatic as it sounded. William was not qualified to fly the C-17 Globemaster. He did however take the controls during the eleven-hour flight and spent three hours on the ground in Kandahar meeting RAF servicemen. While it was nowhere near as hazardous as Harry's deployment it was still dangerous. Two British servicemen had been killed on patrol at the same base earlier that month and William's army mentor Major Alexis 'Lex' Roberts was killed by a roadside bomb there in 2007. As the main hub for British forces on the ground in Afghanistan, Kandahar Airfield was a prime target for the Taliban, but Clarence House defended the decision to send the prince: 'Prince William has learned a lot about the force's role in theory, so it was important for him to see it put into action.' Essentially the trip was to familiarise him with the work of the RAF in a war zone. He also visited RAF personnel at Al Udeid in Qatar. At least William could now say that he too had been to Afghanistan.

When he returned home on 28 April, it was not for long. Having completed his attachment with the RAF, he was busy preparing for a five-week placement with the Royal Navy on board the frigate HMS *Iron Duke*, on station in the Caribbean. Kate, who had quit her job at Jigsaw, was once again left in London bored and alone. She had known that William would spend much of the year overseas on attachment and had accepted it, but his punishing work schedule only served to illustrate how much spare time she had. The media, who until now had always been kind to her, suddenly noticed that she seemed to be doing remarkably little with her days other than wait for William to propose. It was now that, much to her annoyance, she was nicknamed Waity Katie in the British press. This was unchartered territory and Kate did not know what to do. Up until now she had been the subject of only flattering editorials and hailed as a breath of fresh air for the House of Windsor; moreover there was one person in that very house who had also sat up and taken notice of Kate Middleton.

The Queen, who has always been close to her grandson, had taken an interest in Kate in May when she represented William at Peter Phillips' wedding to Autumn Kelly at St George's Chapel in Windsor. William had already accepted an invitation to the wedding of Jecca Craig's brother Batian in Kenya, and when he asked Kate if she would stand in for him, she agreed. Not only did the decision illustrate how close William was to the Craig family, it also served to highlight just how highly regarded and comfortable Kate was in royal circles. Elegant in a black fascinator hat and tailored jacket, she was happy and confident as she mingled with Charles and Camilla and other members of the extended family. Harry had planned to use the wedding to formally introduce Chelsy to the Queen now that their relationship was back on again. Since his return from the front line the pair seemed stronger than ever. They had enjoyed a romantic holiday on a houseboat in the Okavango Delta in Botswana that March, and Harry had excitedly told his grandmother about his African-born girlfriend who wanted to be a solicitor. It was Kate, however, who fascinated the Queen, and when William was inaugurated as a royal knight companion of the Order of the Garter in June that year Kate was there once again watching from the sidelines. As William, in the traditional ostrich- and heron-plumed cap with a blue garter round his leg, processed down the Castle Hill to the annual church service, Kate, supressing a fit of the giggles, watched with Harry from the Galilee Porch. Her appearance at the ceremony of the ancient order generated even more speculation about a possible engagement.

Although they had met several times at formal occasions the Queen knew little of the girl who had enchanted her grandson, and according to sources close to her has never had a one-to-one meeting with Kate. Privately she had grave concerns and believed that Kate needed to have a job and an identity in her own right before an engagement was announced. 'The Queen is interested in Kate,' disclosed one source close to Her Majesty. 'She was having a conversation with a friend and asked "What is it exactly that Kate does?" It was a fair enough question.'

Since leaving her job as an accessories buyer for Jigsaw at the end of 2007 Kate had toyed with the idea of taking up photography professionally and had kept herself busy compiling a catalogue for her parents' online business Party Pieces. But for a bright girl with a good degree the work was mind-numbingly dull. Kate was actually talented behind the lens and at the end of November 2007 helped curate an art exhibition in London at Bluebird on the King's Road. She was not short of job offers, and the American fashion house Ralph Lauren was one of a number of retailers who were keen to appoint Kate as one of their ambassadors. 'Ralph Lauren had an idea to get Kate on board and there was talk of her doing a job that didn't actually involve much more than dressing up in some nice outfits,' so I was told. The job never materialised, however, which meant plenty of time for William, but unfortunately for Kate the newspapers had decided that her life was one long holiday. If she was not with William at Balmoral then the couple were skiing or holidaying on Mustique. Kate was there so often the press dubbed her 'Queen of Mustique', a title that had previously belonged to Princess Margaret. Britain was now in recession and such frivolous displays of wealth were unpalatable to the Queen. She is one of the hardest-working royals, despite her age, and that a future member of the family was without a full-time job was unacceptable to her. While the rest of the world speculated that an engagement was on the horizon for William and Kate, the Queen believed an announcement should be postponed until Kate was settled in a career. 'It is Her Majesty's opinion that if Kate is one day going to be William's consort, then she needs a proper job,' my source insisted. 'Swanning from one five-star holiday resort to another is not the prerequisite for a young woman possibly destined to be queen.'

When the story broke on the front page of the *Mail on Sunday* on 1 June 2008 royal bloggers posted comments on Internet forums noting how the tide had turned for Kate. She was stung by the Queen's criticism, but Clarence House advised her not to react and assured her that the story would go away. On this occasion however Kate ignored their advice and instructed a friend to brief *Hello!* magazine that she was in fact working full-time at her parents' company Party Pieces. Later on a black and white photograph of Kate was posted on the company website, but it was deemed a step too far and within weeks it had been removed from the website. The Queen had quietly suggested that Kate affiliate herself with a charity, and by September she was involved with Starlight, which works with seriously and terminally ill children. William was supportive. He understood better than most the pressures of being in the public eye and was upset that Kate was in the firing line. When she started working for Jigsaw he had told friends he was delighted that Kate was 'finally working in the real world', but he understood it was difficult for her to have a normal job – not least because she chose to be at his beck and call, which made a full-time job impractical. It was something Kate's mother Carole described to family friends as an 'impossible situation'. Meanwhile, as Kate worked on a strategy to get herself out of the news, William had decided that he wanted to join the RAF and become a search-and-rescue pilot.

The news was made official on 15 September 2008, and Clarence House's announcement took everyone, including the Palace, by surprise. William had spent the summer with the Royal Navy. He had been banned from going to the Gulf because of security fears but had enjoyed his secondment aboard HMS *Iron Duke* and within days of his arrival had played a key role in seizing £40 million of cocaine in the Caribbean Sea north-east of Barbados. It had been widely assumed that when he returned he would quit the Household Cavalry and become a full-time working royal, but the young prince had other ideas. 'The time I spent with the RAF earlier this year made me realise how much I love flying. Joining search and rescue is a perfect opportunity for me to serve in the forces operationally.' The British press drew its own conclusions and labelled William a 'reluctant figurehead'.

Joining the RAF meant William could postpone full-time official duties for at least five years. Clarence House was keen to stress that the prince would continue with his charity work, but his commitment would be to his military career. It was a decision he had thought long and hard about and he was certain it was the right one. William had still not ruled out going to war and secretly hoped the job would take him one step closer to the front line. 'In my eyes, if Harry can do it, then I can do it,' he insisted. 'You talk to everyone else and it's impossible. But I remain hopeful that there's a chance.'

He was aware there had been criticism over the brevity of his military attachments. The pressure group Republic had dismissed his secondment with the navy as 'little more than a shallow PR exercise . . . all about selling William to the public and promoting the Windsor brand'. They also asserted, 'There is simply no need for the Windsors to serve in the military.' William disagreed. Now was his chance to prove he was committed to a career in the armed forces. The job was risky and the Palace knew the dangers. William would begin training in the New Year, once he had returned from the Caribbean, where he was due to go on his final attachment with special forces. It would mean transferring his commission from the army, where he was a lieutenant in the Blues and Royals, to RAF flying officer, but William had no doubts. Rescuing people was exactly the sort of worthwhile job he wanted to do and would go some way towards compensating for the fact that he might never serve in a war.

The decision, however, would have serious repercussions for his relationship with Kate. According to her friends she was as stunned as anyone when William announced that he planned to join the RAF. Being an army girlfriend had not been quite what Kate had expected, but then with the future king nothing ever was. For William it was the start of an exciting new career; for Kate it would mean a very long wait indeed. The last time William decided to put his career first, the couple had split up. William told her if they survived this they could survive anything. She could only hope that the pledge they had made in Desroches would be strong enough to keep them together.

Chapter 17

Princes of the future

*For reasons that never cease to amaze Harry and me, we
do seem to be able to bring a spotlight to bear on wonderful
initiatives created by other people to help others in need.*
Prince William, January 2010

The clatter of polished silverware and clinking of crystal filled
the dining room as the din of excited chatter reached a crescendo.
Around the table fifteen young aristocrats dressed in smoking
jackets and bow ties and glamorous evening dresses were drinking
port. The host Arthur Landon, only son of the late Brigadier
Tim Landon and inheritor of a £200 million fortune, liked to
do things in style, especially when it came to entertaining royalty.
William and Harry had arrived, without Chelsy, at his impressive home in north Yorkshire just before eight o'clock on a wet
Friday night in November.

Dinner had been a success. The beef stew had warmed them
all up, and the apple crumble had gone down a treat. Among the
group were William and Harry's best friends Guy Pelly, Jacobi
Anstruther-Gough-Calthorpe and Astrid Harbord, Kate who was
poorly with a cold and her sister Pippa. William, who had just
got back from the Caribbean, where he had spent five weeks
training with the SAS, was deep in conversation with Guy Pelly.
As soon as the last course had been served, Guy's girlfriend

Susanna Warren, the granddaughter of the late Earl of Carnarvon, the Queen's racing manager and close friend, played a recital on the grand piano and when it was over Mrs Landon announced she was off to bed. She reminded them all to be in the Great Hall for breakfast at 8 a.m. – they would need something hot before they went off shooting.

The friends retired to the upstairs games room where Harry was holding court. Some of the group were playing snooker while the prince was busy dispensing shots of vodka to his friends. 'Down the hatch,' he commanded as he poured the alcohol straight from the bottle into Astrid's open mouth. Kate had retired to bed, but William was in no hurry to join her. Arthur had a well-stocked bar and William was regaling his friends with tales of his latest adventure overseas over a pint of lager. He was in high spirits and still sporting a beard, much to Harry's amusement. As midnight approached, Guy Pelly announced it was time for the first game. 'You have to get into each other's clothes for half an hour,' he said, pointing at William and a female guest.

It was no wonder the party felt ill the following morning. Kate however was feeling better, and she and William were up at first light. He had promised to take her deerstalking before they all went shooting and Kate couldn't wait. She had learned to stalk on the Balmoral estate in October 2007 with Prince Charles's gillies and was proving an expert shot. She loved the peace and solitude and it wasn't always the kill she was after. She enjoyed the time with William. After all it had been weeks since they had been alone together.

*　　*　　*

Harry pulled Chelsy towards him and planted a kiss on her lips. They were coming to the end of their nine-day holiday in Mauritius and Harry didn't want it to end. He had flown to the paradise island on Boxing Day after spending Christmas with his family at Sandringham, and splashed out on a £1,000-a-night beachfront suite. Chelsy's parents Charles and Beverley and her brother Shaun were also with them, which helped to take some of the pressure off Chelsy and Harry, who had been arguing recently. Chelsy had been studying hard at Leeds for her finals and they had only seen each other fleetingly. She had decided to stay in London once she graduated in June after being offered a solicitor traineeship with a leading London law firm Allen and Overy, whose co-founder George Allen had advised Edward VIII during his abdication. Chelsy had spent two weeks working in the company's private equity department before Christmas and it was a fantastic opportunity. The problem was, things with Harry weren't going so well. When she returned to Cape Town for Christmas she confided to her best friend Kirsten Rogers that she was beginning to doubt whether she could actually tame Harry. Kirsten liked Harry, but as she pointed out to her best friend it was only a year ago that they last went through a rocky patch and now they were talking about their future again.

Since Harry had returned from Afghanistan the couple had seen little of one another. In July 2008 Harry had flown to Lesotho with twenty members of the Blues and Royals to build a children's school. Then in October he was posted to Canada for a month's training. He rushed home when Chelsy had to have her wisdom teeth taken out in hospital, but before the end of the month he was back in Africa with William taking part in a 1,000-mile motorbike rally from Port Edward on KwaZulu-Natal's southern coast down to Port Elizabeth. The eight-day event, called Enduro Africa '08, entailed motorbiking more than a hundred miles a day in forty-degree heat. It was the perfect chance for the princes to mix adventure with charity work and spend some time together, which they rarely got to do, according to Harry. 'We never really spend any time together – we've got separate jobs going on at the moment.' The boys are both accomplished riders. William drives a powerful Honda CRC Blackbird at home, while Harry owns an £8,000 Triumph, but as Harry observed, 'It's not just a bimble across the countryside . . . We're expecting to fall off many a time. We've got a secret bet with everybody else about who's going to fall off between us.' It was the first time they had joined forces since organising the concert the year before, and it was worth the sweat and toil. Together they helped raise £300,000 for children's charities in southern Africa including Sentebale.

By Christmas Harry was home and about to embark on the next stage of his army career, training as a helicopter attack pilot with the Army Air Corps. When he enrolled at its headquarters at Middle Wallop in Hampshire on 19 January 2009 a few days after he returned home from Mauritius, it was under a cloud. Video footage of him fooling around with his fellow cadets three years before when he was at Sandhurst had found its way into the hands of a tabloid newspaper. The prince had taken the footage himself and could be clearly heard narrating over the grainy footage recorded on his hand-held camera. As he panned over his colleagues sleeping in the airport while waiting for a flight to Cyprus, where they were going on a training exercise, he zoomed in on his fellow cadet Ahmed Raza Khan. 'Anyone else here?' asks the prince. 'Ah, our little Paki friend.'

The *News of the World* published the full transcript of the 'bombshell home video', along with pictures on its front page, nine days before Harry enrolled at Middle Wallop. At one point he could be heard saying to another cadet, 'F*** me, you look like a raghead,' offensive slang for an Arab. During another sequence, filmed at a camp with his fellow cadets looking on, he pretended to be speaking to his grandmother on the phone. 'Send my love to the corgis,' he joked to raucous laughter. 'I've got to go. Got to go. Bye. God save you . . . Yeah, that's great.'

It was only four years since Harry had endangered his army career by dressing up as a Nazi at a fancy-dress party. Now he was at the centre of another race row. His colleague Ahmed, now serving in the Pakistan army, said he had taken no offence, but Harry was still advised by Clarence House to apologise. The story was soon old news. Two days later it was revealed that the Prince of Wales called his good friend Kolin Dhillon, an Indian businessman and member of the Beaufort Polo Club, 'Sooty'. Of course Harry should have known better, but even the press concluded he had committed no real crime. 'In battle all that matters is whether Harry would take a bullet to protect his comrade Ahmed. The answer would be an unequivocal yes,' columnist Jane Moore concluded in the *Sun*, summing up the public mood.

If she was embarrassed by the episode, the Queen did not

make it known. Harry had always been the more troublesome of the two princes and even she had been on the receiving end of his pranks. One Christmas she was given a mobile telephone and asked Harry to activate a standard voicemail greeting. Harry insisted on recording a personalised message. 'Hey, wassup? This is Liz,' he recorded to snorts of mirth from William, who could be heard guffawing in the background. 'Sorry I'm away from the throne. For a hotline to Philip press one, for Charles press two, for the corgis press three.' The Queen was told of the hoax message when her private secretary Robin Janvrin called up and 'got the shock of his life', according to an aide.

With the race row fortunately behind him Harry set to work. He had eighteen months of training ahead of him which started with four weeks of intensive tutorials in the classroom before he was allowed in the cockpit. He was also enrolled on an army diversity course to make him more racially aware. He divided his time between RAF Cranwell, where William learned to fly, and the nearby RAF Barkston Heath. Like his older brother, Harry quickly discovered becoming a pilot meant a lot of hard work, no drinking and little time for girlfriends. For £150 a month he had rented a small room with a single bed and en-suite bathroom. From nine in the morning until 5.30 p.m. he had classes, but he struggled with the theory, according to one officer: 'William is proving to be a good stick monkey. Harry has struggled more with the technical aspects.'

Harry later admitted, 'The flying is fantastic, but there are times I've thought I'm not really cut out for this mentally. It's really intense. I knew it was going to be tough, but I never thought it would be this tough. I hope I've got the physical skills to fly a helicopter. But there are exams and everything. I can't do maths – I gave that up when I left school.' Harry was being trained to fly a Firefly, a small fixed-wing aircraft. Initially he had set his heart on eventually flying an Apache attack helicopter but acknowledged, 'Brain capacity? I don't know if I've got it for the Apache.'

While Kate had been prepared to wait for William as he embarked on his flying carer, Chelsy was not. She was lonely and desperately homesick. As she had feared, things went straight back to how they had been before as soon as they returned from Mauritius. She told Harry she felt the relationship had run its course and removed from her finger the blue topaz ring he had given her as a birthday present. Then she did something which infuriated him: she changed the status on her Facebook page to 'Relationship: Not in one.' The relationship was over in the click of a button. Harry could not believe that Chelsy had done it so publicly, and he was angry and upset when the story broke on the front page of the *Mail on Sunday*. He had not even had the chance to tell his father. 'Chelsy was fed up of just being Harry's girlfriend,' said one of her friends. 'She felt she was making all the effort and he wasn't making enough. She also wants to be her own person, not just Prince Harry's girlfriend. She fully respects his career, but they just don't get enough time together and she's a bit fed up of always coming second.'

Just a few weeks later Harry was photographed with Natalie Pinkham at Kitts nightclub in Chelsea, and this time it was Chelsy who was angry and upset. With his looks and eye-catching red hair, Harry was not short of female admirers. Paris

Hilton had reportedly asked him out on a date, while Harry had secretly exchanged telephone numbers with Australian singer Natalie Imbruglia. They had been introduced through their mutual friend Sam Branson at the singer's fancy-dress thirty-fourth birthday party at the Kensington Roof Gardens in west London in February. Harry had dressed as a surgeon and was, according to guests, immediately taken with Natalie, who he pursued with late-night texts and phone calls. He was back to his partying ways, and started going to all-night raves at warehouses in south London which his cousins Princesses Beatrice and Eugenie told him about. The parties, attended by wealthy young aristocrats, are by invitation only, but just to make sure he wasn't recognised Harry wore a black Rastafarian wig. As a result of his nocturnal activities Harry's work suffered, and unsurprisingly he failed the first of his theory exams in February. Charles was concerned. He had seen the same thing happen in Harry's last year at Eton and knew how much his son needed to concentrate if he was going to pass. Harry was given extra tuition and passed the exam the second time round before the end of the month. He was relieved and elated, and finally qualified to fly the Firefly solo.

While he was making progress with his flying, Harry's private life seemed more chaotic than ever. In March the newspapers were linking him with another glamorous young woman, Astrid Harbord, a twenty-seven-year-old Bristol University graduate and friend of Chelsy. Blond, pretty and single, Astrid was perfect girlfriend material and mixed in the same social circles as Harry. She and her sister Davina had been christened the 'Hardcore Sisters' by society magazine *Tatler* and both are good friends of

Guy Pelly. Astrid was also a guest at Arthur Landon's shoot at which Harry had confided that he and Chelsy were having problems. When they were photographed together on the back seat of Harry's chauffeur-driven car entering the rear gates of Clarence House at three o'clock in the morning, this appeared to be confirmation, to the press at least, that Harry and Astrid were a couple. In fact the friendship has only ever been platonic and they slept in separate rooms that night. Astrid was the worse for wear and had passed out on Harry's bed while he stayed in the spare room. 'Astrid was mortified,' said a friend. 'The next morning she woke up to find William and Kate standing in the doorway offering her a cup of tea. Kate was bright-eyed and bushy-tailed, William was laughing, and Astrid just wanted the ground to swallow her up.'

It was in fact a young TV presenter called Caroline Flack who Harry took a shine to. The pair were introduced through Natalie Pinkham at a poker tournament in London that April. Just weeks later they were pictured leaving Mark Dyer's west London flat, and by June Harry had brought the Sky Sports presenter back to Clarence House. But the fling never got off the ground as Harry was still in love with Chelsy, although there was a problem – she had started dating a thirty-three-year-old property developer called Dan Philipson, and the relationship appeared to be getting serious. Ironically it was Astrid who had introduced them, and Dan had made several trips to Leeds. Needless to say, Harry was riled.

Back in February on Valentine's Day Chelsy had received a number of cards and rather bizarrely a copy of the movie *Crocodile Dundee*, sent anonymously. She immediately suspected Harry. She knew he had always been jealous of her old friend Jabu Kirkland. There were pictures of Jabu on Facebook stripped to the waist with a dead crocodile slung across his shoulders and also holiday snaps of him and Chelsy enjoying a Christmas break with friends in Cape Town while Harry was in Afghanistan. The reality was nothing had ever happened between them, but Chelsy secretly liked the fact that Harry was jealous. 'Chelsy laughed out loud when she got the present in the post,' recalled a friend. 'The card that came with it was anonymous but Chelsy had a feeling it was Harry and she called him up. Harry said he had nothing to do with the present but Chelsy just said, "He would say that, wouldn't he!" and laughed. Ironically that was when they started talking again.'

By early May Harry had graduated from fixed-wing aircraft to the Squirrel helicopter and was about to join William at the Defence Helicopter Flying School at RAF Shawbury near Shrewsbury. After his problems with theory exams he had worked hard to keep up with his studies, and when he graduated from RAF Barkston Heath Harry received the Horsa Trophy, which is awarded to 'the man you would most want on your squadron'. But with their careers literally taking off, there were concerns at the Palace that William and Harry should not just be seen as royal members of the military.

The princes were already regularly appearing in the *Court Circular*, the official record of the royal family's public activities, and in January 2009 the Queen allowed them to set up their own household in Colour Court within the St James's Palace compound. Charles had been given a private office after his investiture at Caernarfon Castle in 1969, when he was twenty years old, and the decision to give William and Harry their own was seen as an important part of their gradual move into the public arena. It also gave them some independence from their father, who financed the cost of setting up the office through his estate, the Duchy of Cornwall. The princes had stationery embossed with their personal crests and their own team of staff, which included private secretary Jamie Lowther-Pinkerton, personal secretary Helen Asprey and, at Harry's suggestion, Miguel Head, the bright and astute Ministry of Defence press officer who had helped coordinate his trip to Afghanistan, was appointed assistant press secretary. Until now Charles's long-standing press secretary Paddy Harverson had always commented – or more often not – on stories concerning the princes. Now William and Harry would be briefing their own aide. The Queen insisted on one condition: that Sir David Manning, former British ambassador to the United States, was appointed as a part-time adviser. Sir David was regarded by Her Majesty as a safe pair of hands who would have the authority to intervene as and when he felt it was necessary.

Juggling William and Harry's charitable commitments with their careers and private lives is no easy feat. Among other organisations, William is patron of the English Schools' Swimming Association, Mountain Rescue England and Wales, Skill Force, HMS Alliance Conservation Appeal, The Tusk Trust and the Royal Marsden Hospital – which his mother also had close connections with – as well as Centrepoint charity for the homeless and The Child Bereavement charity. He is also president of the Football Association and vice-patron of the Welsh

Rugby Union and most recently was made the president of Bafta, the British Academy of Film and Television. In addition to Sentebale, Harry's portfolio includes Dolen Cymru, MapAction, and WellChild of which he became the first royal patron in March 2007. He is also vice-president of the England Rugby Union, which inevitably leads to a spot of healthy sibling rivalry with William sporting a daffodil at matches and Harry a red rose for England.

But despite their numerous patronages the boys still faced criticism. On 23 February 2009 the investigative TV programme *Dispatches* accused them of being lazy and pointed out that William had only carried out fourteen royal engagements in 2007 while he was serving with the army, five of which were linked with either rugby or football. The programme noted that when Charles was the same age he carried out around eighty-four royal engagements a year while in the Royal Navy. William was incensed. In 2008 he and Harry had carried out close to sixty engagements between them despite having full-time careers with the armed forces. According to one senior aide, 'No other member of Her Majesty's forces would ever be regarded as lazy, so the criticism is wrong at best, at worst insulting to Prince William's colleagues in the forces, who work as hard as he does.' Despite his punishing work schedule, William told his grandmother he wanted to increase his charitable engagements, although he complained to friends that he wished he had more siblings to share the workload with.

Keen that Harry should also be established as a working royal, the Queen agreed to allow her grandson to visit New York in May. Harry had come up with the idea, having been invited to play in a charity polo match to raise money for Sentebale. Both William and Harry had given up playing the game regularly as neither had time, but they were delighted to compete in charity matches. With Britain in the middle of its worst economic recession since the 1930s, the Queen decided to finance the £25,000 trip from her own purse. 'As it's not a full-fat royal trip, the Queen has very graciously offered to foot the bill, which is very kind of her,' explained Jamie Lowther-Pinkerton.

Harry arrived at John F. Kennedy International Airport on Friday 29 May. While visiting Ground Zero he met families who had lost loved ones in the 11 September terrorist attacks, and planted a tree at the British Memorial Garden in downtown Manhattan, where screams of 'Marry me, Harry' greeted his arrival. Harry mania gripped America. 'He's so handsome,' cried one fan as she reached out for an autograph. 'Cuter than William – I love his ginger hair,' remarked another. The trip generated huge interest in the American media, which wanted to know everything about him. Ahead of his arrival, *Time* magazine had written about Harry's 'long alcohol-fuelled nights' while the *New York Daily News* recalled his 'hard partying ways'. I was invited on to *The Early Show* on CBS and asked where Harry would be drinking during his visit. He wouldn't. He had already been warned in no uncertain terms that he was expected to be on his best behaviour – there were to be no incidents outside night-clubs – and Harry was determined not to let his grandmother down.

He was genuinely moved by the stories of war veterans he met and in his element when he visited the Children's Zone in Harlem, an echo of his mother's famous visit in 1989 during which she famously hugged a child with Aids. As he raced around an assault course with the youngsters popping balloons during a relay race, Harry could not hide his glee. The weekend ended victoriously on Sunday afternoon when Sentebale won the Veuve Clicquot Manhattan Polo Classic on Governors Island 6–5 and raised £100,000 for his charity. Harry's whistle-stop tour proved that the American public's adoration for the British royal family had only increased since Diana's death. The trip had been a wise investment for Her Majesty.

It was clear from New York just how valuable both boys were in promoting the House of Windsor overseas. By now William had just turned twenty-six and Harry was twenty-four. At William's age the Queen had already come to the throne, while Charles and Diana were married and well established in their public roles, and there was a growing feeling within the upper echelons of the Palace that William and Harry should start taking on more high-profile engagements. Charles, who was declared the hardest-working royal in 2008 ahead of the Princess Royal, agreed. Previously he had wanted to protect his sons from the limelight, but now they were older there was a strong argument for them to raise their public profiles.

The princes agreed to give the media access to their professional lives in return for privacy the rest of the time, and in June 2009 they gave a rare joint interview at RAF Shawbury, where they were living together in a rented cottage close to the airbase. It was as normal a life as they could expect to lead save for the presence of their usual round-the-clock protection. They did the housework themselves and ironed their own shirts. During the televised interview they joked and teased one another.

'Bearing in mind I cook – I feed him every day – I think he's done very well,' said William. 'Harry does do washing up, but then he leaves most of it in the sink and then I come back in the morning and I have to wash it up . . . I do a fair bit of tidying up after him. He snores a lot too. He keeps me up all night long.' Harry pulled a face and groaned, 'Oh God, they'll think we share a bed now! We're brothers not lovers!' He vowed it would be the 'first time, last time we'll live together', while William drily observed, 'It's been an emotional experience.' It was a far cry from the strained press conferences that their father so dreaded.

Joking aside, there were serious points they wanted to make. Harry reiterated his determination to get back to the front line: 'To get out to Afghanistan again would be fantastic and my best chance is to do it from a helicopter . . . I'm a bit of Lynx lover since I started this course. Lynx is more challenging, it's more my cup of tea.' William said he remained 'hopeful there's a chance' he too will make it back to Afghanistan. 'I didn't join up to be mollycoddled or treated differently. As far as I am concerned, in my eyes, if Harry can do it, then I can do it.' It was a fascinating insight into William. Some called him naive for holding out hopes of ever serving on the front line, but most respected his willingness to fight for his country.

With so many charitable commitments and so little time, the boys agreed that they would be more effective if they combined forces. In September 2009 they set up the Foundation of Prince William and Prince Harry. Charles had created The Prince's Trust with his £7,500 severance pay from the Royal Navy and William and Harry wanted to establish their own charitable forum. So in

2006 they created The Princes' Charities Forum in order to team up their assorted charities. Between them they are presidents or patrons of over twenty charities and the foundation, which is the culmination of their charitable work so far, will become a grant-giving body in years to come. William said that he and Harry derived inspiration from both their parents, who had 'instilled in us from the word go that with these great priviliges goes an absolute responsibility to give back'. The princes invested a six-figure sum from their personal fortunes into the foundation and decided that at least a third of all the money it raises will go to the armed forces. As head of the armed forces, the Queen backed the decision whole-heartedly. She appointed her trusted former secretary, now Lord Janvrin, chairman of the board of trustees, while Sir David Manning was also drafted in to work alongside Jamie Lowther-Pinkerton, president of the Historic Houses Association Edward Harley, City financier Guy Monson and the Prince of Wales's divorce lawyer Fiona Shackleton.

It was clear that their parents' prodigious campaigning talents had rubbed off on both of them, and in May William and Harry appeared in a ninety-second advert produced by the Prince's Rain-forests Project with their father, the Dalai Lama and a host of celebrities to draw attention to the climate crisis. 'I've been trying to take the best bits of both of their [Charles and Diana's] charit-able lives and trying to amalgamate them into making them even better,' said William. 'I'm not in their league, but I'm warming up, hopefully, and I'm trying to do what I can. My grandmother inspires me obviously. I think she has done a fantastic job. I wouldn't say it's a third way. I think it's just trying to find your own way.'

They were already joint patrons of the Henry van Straubanzee

Memorial Fund, set up in memory of Harry's schoolfriend killed in a car accident during his gap year, and the princes had seen how successful they could be when they worked together. 'We feel passionately that, working closely together with those who contribute to our foundation, we can help to make a long-lasting and tangible difference,' said William. The memorial concert for their mother had been a huge success, and in May 2008 they had staged the City Salute, a pageant in the heart of London which raised £1 million for the Headley Court military rehabilitation centre and the Soldiers, Sailors, Airmen and Families Association to support injured servicemen and their families. In July the following year William visited the Lake District to join an expedition up Helvellyn, the third-highest mountain in England, with a group of homeless people. It was a novel way of combining his work with Mountain Rescue and Centrepoint, and it worked. Among those he climbed with was a former homeless eighteen-year-old called Jonny Glendinning. 'People see him for the fact he's got nineteen piercings, but he's nothing like he looks,' said William. 'It's people like that I want to relate to. They have fantastic characters and they just need opportunity and hope and confidence.'

It was an echo of their mother's empathy and philanthropy, according to Diana's friend Vivienne Parry.

Diana was involved with Aids charities and landmines – she didn't want to do the fluffy stuff – and I think William and Harry are very like her in that respect. She overcame all sorts of social barriers, and Harry and William are doing the same. Like her they also identify with people on the margin. They want to do the difficult work. We all remember Diana holding an Aids patient in her arms at a time when people thought you could get the disease through touching. The boys' trajectory is very similar, and Harry has his mother's gift – we've seen it with him in Africa.

Although William loves Africa, in terms of charitable work this is very much Harry's domain, and in March 2009 he made his most political public speech to date on Sentebale's third anniversary. 'Prince Seeiso and I founded Sentebale in memory of our mothers. They worked tirelessly to help the deprived and the afflicted and – in our own way – we aspire to follow their great example.' He called on the British public to help: 'Unless we help Lesotho . . . these wonderful people will be decimated and their society destroyed.' It was an emotive speech and every word was his own. The charity had nearly been forced to close down because of insufficient funds, but was rescued when Lord Ashcroft, one of the Conservative party's richest benefactors, made a £250,000 donation in 2009. At Harry's request and to save money, the charity moved into the princes' private office at St James's Palace, and Harry speaks to Kedge Martin, the charity's chief executive, on a daily basis.

Like their mother, who famously said she didn't want to 'just be a name on a letterhead', neither William nor Harry wants to be figureheads. 'There is a time and a place for being an ornament, or shaking people's hands and being at an engagement. But I think there's an awful lot more from actually doing stuff,' William explained at a press conference at St James's to discuss the work of the princes' foundation at its biannual meeting in September 2009. 'You could just turn up and open things – and don't get me wrong, there's always a good reason to do that – but it's about bringing some other things into it as well.' This was why William had chosen to spend his twenty-seventh birthday in June meeting former gangsters in an attempt to understand street culture in Britain and why he spent a night before Christmas sleeping on the streets of London in minus-four-degree temperatures. 'I hope that by deepening my understanding of the issue I can help do my bit to help the most vulnerable on our streets,' he said. 'I cannot after one night even begin to imagine what it must be like to sleep rough on London's streets night after night.' According to Vivienne Parry, this was something Diana would have been immensely proud of.

Diana was always passionate about her work with homeless people and William is the same. It was amazing when he slept rough on the street and quite extraordinary that he was able to do that. Diana would have loved it. William and Harry have had more choice than Diana in terms of choosing their patronages. Diana was under the Palace's direction for many years and came to her charities relatively late in life, but the boys have been able to pick and choose the charities they want to work with. She often said to me that she felt like an outsider and she identified with people who were struggling. I see that in William and Harry too.

Ironically it is in the company of strangers that William allows his guard to slip. When, as their new patron, he addressed The Child Bereavement Charity in London on Mother's Day in March 2009, he drew on the most painful experience of his life in order to connect with ordinary people. 'Never being able to say the word "mummy" again in your life sounds like a small thing. However for many, including me, it's now really just a word – hollow and evoking only memories.'

Chapter 18

Shadow king

The monarchy is something that needs to be there — I just feel it's very, very important. It's a form of stability and I hope to be able to continue that.

Prince William on his twenty-first birthday

Kate Middleton sat at the kitchen table and turned the pages of the Sunday newspaper in horror. It was 19 July 2009 and in the Middleton household the mood was one of panic. As Kate's mother Carole boiled the kettle to make another pot of tea, William's girlfriend could only stare at the front page of the *News of the World*. I CALLED WILLS A F***ER! was the headline above a grainy black and white picture of her uncle Gary Goldsmith preparing to snort a line of cocaine through a one-hundred-euro note, his oversized gut spilling onto a kitchen worktop. 'Tycoon who boasts of hosting Wills villa holiday supplies cocaine and fixes hookers', ran the strap line. Gary Goldsmith had unwittingly invited two undercover reporters into his £5 million villa, the dubiously named Maison de Bang Bang, and told them all about his niece and her royal boyfriend. Worryingly, and rather embarrassingly for William's police protection officers who have to make a detailed reconnaissance of everywhere the prince stays, William and Kate had been guests at the villa on Ibiza, where Mr Goldsmith has his initials daubed in gold on an outside wall, in 2006. 'My first words to Prince William were, "Oi you f***er! Did you break my glass pyramids?" He and a pal had been throwing balls around and broke all these ornamental pyramids I had loads of them,' recalled Mr Goldsmith.

Kate could not believe what she was reading. Her uncle claimed that she and William planned to get married at the end of the year and that Prince Philip had taught her to shoot: 'When William was away one Christmas, she was invited over.' He also boasted that he could score drugs and procure Brazilian call girls for visitors to the island.

The Middletons had always known that Gary was the black sheep of their otherwise faultless family, but they had never imagined how much trouble he was capable of causing. This was far more serious than when Kate's younger brother James had embarrassed the family when he was photographed urinating in the street after getting drunk on his twenty-second birthday – fortunately the pictures were only published in an Australian magazine.

Kate had received several messages of support that morning, including a call from William, who told her not to worry. Even Charles had rung to assure her it was a storm in a teacup that would soon blow over. Kate wasn't sure whether Charles had even read the story. He dislikes newspapers in general and only reads the *Week* magazine to keep him up to date. Upstairs Kate could hear her father packing. The family needed privacy, and the only place to get away from the media storm and the paparazzi camped on the doorstep of their home was Mustique. William's friends jokingly refer to the close knit family as the 'OM Middletons' meaning the 'On Mass Middletons' because they are always together, and it was en masse that they flew to the private island while the furore blew over. The Robinson family had once again offered the loan of their villa and the Middletons had gratefully accepted. Within a fortnight Kate would be back, tanned and on William's arm at the wedding of their friend Nicholas Van Cutsem. As Charles had predicted, the story had blown over, but as far as wedding bells between Kate and William were concerned, everything was on ice.

William had signed up for eighteen months of training with the RAF and there was simply no time to even think about a wedding. Besides, he had used up all his holiday that year skiing with Kate's parents in the French Alps and seeing the New Year in with Kate at his father's Scottish holiday home Birkhall. It was the first time the pair had been invited to stay with Charles and Camilla in residence, and Kate had felt very much at home. According to one aide she had laughed 'until she had tears in her eyes' when Camilla told her how much she hated the heavy moth-eaten tartan curtains that Charles refused to change because they were his grandmother's favourite. She had joined William and Charles shooting, and at the end of the day the four of them enjoyed family dinners. It was William's way of assuring Kate that he was more serious about her than ever. Right now though his focus was on his course. He had graduated from flying a single-engined Squirrel helicopter to a double-engined Griffin and was proving to be an accomplished helicopter pilot.

He was based at RAF Shawbury, and although they managed to see each other most weekends their time together was fleeting. It was a difficult period for Kate, who was dividing her time between her flat in London and her parents' Berkshire home, where she still slept in her old bedroom. William had asked her to keep a low profile after their last visit to Boujis, and Kate didn't go out much these days. She had lost touch with many of her old schoolfriends from Marlborough, and most of their friends from St Andrews were married. Fergus Boyd and Sandrine Janet – one of Kate's best friends at university – had got married in May at the fifteenth-century Château de Boumois in the Loire Valley, but Kate and William had pulled out at the last minute. Their absence was the subject of speculation among their friends Alasdair Coutts-Wood, Olli Chadwick Healey and Oliver Baker, who they had lived with during their third and fourth year and who had recently got engaged to another St Andrews graduate. William was said to be concerned that the wedding would be full of guests they didn't know, while Kate was said to be dreading the inevitable 'When will you two be next?' question

However, in the summer Kate's spirits were lifted. She had a contact at Harrods, who told her there was a vacancy for a buyer's assistant in the fashion department. Kate had always wanted a job in fashion, and was keen to pursue this new opportunity. 'It was discussed,' a senior source at the store told me. 'Kate is a regular shopper at Harrods and the chairman had an idea to approach her to do something but it never came to anything.' The Knightsbridge store is owned by Mohamed Al Fayed, who has installed a shrine to his son Dodi and Diana in the lower ground floor of the store, and according to sources close to Kate she was worried that the job could turn into a potential PR disaster.

She kept as busy as she could at Party Pieces and raising money for the Starlight children's charity. In September 2009 she hosted a charity dinner at the Saatchi Gallery in London, which William attended. It was the perfect opportunity for them to step out together with Kate secure in her own role, but she refused to have her picture taken with William. Society photographer Dominic O'Neill remembers being asked to stay away from the event.

I got a note from the princes' office saying that Kate wouldn't attend the dinner if I was there. She was upset that I'd photographed her flat on her back at a charity roller-skating disco because the pictures had made the front pages. I've photographed her and the boys a lot at social events like the Boodles Boxing Ball but things have changed. There's definitely been a tightening up over the past year and I suspect it is all preparation for a royal wedding between William and Kate. The problem is they seem petrified about getting bad publicity. Kate used to be pictured coming out of Boujis all the time and she'd always be smiling, but not any more. William and Harry have both also grown up a lot. We don't see them falling out of nightclubs any more.

It was not just William and Harry who were increasingly wary of prying cameras. For the first time the Queen was also taking an active interest in the paparazzi, and before Christmas she met the Press Complaints Commission and a leading privacy lawyer in a concerted effort to protect her family and their friends. Every year the paparazzi stake out Sandringham and the Queen wanted the practice stopped. William, Charles and Harry all supported the Queen's intention to take action against newspapers if they printed pictures of the family in private situations. 'Members of the royal family feel they have a right to privacy when they are going about everyday private activities,' explained Paddy Harverson. 'They recognise there is a public interest in them and what they do, but they do not think this extends to photographing the private activities of them and their friends.' Inevitably the Queen's initiative triggered engagement rumours, but Christmas came and went without any photographs of the family on their traditional Boxing Day shoot and without news of a forthcoming royal wedding. There was, however, still huge interest in their holiday plans and on Christmas Day Kate Middleton was photographed playing tennis during a family holiday at Restormel Manor, a Duchy of Cornwell owned mansion complete with its own tennis courts in Cornwall. Fearful of the repercussions, none of the British newspapers printed the set of pictures which had been taken by Niraj Tanna, a well-known photographer who claimed he was standing on a public footpath when he took the images. When a German newspaper published the pictures Kate instructed the Queen's solicitors Harbottle and Lewis to pursue action on her behalf. Months later, in March she reportedly received £10,000 in damages for breach of privacy. It was a victory for Kate and the royal family, and a warning to the world's media.

As the Range Rover with tinted windows sped through the gates of Clarence House, Chelsy Davy hid beneath a blanket on the back seat. But there were no photographers: the late-night clandestine meeting had been carefully planned. Inside the palace Harry was waiting for her with dinner and a bottle of wine. It was early August and Chelsy was still tanned and relaxed from a recent holiday to Portugal. From her Facebook pictures, it had clearly been a great two weeks. One particular snap – a candid shot of Chelsy in a swimming pool, sitting in a giant inflatable ring with a nightclub promoter called Dominic Rose – had stuck in Harry's mind. Back in the UK, Chelsy had received a flurry of emails and texts from Harry. In fact they had been in constant touch since Valentine's Day, but until now there had been no talk of getting back together. 'Chels was devastated when they split up, but she knew they needed some time apart,' recalled a girlfriend. 'Initially she loved the attention that came with being Prince Harry's girlfriend, but she came to resent it. She's actually quite a private person and she hated the cameras following her all the time. Harry begged her many times to get back together – he told her he had lost the best thing in his life – but she stuck to her guns.' Now, after a summer of meaningless flings, they realised they had missed each other, and over drinks they decided they would give their relationship another chance. Chelsy stayed the night for the first time in months.

On the night of Harry's twenty-fifth birthday they were together again – at Raffles nightclub on the King's Road. Chelsy had cooked dinner for them before they sneaked into the club un-noticed. They had spent the night drinking vodka Red Bulls and at one point hit the dance floor together before leaving separately at the end of the night. The ruse fooled no one, and by October their secret was out. Harry and Chelsy were pictured leaving Beach Blanket Babylon, a fashionable bar and restaurant in west London, where they had spent the night celebrating. Harry had passed the the latest part of his helicopter course and was just one step from getting his wings. As they sat in a private booth sipping Porn Star Martinis, a cocktail of vanilla vodka, passion fruit and champagne, they discussed their futures. Chelsy had decided to defer her trainee solicitor's job so that she could take another gap year – the fact that they were prepared to give the relationship another chance when they would be thousands of miles apart was testimony to their closeness. Harry had inherited £6.5 million of his late mother's fortune when he turned twenty-five, and when he treated a group of friends which included Natalie Pinkham to a water safari in Botswana in October, Chelsy didn't object. She was once again wearing the topaz ring Harry had given her, safe in the knowledge that this time they were both committed to making things work.

The Way Ahead group had met in summer 2009 as it always did in the Queen's private sitting room at Balmoral. Privately Charles referred to these twice-yearly meetings as the 'trailing behind group'. When the Way Ahead was started by former Lord Chamberlain the Earl Of Airlie in 1994, it was suggested that the in-house forum should consist of the Queen, Philip, Charles and their private secretaries, but at Philip's insistence Anne, Andrew and Edward also sit in on the meetings. Male primo-geniture, royal marriages to Catholics and public access to palaces are all regular subjects on the agenda, but according to one of the Queen's aides,

Charles would much rather discuss how to save the planet. The Queen and Prince Philip keep the focus very much on the family and getting the young generation to think about the future. Philip traditionally chairs the committee and there is always a two-fold plan, the immediate future and the long-term future, which Charles steers away from as much as possible. It's the same when he meets with the private secretaries. When issues like the Queen's funeral come up, he refuses to discuss it because he considers it 'impertinent'. It can make the meetings very tense.

William has been attending the meetings for several years and now Harry sits in too. He may be the spare, but William has made it clear how much he depends on his younger brother, and the Queen recognises the importance of Harry in shaping the future of the House of Windsor. The purpose of this particular gathering was to discuss the Queen and Philip's overseas engagements over the coming months. The Foreign Office had pencilled in trips to New Zealand and Australia, Bermuda and Canada all in the space of several months, and the Queen was concerned about the number of long-haul trips in her diary. She was eighty-three and had carried out 400 official engagements including two overseas tours the previous year, but the trips were perhaps beginning to take more of a toll on the eighty-eight-year-old duke, who had been troubled with ailments. In April 2008 he had spent a fortnight in hospital with a serious chest infection, and that February the Queen had cancelled a state visit to the Middle East because she and the duke had 'too much on their plate'. It was the first time she had abandoned a trip because of her workload.

It had already been agreed that Charles and Camilla would represent the Queen on the visit to Canada in November 2009, and because the Prince of Wales would be away for Remembrance Sunday it was decided there and then that Harry would lay a wreath at the Cenotaph in his father's place. This was entirely appropriate – it was after all nearly a year since Harry had served on the front line. The Queen and Philip were determined to go to Bermuda to celebrate the 400th anniversary of the island's settlement by the British at the end of November, but the New Year trip to New Zealand and Australia was still undecided and now was an opportune moment to propose that William should go. The Foreign Office was in full agreement; now it was down to William. He had last been Down Under in 2005 after he graduated from St Andrews, and to his grandmother's delight was enthusiastic about the idea of returning. There were some logistics to sort out because of his commitments with the RAF, but there was a break between him graduating from RAF Shawbury and going to RAF Anglesey in Wales after Christmas.

By October all the plans were in place. Clarence House was keen to keep the trip a secret as sending Prince William in place of the Queen was a momentous decision that needed to be carefully presented. The story had all sorts of implications. Prince Philip had started to cut down on his public engagements after his eightieth birthday; was the Queen now finally starting her retreat from public life? It was highly significant that she had asked William rather than one of her children to represent her. So was this the start of William's career as a fully paid-up member of the firm? When the *Mail on Sunday* revealed the plans for

William to travel to New Zealand in the Queen's place in October, Clarence House declined to comment such was the sensitivity of the scoop. William had already let it slip to an Australian tourist in July that he was heading to the southern hemisphere during an engagement at the Tower of London. 'I'm visiting there soon,' he told Camilla Doyle a fifteen-year-old from Melbourne.

When the Palace eventually confirmed the state visit there was much speculation on both sides of the globe about how William would be received. Opinion polls showed that 40 per cent of New Zealanders and 60 per cent of Australians were in favour of republics, and there were already stories in the local press about the £88,000 bill to taxpayers for William's security. Sending William was a way of testing the water. Charles and Camilla's reception in Canada had been lukewarm. Camilla had caused controversy by wearing a real rabbit fur stole, and when the prince and duchess toured the country's oldest permanent English settlement they were greeted by a crowd of just fifty people. Although swine flu was blamed for the poor turnout, the suggestion seemed to be that the Canadian public had yet to embrace Camilla as their future queen.

Such a reception in New Zealand and Australia was potentially disastrous for the monarchy and it was forward thinking on the Queen's part to send William. It was also a key step in a behind-the-scenes plan to move William to the centre of the public stage alongside his father. Although the Palace strenuously denied that the Queen was planning to cut back her public engagements, she had issued instructions to private secretary Christopher Geidt and trusted aide Robin Janvrin. According to one of her key advisers, 'She has two substitutes on the bench, Charles and William, and she wants to use both of them.' It was not an unreasonable strategy, and plans were already being drawn up for William as well as Harry and other members of the family to be involved in the diamond jubilee celebrations of 2012, thus easing the pressure on the ageing royal couple. According to Her Majesty's dedicated team of staff, the Queen's brief in the run-up to her diamond jubilee is clear: 'Do not overburden me.'

Then in December, just weeks ahead of William's state visit, the *Mail on Sunday* obtained a confidential Treasury document which for the first time revealed plans for William and Harry to undertake engagements on behalf of the Queen. The papers referred to spring 2009 and had been submitted ahead of the April Budget, but the message was simple and clear: 'from next year, it is expected that HRH Prince William will spend a significant part of his time on official engagements'. In another uncensored paragraph the document stated, 'The Princes (William and Harry) will increasingly incur expenditure when undertaking engagements on behalf of The Queen.' The document had been obtained under the Freedom of Information Act and essentially concerned tax arrangements in relation to Prince Charles and the new office that he had set up for William and Harry that year. The idea had been that Charles would receive tax relief worth hundreds of thousands of pounds by allowing him to deduct his sons' official expenses from his tax return. The document, written by Chancellor Alistair Darling's Treasury officials, had been blacked out in certain sensitive parts, but the *Mail on Sunday* had been given an uncensored version.

For the first time here was tangible proof that within the

corridors of Buckingham Palace a handover of power was beginning. The revelations suggested that William was being lined up as a 'shadow king', and fuelled speculation that the crown could skip a generation when the Queen dies, passing directly to William. It was certainly not the first time this theory had been aired, but the Palace seemed horrified and rebutted any such suggestion: 'There are no plans for the Queen to carry out fewer engagements and there are no plans for the prince to take her place.' Prince William's press officer also waded into the row: 'Prince William will not be "shadow king". Over the next few years Prince William will be concentrating primarily on a military career while also slightly increasing his charity patronages and the other interests he pursues.' The article had clearly rattled both Buckingham Palace and Clarence House, and as is always the case with such stories, there was no smoke without fire. The document may have been a few months old, but the fact that William and Harry would be undertaking engagements on behalf of the Queen was there in black and white.

Privately William was worried. In the past he had made it clear that he did not want to be hurried into a life of royal duty. 'There are obviously areas that I am being pushed in to do but I can be quite stubborn if I want to,' he had said in his final year at St Andrews. 'I'm very much the person who doesn't want to rush into anything without really thinking it through. It's not that I never want to do it, it's just that I am reluctant at such a young age, I think anyway, to throw myself into the deep end.' He may have made the comments six years before, but he felt the same way now. According to his aides he was also upset by the suggestion that he might in some way be trying to leapfrog his father. William could not think of anything worse. While he was destined to be king, it was his father's turn first, and William had more immediate concerns. He had set his heart on becoming a search and rescue pilot – it was his dream, and he was not prepared to give it up. He also had his charitable commitments to factor into his already packed timetable. He was happy to represent his grandmother and in no position to question her requests, but he was still not ready to become a fully fledged ribbon-cutting royal.

As the scheduled Air New Zealand flight taxied on the runway in Auckland, Prince William folded away his newspaper and took a deep breath. The coverage ahead of his arrival had divided editorial commentators, who were expectant, curious and pessimistic in equal measure. The *Sunday Star Times* had described the monarchy as rotten, with Charles labelled a 'prat who cheated on his glamorous young wife from the start of his marriage'. William was not discouraged, but he was tired. It had been just forty-eight hours since he had graduated from RAF Shawbury, where once again Kate had been there to support him as he received his helicopter wings. Now he was on the other side of the world and had an intensive five-day tour ahead of him, which Jamie Lowther-Pinkerton had described as a chance for him to 'learn the ropes'.

The prince had wanted the trip to be as informal as possible, and when he wasn't required to be in a suit wore his favourite brown cords and an open-necked shirt. He didn't want to be entertained at fussy state dinners; instead the emphasis was on barbecues washed down with bottles of beer. The state visit got off to an auspicious start in Auckland, when William met the All Blacks at the Eden Park Stadium. After that he enjoyed beer and sausages with Prime Minister John Key. The next day he was in Wellington to carry out his first walkabout – at the new NZ$80.2 million (£36 million) Supreme Court building in Wellington. The excitable crowd of 2,000 that turned up to meet him was far bigger than William had expected, and as he shook hands and chatted happily to well-wishers it was hard not to think of Diana. The Prince of Wales's fresh-faced bride had won over the New Zealanders the same way when she visited in 1983 with the baby William. As a grown man it was evident that William had inherited his mother's empathy although he was loath to admit it. 'I would not say I was anywhere near her level,' he told locals at a children's hospital in Wellington. With his thinning hair he was beginning to resemble his father more than his late mother, but his personality and warmth were winning assets, and his team of advisers knew it. He had all the humility of his father when he greeted Maoris with the hongi, the traditional pressing of noses, and he knew how to deal with awkward moments. When he landed in Sydney and visited a community centre, William handled with aplomb a six-year-old girl who asked if his mummy had died. 'Yes, she did,' he said bending down to her height. 'It was pretty sad.'

The Australian press concluded that William had the common touch even though it occasionally meant he came in for criticism. When he chatted to four rappers in front of Prime Minister Kevin Rudd, William said that he had 'the piss taken out of me for my taste in music'. This colloquialism was viewed as a step too far by some, but despite the faux pas, William had more admirers than detractors. Even the secretary of the Republican Movement Mike Smith declared, 'He's a nice chap.' When he arrived at Government House in Melbourne at the end of his tour he was again swamped by female fans, one of who fainted when he arrived. Like his father, William has been kissed countless times by female admirers. These ones waved 'We Love Wills' banners and cried out for the prince's autograph. When one elderly woman asked when he planned to marry Kate, William coyly replied 'As I keep saying, just wait and see.' It was a surprisingly playful response – a tease from a young man who loves to keep the papers and his public waiting – but there would be little need to wait and see when it came to the verdict on his tour.

The tabloid *Herald Sun* printed a collector's souvenir edition and a front page that said it all: MUM WOULD BE PROUD. Back at St James's Palace, the debrief could not have been better, according to one senior aide. 'We were absolutely delighted with the tour: all the feedback we had was so positive. William did what he set out to do, which was to meet as many people as possible and, yes, they warmed to him more than we could have hoped.' At Buckingham Palace the mood was one of delight, but the very fact that the trip had been such a success posed a problem. Might William's charisma eclipse his father's too soon? And with Kate by his side, might this royal couple overshadow one that has always been controversial but which remains next in line for the throne – or thrones?

In New Zealand and Australia William was a breath of fresh air, just as the Queen expected. He was youthful and charming and, many argued, more appealing than his father. His presence and his words evoked thoughts of a future in which Charles already seems too old. William is a young man thinking of his future, thinking of his career, thinking of his responsiblities, thinking of holding on to what freedoms he can. Thinking, his comments suggested, of marriage. He had never publicly acknowledged his long-term girlfriend as openly as he did to that elderly fan in Australia. I was told that William was finally thinking about settling down with Kate, but he wanted to finish his military training first. According to those close to William he was playing his cards close to his chest when it came to the subject of marriage. 'When it comes to Kate and William and a wedding date, there's only one thing you can safely put your money on,' I was told. 'If the truth about any date ever did leak out, he would change it.' But the truth of the matter was that William wasn't only being coy when pressed over his intentions. He just wasn't sure.

When he returned from Australia in late January, William began an eight-month long Sea King Operational Conversion Unit course at RAF Anglesey in Wales. He also spent several weeks completing the Sea King ground-school course at the Royal Navy Air Station Culdrose in Devon in March, which he passed. He had set his heart on joining Number 22 Squadron as a fully-qualified pilot flying the Sea King MK3 helicopter. He had also decided that he wanted to be stationed at RAF Valley, one of the most challenging RAF bases in the country because of its remote location. On the windswept island of Anglesey he and Kate were able to enjoy all the privacy in the world. All he needed to do now was pass his exams.

Chapter 19

Out of Africa

When I step off the plane I'm like, 'Yes I'm back,' I know I'm here to work but you can't help feeling like that. Africa is my second home.

Prince William

William and Kate could barely contain their laughter as they put yet another giant tick through the colourful chart that hung in their bedroom at Clarence House. They were running out of space on the piece of scrap paper on which they had drawn a tally of the times the press had speculated that the two were set to marry. Hastily cobbled together, William had made the chart as an after-dinner party joke, but the couple, who secretly rather enjoyed the game of cat-and-mouse with the press, found it so amusing that it had become a permanent fixture on the wall. The latest tick was extra large. It was early April and reports were coming in from America that a royal wedding was imminent. According to the highly credible New York-based author and journalist Tina Brown, who had enjoyed a close friendship with William's mother and wrote an acclaimed book about Diana's life, Buckingham Palace had 'cleared its diary' for a June announcement. According to Brown, 3 and 4 June had been earmarked as dates for the announcement while a wedding was being planned for November that year. The information seemed too specific to be just a rumour and caused a tremor of excitement and fresh talk about a wedding. Brown insisted that the scoop had come from an anonymous but reliable royal contact. She pointed out that Queen Elizabeth had also married Prince Philip in November, and of course June was the month William would turn twenty-eight, the age to which he gave unwitting importance when he announced many years ago that he was 'not going to get married before I'm twenty-eight'.

The story was published on Brown's website the *Daily Beast* and within twenty-four hours it was headline news in every national newspaper on both sides of the Atlantic. Clarence House declined to comment but they also refused to deny the story. Privately they insisted it was pure speculation and pointed out that the only thing being planned for June was William and Harry's first joint overseas tour to Africa. Sure enough June came and went without an announcement but there was no denying the fact that William and Kate seemed closer than ever and that an engagement really was just around the corner.

By now the couple were pretty much living together. After completing his ground-school course in Devon, William returned to Anglesey but he decided to move out of the single room he was renting on the rather austere RAF base and into a cottage so that he could spend more time with Kate. He was in the final stages of his intensive 'Star training' programme and life on the base was not conducive to a relationship. William had worked hard to impress his senior officers but he would have to wait until September to find out whether he would successfully qualify as a full-time search and rescue pilot. At the rented farmhouse, which is surrounded by trees and not visible from the road, William could enjoy all the quality time he wanted with Kate without the fear of being spied on or photographed. It was an ideal bolthole and, some speculated, a perfect marital home. Kate seemed keen to road test life as an army wife–in–waiting. By now most of her friends were married or fulfilling busy careers in London but she was happiest in Wales with William. At the weekends they would drive to Highgrove and catch up with friends or stay with Kate's parents at the family's five-bedroom home in Bucklebury. William loved these weekends and over the years he had become close to Kate's parents, and vice versa. On one occasion shortly before Christmas, Carole, who is said to keep a picture of William on her mobile phone, voiced concerns about William's reluctance to propose. She was worried that Kate was getting closer to thirty and there was still no ring on her finger. According to one source, 'Carole felt like she was treading water as far as her daughter's relationship was concerned. She put some pressure on William to let the family know where it was all leading. William spoke with her and assured her that the relationship was very much on track and that there would be an engagement soon.' It was enough to satisfy Carole. She knew about the pact that the couple had made in the Seychelles when William had promised Kate she was the one, and Carole, like her daughter, had put her trust in William.

Whenever William came to stay he was warmly welcomed. While Carole and Michael enjoy drinking cider, they would make sure they had plenty of William's favourite red wine in the cellar ahead of his arrival. On Sunday mornings William would drive to the local Spar, half a mile away to get the papers, much to the surprise of the regulars of the sleepy town who would do a double take as the future king strolled in wearing a baseball cap. 'He is often in here buying the newspapers,' I was told by one cashier. 'He's always pleasant and very low key.' Often William and Kate enjoyed a stroll through the woods where Kate and her siblings used to play when they were little, and sometimes the couple would stop in at the Bladebone Inn in the pretty village of Chapel Row before returning home for Carole's delicious Sunday roast dinner.

When she wasn't in Wales with William, Kate was spending more time in Bucklebury. She had moved out of her parents' fashionable flat in Chelsea and according to close friends she was still feeling the sting from criticism that she didn't have a full-time job. When she was in Anglesey she indulged her passion for photography and would spend hours capturing the dramatic Welsh landscape. According to photographer Alistair Morrison, for whom Kate compiled an exhibition in November 2007, 'she takes beautiful detailed photographs. She has a huge talent ... I'm sure she will go far.' Her parents, however, were keen for her to continue working at the family firm, Party Pieces. The offices are just a fifteen-minute drive from the family home and it was an opportunity for Kate to spend time with her brother and sister. Pippa had recently set up *Party Times*, an online magazine under the umbrella of Party Pieces, while James was busily building up his own cake-making business, Cake Kit, and was looking for a London outlet. William was happy that Kate was working for the family business even though she sometimes complained she was bored. It was not the career she had plotted when they were students at St Andrews – she had actually wanted to work in fashion – but working for the family business where she was protected fitted in with their lives. Kate could flit between Anglesey and home and now she was spending less time in London the spotlight was off her. Neither she nor William missed the bright lights of the city and it had been many months since they had been spotted out on the town. Instead they preferred to stay in and watch DVDs and cook supper together. In Anglesey it was almost like being back at St Andrews again, although this time it was just the two of them.

Any doubts William may have had in the past about his future with Kate were a thing of the past. Although Kate didn't have a ring on her finger I was told by close friends of the couple that the pair were 'as good as engaged.' The press had dubbed her Waity Katie, but Kate knew that she wouldn't be waiting much longer. Earlier in March, they were photographed on the slopes of Courchevel in France, enjoying a skiing holiday with Kate's family and a group of friends. The images of William and Kate zooming around the mountains on snowmobiles, shrieking with delight, were published around the world and this time there were no complaints from St James's Palace about privacy. Certainly the couple, in their matching 'his and hers' red salopettes, looked blissfully happy and in love. At one point during the trip William affectionately referred to Kate's father as 'Dad'. According to a friend 'it was a tongue in cheek reference to the assurance he gave Carole just before Christmas. The holiday was very low key and relaxed. Kate's family is very normal which William loves. They make him feel incredibly comfortable and William and Kate are really happy.'

The African sun shone down from the cloudless sky, bathing the mountainside in some much welcome warmth. It was winter in Lesotho and the surrounding countryside was covered in snow. Harry, wrapped up warmly in his fleece, lay on the ground next to William, trying his hardest not to giggle. The schoolchildren they were visiting from the Mamohato Network Club, one of the organisations Harry's charity Sentebale supports, were gathered around them. The princes were lying in a most un-regal-like pose on giant pieces of paper and had been asked to keep still while the pupils, many of whom were orphans infected with HIV, sketched their outlines. Then it was William and Harry's turn to contribute. They were asked to write their feelings and dreams on the sketches. William shot his aide a look of concern. The eyes of the world's press who had been invited on the tour were upon him just waiting to see what he would write. Unperturbed Harry was already busy scribbling away. 'Professional surfer, wildlife photographer, helicopter pilot.' Harry's pen hovered over the page. 'Live in Africa.'

William guffawed at Harry's pipe dream before jotting down his own feelings. 'Happy, lucky, strong, caring, the funniest, friends/family, successful pilot.' Harry suddenly jotted 'Loser!' onto the page, to much laughter and applause. While he was comfortable with the children and clearly delighted to be in Africa with his brother, William had been careful not to let his guard slip. Harry had been more candid. He loved training with the Army Air Corps, but he really did want to live in Africa with Chelsy. They had just spent two amazing weeks in Zambia where Chelsy's family had recently relocated and it had been a wonderful holiday. Wouldn't it be fantastic, they had mused, if they could live together in Africa? The reality was rather different. Chelsy had decided to move back to South Africa to complete her training to be a solicitor while Harry, who had surprised everyone by qualifying to fly the Apache air attack helicopter, was to be posted at RAF Middle Wallop in Hampshire at the end of the summer. Once again the couple faced a long-distance relationship and when Harry kissed Chelsy goodbye in Zambia, he genuinely didn't know what the future held for them. He planned to meet up with her in Cape Town, where he and William would be watching England play Algeria in the World Cup, and they would discuss things in more detail then.

It was day three of the brothers' six-day whistle-stop tour which had started in Botswana and would culminate in Cape Town where William, who is president of the Football Association, would be addressing FIFA executives to support the FA's bid to host the 2018 World Cup. In Lesotho, the brothers had been welcomed like kings. They arrived on horseback, the traditional mode of transport in Semonkong, one of the poorest areas in the mountains of Lesotho, to a hero's welcome. Harry had wanted William to see the school that Sentebale had set up for the country's poor and deprived herd boys. It was freezing cold and there was no heating or electricity, but wrapped up in blankets which had been handstitched with their names, William and Harry did not seem to mind at all. In an interview with ITN's Julie Etchingham they said that Africa was a place close to both of their hearts and it was here, in the African wilderness, where they felt closest to their late mother. 'Every day, whatever we do, wherever we are and whoever we're with I always wonder what she'd think – what she'd be doing – if she was with us now. If she'd be sitting here having a laugh, whether she'd be in the background sticking her tongue out – or whether she'd be playing football with the children,' said Harry. 'That's what keeps us going every day – that thought of what she would be like if she was around today. It's refreshing because we both have our opinions of what she'd be like – and "mad" would be one word to describe her.' It was a deeply moving interview. 'We'd like to think she's proud of us,' said William. 'She'd be very proud of what

Harry's done with Sentebale.' In a rare moment of openness, William spoke of his love for his brother describing him as a 'free spirit . . . he's got a big heart and he wants to make a difference.' For the first time Harry acknowledged that his role in life would be to support William. 'I will always give him as much support as I can,' he said. 'Sometimes it's probably not valued which is understandable as the older brother always thinks they know best!'

Back at home their debut tour was seen as a way of testing the water and the general consensus was that it had been a huge success. I was there as the princes swept into the Mokolodi nature reserve just outside the capital of Gaborone in Botswana in a fleet of black BMWs. To a backdrop of beating African drums and native dancing, the excitement at the royal arrival was audible. The world's press were already assembled and as the photographers jostled for prime space one remarked that this tour was 'just as big as Diana.' It was true and, although William privately noted the media was 'a bit excessive', this was an historic occasion. If they were nervous, the brothers didn't show it and, in a nod to how they see the monarchy modernising, both William and Harry insisted on being called by their first names. There was to be no bowing –a handshake sufficed. They became know in the press as 'Team Wales' and there was plenty of joshing around for the cameras. When they attended a snake-handling lesson Harry mischievously pointed the head of an eight-foot long African rock python at William. 'Whoah! Don't put it in my face,' exclaimed William as Harry burst out laughing when the reptile relieved itself on William's shoulder. Dressed in chinos and wrapped up against the bitter cold in navy blue fleeces, the princes couldn't contain their delight when they got to stroke the reserve's two orphaned cheetahs. There was just enough time to see some of the wildlife in situ before they had to leave Botswana. William, who was keen to promote the work of Tusk, the conservation charity of which he is patron and which was celebrating it's twentieth anniversary, had agreed to make a film while on safari in the Okavango Delta with TV presenter Ben Fogle. *Prince William's Africa*, which was screened on Sky 1 several months after the trip, showed a relaxed prince who clearly felt at home in the vast African plains which he described as 'my second home'. He was uncharacteristically open about the pressures he faces and when asked how he coped with the intense interest in his life he admitted: 'My life is not always like this. It is difficult flitting between military life and public life. There's loads of things I need to keep track of.' He refused to talk about his private life and his relationship with Kate insisting, 'There's always speculation but it comes with the job. That doesn't mean I would be as polite talking about this behind closed doors . . . but you know, it's one of those things. The way I see it is that everyone has their own problems. It's a slight disadvantage but I'm very lucky to be in my position so I won't complain.' When asked by Fogle whether he has to 'accept there will always be people who dictate what you can and cannot do' William responded emphatically. 'No. That's the thing. I like to disagree with them deliberately because many of the things they come up with are very old-fashioned and don't work nowadays, or are just wrong. People have the wrong views on what it's like to be in this family, for instance. I want to correct them and I want to make people aware that there's new stuff and there are other ways and there's no reason why you can't be different. Sometimes I listen to people but I like to take in lots of opinions and then make my own judgement.' His words were confident and no doubt riled the senior courtiers for who they were intended. William who is known for being stubborn had made it clear that he has his own ideas about the future of the monarchy. He also said he was ready for the life of duty that lies ahead of him. 'I am obviously slightly nervous and anxious about it but at the same time it's where my life is heading and I hope I'm ready for it. I have a good basis of knowledge and I've managed to understand a lot more through my experiences.'

When he represented the FA's bid for England to host the World Cup in 2018 he also proved he was an excellent ambassador both for football and England. Despite the country's humiliating defeat on the pitch by Algeria, William was full of optimism for the bid and, with his brother and the former England captain David Beckham to support him, he delivered a sparkling address full of promise to the FIFA executives who had gathered in Johannesburg. It was the day before William's twenty-eighth birthday and after the conference he flew home to celebrate quietly with Kate. Fortunately much of the speculation about a pending wedding that was expected to overshadow his birthday was deflected by Harry who had secretly travelled from Johannesburg to wartorn Mozambique. In images that brought memories of his mother flooding back the prince was photographed working with the Halo Trust in the very same flak jacket and protective visor his mother had worn when she brought the work of the British charity to the world's attention back in 1997, just before her death. Like Diana, Harry was taught how to detonate a mine and met with some of the country's victims. It was his way of fulfilling the pledge he made when he was eighteen years old to continue his mother's humanitarian work because she was no longer around to do it.

Chapter 20

A Royal Wedding

'It was very romantic. There's a true romantic in there. I really didn't expect it. It was a total shock . . . and very exciting'

Catherine Middleton

The waves crashed onto the white sand at the exclusive Grand Café in Granger Bay in Cape Town, where Harry and Chelsy were sipping diet Cokes and smoking cigarettes. Harry was back from Mozambique and ready to head back to RAF Middle Wallop, where he was to start training to fly the Apache, but he wanted two days with Chelsy before he returned home. He knew it would be some time before they saw each other again and this would be a difficult parting. Chelsy had made the decision not to return to England. The recent holiday in Zambia with her family had confirmed just how much she missed home and she had decided she wanted to move back to South Africa. Now all she had to work out was whether to live in Cape Town or Johannesburg where some of her closest friends had recently moved to. It was a blow to Harry and despite the success of the tour he was miserable. He loved Chelsy and he worked hard to try to convince her that they could make a long-distance relationship last. They had done it in the past, he reasoned, why not give it another go?

After their last split in the autumn, Harry and Chelsy had enjoyed the most incredible fortnight in Zambia. They went on safari every day and it had been an adventure, especially when their Land Rover had run out of petrol in the middle of the bush. Harry had spent days playing polo with Chelsy's brother, Shaun, and enjoying al fresco dinners with Chelsy's parents. Both of them knew when he qualified to fly the Apache in May that it would mean a big change for them. Harry was about to undertake one of the most demanding jobs in the Army. Flying the air attack helicopter was his ultimate goal and the career move he desperately hoped would get him back to the frontline. Chelsy knew how important it was to him. She had been at the graduation ceremony to support Harry who was awarded his wings by his father. Shortly before the ceremony, St James's Palace announced that twenty-five year old Lieutenant Harry Wales had been selected to fly the Apache attack helicopter. 'The decision has been taken by the Army Air Corps commanders who judged that Prince Harry's skills and flying abilities best suited the Apache,' said a Palace spokesman. It was a great achievement, only two per cent of the trainees had been selected and, as much to his surprise as everyone else's, Harry was one of them. He was 'honoured', he said, to be flying 'an awesome helicopter. There is still a huge mountain for me to climb if I am to pass the Apache training course. It's a seriously daunting prospect but I can't wait.' Dressed in an elegant cream frock, her blonde hair freshly blow dried and with just a hint of make-up, Chelsy looked quite the princess-in-waiting. She kissed Charles and Camilla after the ceremony and she and Harry looked happier than ever. But as the reality of his future training set in, Chelsy soon realised she would be seeing much less of Harry. He had been told by his commanding officers that his sixteen-month long course would be intensive. He was to start a conversion course at Middle Wallop at the end of July followed by eight months of tuition at RAF Wattisham in Suffolk. He would be posted to Arizona for several weeks as part of his training on the 227mph helicopter and there was a chance he could be back on the front line by the end of 2011. When he visited New York for a three-day charity visit at the end of June he gave an interview to ABC's *Good Morning America* in which he said that he would 'love to go back' and fight with British forces. 'At the end of the day you train for war, it's as simple as that,' he said. 'If we could be at peace then fantastic but if you're at war then you want to be with your brothers in arms. As long as my military career allows it, and politically it's allowed, then I will serve my country as any other soldier. You train for a reason and you want to be there, you want to help your buddies left and right of you.'

While Kate had been prepared to make the ultimate sacrifice and put her career on hold to be with William, Chelsy was not. Her heart was in Africa and that was where she planned to stay.

It was a clear cold night at the Il Ngwesi lodge in Lake Rotunda in Kenya and William and Kate were grateful for the extra layers they had packed. They had enjoyed a simple supper prepared over a fire and the embers were keeping them warm as they drained the last of the celebratory bottle of chilled champagne. Apart from the candles and the campfire that William had kept well stoked throughout the evening they were in total darkness. From the verandah of their remote log cabin they could see the glittering peaks of Mount Kenya. Around them on the edge of the Mukogodo hills they could hear the constant calling of crickets and the deep, contented croaking of lake frogs settling down for the night in the cedar trees. It was just the two of them and as Kate looked disbelievingly at the enormous sparkling sapphire and diamond engagement ring which fitted her finger perfectly, she reflected on the most special day of their lives.

It was 20 October and the last day of what had been a perfect holiday when William finally summoned the courage to ask Kate to marry him. He had been carrying the gem, his mother's prized engagement ring, in the bottom of his rucksack ever since they left London, knowing that he would ask Kate to marry him during the holiday. Protected in bubblewrap and safely hidden, William later admitted that he had been terrified of losing the £250,000 oval sapphire which is set in fourteen diamonds. 'I had been carrying it around in my rucksack for about three weeks before that and I literally would not let it go, everywhere I went I was keeping hold of it because I knew if this thing disappeared I would be in a lot of trouble,' he revealed. Before leaving London he had gone to the safe at St James's Palace in what would be the first of several cloak–and-dagger operations. He knew where his late mother's jewellery was kept and he specifically wanted the engagement ring. As he would later explain, it was his way of making sure Diana could still be a part of his special day.

William had planned the three-week African adventure meticulously, with the help of his close friend Jecca Craig's father, Ian, at whose Lewa Downs reserve in Kenya he had stayed many times. The vacation began in the northern rain lands of Kenya, known in Swahili as Ishak Bin, where the couple camped in tents. It was very basic – there was no running water and supper was cooked over a campfire made from forest wood. From Ishak Bin William and Kate, accompanied by two protection officers, returned to the Craig family home where they had holidayed after they graduated from St Andrews. William had paid for one of the £2,000-a-night five-star lodges which boasts a four poster bed under the stars and panoramic views of the breathtaking countryside. They spent their days enjoying game drives with Ian Craig and one day they spotted a black hook-lipped rhino which was tranquilised, marked and named in William's honour. The future king decided he wanted to pay £6,000 to sponsor the animal, which he and Kate had touched as it lay sleeping on the scrubland. From the Lewa Downs they flew in Mr Craig's private jet to Sarara for another safari, this time with two friends from South Africa. Here they camped near a watering hole richly populated with giraffe, elephants, wild dogs and buffalo before flying out to Lake Rutundu. Apart from a solitary cabin next to them they were alone at the Il Ngwesi lodge – there was nothing except dense forest and wild animals around them for miles. William had stayed at the lodge before and had been keen to return. It was the most private place he had found in the world and perfect for a proposal.

That afternoon the pair had driven to the lake to fish for rainbow trout but they didn't catch so much as one, not that it mattered. William had made Kate the happiest girl in the world by getting down on one knee and proposing. With the magnificent lake glistening in the background and not another soul to witness the magical moment, Kate knew that every year she had waited was worth it for this. William had already arranged for a bottle of champagne to be put on ice back at the lodge. As they checked out they each wrote messages in the well-thumbed guest book saying that they had had the time of their lives and hoped to return soon. 'Thank you for such a wonderful twenty-four hours!' Kate wrote. 'Sadly no fish to be found but we had fun trying. I love the warm fires and candle lights – so romantic. Hope to be back soon.' She signed the book Catherine Middleton. Dating his note 20–21 October 2010, William wrote in blue ink, 'Such fun to be back! Brought more clothes this time! Looked after so well. Thank you guys! Look forward to next time, soon I hope.'

When they returned to Lewa Downs the couple told Ian and his wife Jane the news, but made them promise to keep it a secret. Before they left, William gave the maid Margret Lekartgi, a twenty-two-year-old member of the Masai tribe who had cleaned their room and looked after their laundry, a one hundred dollar bill, the equivalent of a month's salary. Astonishingly she was one of the few people in the world who knew the couple were engaged. 'They were having the times of their lives,' she told the *Mail on Sunday*. 'They would say hello, were always smiling. They were just so very happy all the time.' William wanted to do the right thing and ask Kate's father for her hand in marriage. As soon as they were back in England he invited Kate's parents to Balmoral for a shooting weekend. Although Kate had been many times, it was the first time her parents had been invited to the Queen's Scottish retreat. Although he was not in residence, Charles had said that Kate's parents were welcome to stay at Birkhall and allowed them the use of his personal driver to escort them around the estate. On Saturday night, just before dinner,

William took Michael aside. In the tartan-furnished drawing room he asked him for permission to marry Kate. It was granted immediately and, by all accounts, with great delight, but once again William made Michael swear a vow of silence. The couple did not want the news to leak out before he had spoken with his father and the Queen. Royal protocol dictates that Her Majesty must be informed of any wedding plans within the immediate family ahead of an official announcement.

Michael gave William his word. Keeping the press quiet was evidently going to be more of a challenge, however. When pictures of the Middletons shooting at Balmoral were published on the front page of the *Daily Mail* the engagement rumour mill went full throttle once again and there was much speculation about an announcement in the press. The palace refused to comment, but there was no denying the significance and importance of Kate's family being invited to shoot on the Queen's estate. They had been welcomed into the royal fold, so was Kate about to join the firm? The *Daily Mirror* took a gamble and predicted a summer wedding, splashing the story on the front page. At St James's Palace, aides insisted that they knew of no plans for an announcement, but when the *Mail on Sunday* ran a front-page story about the Royal Mint commissioning a mould for a commemorative coin to celebrate the royal wedding, all signs pointed to an imminent announcement. This time the wedding rumours would not go away. I published an article in *Vanity Fair* predicting a 2011 wedding and suggesting that an announcement was just around the corner, while an American tabloid magazine used the bold headline 'Royal Wedding is on!' This time the Palace changed tack. 'Only Prince William and Kate Middleton know their plans,' they insisted. On 24 October, which was in fact four days after William had popped the question, I wrote an article in the *Mail on Sunday* under the headline. 'Kate appears in public for the first time in 104 days . . . will an engagement be next?'

Kate had not been seen since she attended a polo match in July. I had spotted her shopping at designer discount store TK Maxx on Kensington High Street and she had also been seen playing tennis with Pippa and William at the Harbour Club in Fulham, but she had been keeping a low profile. When she was pictured on Saturday 23 November at the wedding of Harry Meade and Rosie Bradford in Gloucestershire she displayed a new confidence. Unusually, she and William entered the church in the picturesque village of Northleach together and through the front entrance, flashing broad smiles for the waiting cameras. At previous weddings they would often arrive separately and sneak in through the back so as not to attract attention. Tanned from their recent holiday and walking side by side they looked content and it didn't seem to bother Kate that several of William's ex-girlfriends were in the congregation. Rose Farquhar, who William had romanced the summer he left Eton and was part of the 'Glosse Posse', had been invited, along with Jecca Craig and Olivia Hunt, the sister of Chiara Hunt whose wedding in Austria William and Kate attended in September 2008. The statuesque Edinburgh University graduate was rumoured to have dated William briefly while he was at St Andrews, but the fling was short-lived and she went on to date William's best friend William Van Cutsem. In her elegant hat, tailored jacket and peacock blue frock Kate upstaged them all. 'When they turned up together and went through the front door where there were obviously photographers no one could believe it,' recalled one spectator. 'It was very unusual and very significant.'

It was also significant and noted in my story that Kate was wearing a tailor-made blue dress by her favourite designer, Brazilian-born Daniella Issa Helayel, whose signature jersey wrap dresses Kate has worn on many occasions. This, however, was the first time Daniella had designed a one-off couture frock for her. Such a dress would have cost upwards of £1,000. I was told that Daniella was hard at work designing an entire wardrobe for Kate so that she never risked the embarrassment of turning up to an event in the same outfit as someone else. It was a tell-tale sign that Kate was preparing herself for more future public engagements, and it just so happened that Issa had recently started designing bridal wear.

As they danced the night away at the reception their friends joked that next time it would be William and Kate walking down the aisle. This was, after all, the tenth wedding she and William had attended as a couple. Kate smiled and diplomatically told one inquisitive guest, 'Maybe he'll get round to it some day,' while William laughed off the comments good naturedly. Only the two of them knew the truth – they were already engaged to be married, the problem was finding the right time to tell their families before they could make the happy news official.

They had wanted to make the announcement that very week and Wednesday 3 November, they decided, was as good a time as any. But an unforeseen tragedy in the Middleton family meant the announcement had to be postponed. Kate's paternal grandfather Peter Middleton, a retired airline pilot, died suddenly on

1 November at the age of ninety. The Middletons were in mourning and both William and Kate agreed to postpone the announcement. William accompanied Kate to the funeral at the West Berkshire crematorium the following Friday and the very next day he was flown to Afghanistan on a secret mission to visit the troops on Remembrance Sunday. When he returned home on Monday he and Kate met at Clarence House. They both agreed they could not keep the secret for much longer so that night they decided to call their families. From the living room of his quarters at Clarence House William called his grandmother who was in residence at Windsor with Philip. His next call was to Charles who was at Highgrove with Camilla preparing for an engagement the next day. 'They were both delighted,' said a family friend. 'They are very fond of Kate and over the years have got to know her very well. They popped open a bottle immediately.' When William called Harry to tell him he had a sister there was a momentary silence before Harry let out a string of expletives. 'It took you long enough,' he finally mustered, to laughter from Kate in the background. Of course, her father already knew, but Kate wanted to call her mother – this had been the longest and hardest secret she had ever kept from her. 'We had quite an awkward situation because I knew that William had asked my father but I didn't know if my mother knew,' Kate later explained. 'So I came back from Scotland and my mother didn't make it clear to me whether she knew or not, so both of us were there sort of looking at each other.'

The couple were so excited they could barely sleep that night. They arose early the next day and made their way across the courtyard to William's office at St James's Palace to inform Jamie Lowther-Pinkerton and William's team of press secretaries so they could prepare a statement. 'We were ecstatic when they came in to tell us,' recalled an aide. 'We genuinely had no idea they were secretly engaged and they looked so happy when they told us. There was a palpable sense of relief. Then the hard work started and there was an awful lot to organise in a very short time. Two hours later, we made the announcement.'

William had always wanted it to be this way. Unlike his father's wedding to Camilla which was revealed by the press before Clarence House had made the official announcement, he was determined that his engagement should not be leaked. By shrouding it in secrecy William had been able to orchestrate the announcement exactly as he wanted. At 11 a.m. on Tuesday 16 November Clarence House issued a press statement via the royal family's newly launched Facebook page and sent out a 'tweet' to its followers on Twitter. 'His Royal Highness Prince William of Wales and Miss Catherine Middleton are engaged to be married,' it said. 'The Prince of Wales is delighted to announce the engagement of Prince William to Miss Catherine Middleton. The wedding will take place in the spring or summer of 2011 in London.' Although the couple had only just made the announcement, they wanted to make it quite clear that William's career at the RAF would not be affected. 'Following the marriage the couple will live in north Wales where Prince William will continue to serve the Royal Air Force.' The Queen, who was at Windsor Castle hosting a reception, was the first to be quoted that day. 'It is brilliant news. It has taken them a very long time,' she said while Charles who was on an engagement in Dorset quipped 'They've been practising long enough.' Harry spoke of his delight; 'It means I get a sister which I have always wanted,' he said touchingly. Kate's parents, Michael and Carole, also addressed the press from the driveway of the family home. Dressed in cords and a casual blazer and clutching a piece of paper with some notes Michael declared that he and Carole were: 'absolutely delighted by today's announcement and thrilled at the prospect of a wedding.'

As news organisations around the world headed to Canada Gate outside Buckingham Palace to broadcast the news and speculate on where and when the wedding might take place, William and Kate were getting ready for their first ever joint photo call and an exclusive interview at St James's Palace with ITV. They had chosen to speak with ITN's political editor Tom Bradby because they had met him several times and got along well. By coincidence Kate had worked with Tom's wife Claudia, a jewellery designer at Jigsaw. The fifteen-minute interview which was screened to a record three billion people around the world later that night was history in the making. It was the first time the world had been properly introduced to William's girlfriend of nearly nine years. Until now they had never even heard her speak. This was effectively day one of her new life, and the public seemed suitably impressed by the glossy brunette who had captured the prince's heart and spoke so beautifully. The media training that Kate had quietly been receiving over the years had stood her in good stead. When I met Kate, who said she preferred to be called Catherine, at the palace afterwards she admitted to me over a cup of tea served in bone china that she was nervous about the photo call. She needn't have worried – her poise was nothing short of regal and she seemed confident and, above all, happy. Naturally she had chosen one of Issa's couture dresses for her first public appearance and the deep shade of blue perfectly complemented the sparkling sapphire which she showed off in public for the first time. In the flesh she looked flawlessly beautiful and incredibly slim. Her long tresses had been expertly blow dried and with just a touch of professionally applied make-up she dazzled in front of the cameras. Kate knew that every gesture and nuance would be analysed and that the eyes of the world were on her, but despite the pressure she looked radiant. As they walked into the state room to greet the world's press the flashing of hundreds of cameras blinded them. William took Kate by the arm and neither could contain their enormous smiles.

There was a strong sense of déjà vu. With her arm linked lovingly through William's, her engagement ring on display, Kate bore more than a passing resemblance to Lady Diana Spencer in 1981. But there was to be none of the awkwardness of that infamous engagement interview when Prince Charles was asked if he was in love with his fiancé and famously responded 'whatever in love means.' It was clear from their body language and the smile on his face that William absolutely knew the meaning of love. Kate also echoed Diana's sentiments when she was asked about the future. 'It's quite a daunting prospect but hopefully I'll take it in my stride, and William's a great teacher so hopefully he'll be able to help me along the way . . . It's obviously nerve-wracking. I don't know the ropes, William is obviously used to it, but I'm willing to learn quickly and work hard.' At one point when she was asked how she would cope in the shadow of Diana's legacy William tenderly put his hand on Kate's knee.

'It is about carving your own future,' he said. 'No one is trying to fill my mother's shoes, what she did was fantastic. It's about making your own future and your own destiny and Kate will do a very good job of that.' The couple were candid and honest when asked about their courtship and when asked why he had taken so long to propose William explained that he had wanted to finish his military training and bide Kate some time. 'I wanted to give her a chance to see in and back out if she needed to before it all got too much. I'm trying to learn from lessons done in the past and I just wanted to give her the best chance to settle in and to see what happens on the other side'.

They acknowledged that they had had ups and downs. Speaking about the very first time they broke up in the summer of 2004 when they were at St Andrews William explained: 'We were both very young, it was at university, we were both finding ourselves as such and being different characters. It was very much trying to find our own way and we were growing up.' It was clear, as I had revealed that summer when William had taken a boys-only holiday and pursued a pretty young aristocrat, that Kate was not happy about the break up. 'I think at the time I wasn't very happy about it but actually it made me a stronger person. You find out things about yourself that maybe you hadn't realised,' she said. There was laughter when Kate dispelled the well-documented story that she once had a picture of William on her bedroom wall. 'He wishes,' she said, playfully patting William on the leg. 'No, I had the Levi's guy on my wall, not a picture of William, sorry.' Speaking about the first time she met the prince she admitted that she had gone 'bright red and scuttled off feeling very shy' but they soon became good friends. 'Kate's got a really naughty sense of humour which kind of helps me because I've got a really dry sense of humour, so it was good fun,' William recalled. When asked about their plans for the future they said they were looking forward to starting a family soon. 'Obviously we want a family so we'll have to start thinking about that,' said William.

The couple had not yet confirmed where they would be married. The announcement had been so sudden that neither a venue nor date had been confirmed although it was reported that the couple wanted to marry as soon as possible, either in March or April. Palace aides immediately started talks with the Queen's private office, the British government, heads of state around the world, diplomats and other royal families who all needed to be consulted about the date. It was over a week before Friday 29 April 2010 was decided upon and the British Prime Minister David Cameron announced that it would be a national holiday in the UK. Just hours after the announcement, Kate was photographed leaving Westminster Abbey after being given a private tour of the world famous church. Steeped in one thousand years of royal history the ancient church which can hold 2,000 people was where the Queen married Prince Philip on 20 November 1947 and where the Queen Mother married the future George VI, then the Duke of York, on 26 April 1923. It is also where the funeral of the Princess of Wales took place in 2007. William thought it a fitting tribute and Kate agreed. It was perhaps no coincidence that William had chosen to marry Kate in 2011. It is the year his mother would have turned fifty had she been alive and marks what would have been the 30th wedding anniversary of his parents' ill-fated marriage. William was determined that Diana should not be forgotten on his wedding day. It was why he gave Kate her sapphire engagement ring. 'It's very special to me. As Kate's very special to me now, it was right to put the two together,' he explained. 'It was my way of making sure my mother didn't miss out on today and the excitement and the fact that we are going to spend the rest of our lives together.'

Royal weddings may seem like fairy tales to the public, but they are in fact all about timing and dates. William and Kate are determined to make their wedding as much their own as a state occasion. While the Queen and Prince Charles will be picking up the bill, with some help from the Middletons who are being allowed to contribute, William and Kate are overseeing every last detail. Aides at Buckingham Palace who traditionally oversee the ceremonial aspects of royal weddings have complained about being 'kept in the dark' but it is, say friends, William and Kate's way of putting their stamp on the most important day of their lives. From their wedding day and beyond Catherine Middleton, the girl from the home counties who happened to fall in love with a prince at university will have to work at being 'royal'. It was a transition Diana often struggled with and one that Kate describes as daunting. But in William she has a loving future husband who has vowed to help her every step of the way. As he has said: 'I'm trying to learn from lessons done in the past' and so it seems are the rest of family. From early on in their relationship, Kate was made to feel at home at the royal residences of Highgrove, Balmoral and Clarence House and she has received training and guidance to help her prepare for the next stage of her life. William, for his part, seems to be a royal genuinely in love. A young man who watched his parents' marriage crumble, he is determined that his marriage will be for life. It is why he slipped his beloved mother's sapphire ring on Kate's finger in Kenya. Now that he has, Kate's life has changed forever. She has been assigned a team of personal protection officers and will soon, one suspects, become one of the most photographed women in the world.

Once they are married, William and Kate want to continue enjoying a 'normal' life in Anglesey. She is happy to be an army wife while William is determined to serve at least another two years with the Royal Air Force who have invested nearly £1 million in his training. When he announced he was going to join the RAF back in September 2008 William surprised everyone, but it was a canny move. He wants a sense of purpose, not just a sense of duty. William knows how much his father agonised over how to live his life as king-in-waiting and he is determined to carve his own future. William has said he intends to serve as a search and rescue pilot for the next two, possibly three, years. It is a commitment that suits him and Kate and given the longevity and good health of the Windsors, he has every reason to believe it will be some time before he is king.

That said, as he embarks on married life, he has reached an axis at which his life will change. At a time when the Royal Family is continually under the spotlight over its future, it recognises the value of a telegenic young royal couple. Plans are already in place for them to take centre stage on the balcony of Buckingham Palace at the Queen's Diamond Jubilee in 2012.

And while William continues to undertake patronages and keep up his charitable commitments, there is an expectation that Kate will also take on some of her own, first with William and then in her own right over the coming months. The household of Prince William and Prince Harry at St James's is currently being divided up so that William and Kate will have their own office as soon as they are man and wife. It is part of a carefully calculated induction to public life which the palace has no intention of rushing. They have worked hard at establishing William as a public figure in his own right and the lessons of the past have been learned by courtiers too. Diana so often eclipsed her husband but Kate has made it clear she plans to follow William's lead. The signs for the future are promising; Kate has so far displayed a maturity, confidence and level headedness that will endear her to the public. One hopes that her working class roots and the Middleton's family ethos of hard work will stand her in good stead.

But while William and Kate promise to be the bright hope of the future, they simultaneously present a problem for the British monarchy. Opinion polls following the news of the royal engagement showed that sixty-four per cent of the British public were in favour of William and Catherine succeeding the throne, while less than one in five wanted the crown to pass to Charles and Camilla. It was an alarming statistic and although aides were quick to insist that William has 'no desire to climb the ladder of kingship prematurely' the poll had clearly been noted at the Palace. Charles and Camilla, whose car was attacked by students protesting about a rise in tuition fees as they were driven through central London just weeks later, have every reason to be concerned.

Being Royal – whether born or married into it – is always, in part, a waiting game. For Charles – who at sixty-two is the oldest Prince of Wales in history, the wait has been long and continues. The Queen is in good health. She may well have another decade on the throne and one has to wonder how effective a ruler Charles will be then. He is finally recognised for his tireless work with The Prince's Trust for the young and disadvantaged, and celebrated for his global campaigning. While he was once ridiculed for his statements about organic farming, the prince has now been proved right in many of his arguments for preserving British agriculture and traditional farming methods. But he still has a reputation for meddling in political issues and interfering with planning applications that should not concern him. As an avid letter writer, his personal correspondence and the diaries he writes and sends out to a select group of politicians and influential friends have landed the royal family in controversy – most notably the time he referred to the Chinese as 'appalling waxworks' during the handover of Hong Kong.

Whether Charles is fit to be the country's next King is something that continues to divide the nation. But it will be down to him, and then William, to justify the existence of the monarchy. 'The world is changing, as everybody knows, and we've changed with it,' Harry once observed. 'I think everybody can see that.' His confidence is touching. It is true that when set against their forebears William and Harry, at least, stand apart. As siblings they have a closeness that their father never enjoyed with his own brothers and sister. Harry wants to take on more official engagements and his work with the Armed Forces is tireless. His willingness to share the load with William will no doubt be to the benefit of them both. My personal view is that Charles will be king, but William with Catherine at his side is the true future of the monarchy and the key to the success of the royal family.

The boy who rattled around the corridors at Balmoral, bumping into skirting boards and playing merry havoc with stuffy notions of decorum, who stood on unfamiliar school steps as anxious as any new boy, who suffered a near unbearable loss and carried himself with dignity beyond his years, who has won over hearts and no doubt broken a few – that boy, now a man, carries more on his shoulders than most would care to imagine. Throughout his life and until now Harry has been by his side to support him. His future is less certain, his role less defined – something which must be at times both liberating and troubling.

Behind the palace walls it is William who is being groomed as Shadow King. As 2010 came to a close the Duke of Edinburgh announced that he would be scaling down his official engagements ahead of his ninetieth birthday. There is now a natural gap for William and Catherine to fill. The tutelage William received from his grandmother more than ten years ago is constantly being updated and refined. The look on William's face as he posed next to an empty throne at Government House in Melbourne said it all. It was an echo of the feeling of awe he tried to convey to his friends many years ago on a mountain-side in Chile. In reality it is an emotion that words cannot capture. He knows the task ahead of him, and he is slowly preparing himself for it. With Catherine, the love of his life, at his side to help guide him it is finally a journey he is ready to embrace.

Acknowledgements

Andrew Morton, arguably the most controversial royal biographer of all time once wrote: 'The eternal problem facing royal writers is that of authenticity. How to convince the world of the truth of your account, and the veracity of your sources when so many interviews are conducted on a confidential basis.' My entire career as a journalist and royal reporter has depended on sources, none of whom I have ever been able to name or acknowledge. Understandably you all wish to remain confidential and it is my duty to keep you so. Please know that I am indebted to every one of you – thank you for all your time and trust. Without you this book could never have been written.

Some of the contributors to this book, however, have kindly agreed to be named. I would like to thank the Queen's cousin Lady Elizabeth Anson for generously sharing her wealth of knowledge about William and Harry's early lives. Having worked closely with the Prince and Princess of Wales for many years I must also thank Dickie Arbiter for his time, memories and archive footage. I would also like to thank Camilla Fayed for agreeing to speak with me about the summer of 1997 for the very first time.

My thanks also, in no particular order, to Tara Palmer-Tomkinson, Simone Simmons, Vivienne Parry, Emma Sayle, Sam Young, Ian Jones, Alan Davidson, Dominic O'Neill, Ingrid Seward, Darren McGrady, Mark Fuller, Andrew Neil, Kitty

Dimbleby, Garth Gibbs, Mike Merritt, Niall Scott (Head of Communications at St Andrews), Dr Declan Quigley, Carley Massy-Birch, Ben Duncan and Katherine Witty. My gratitude and sincere thanks also go to Lieutenant Colonel Roy Parkinson and Major David James-Roll for inviting me to Sandhurst. Thanks also to the Ministry of Defence Press Office for their assistance and also the Royal Air Force press office, especially Martin Tinworth for his time.

Special thanks to my agent Jonathan Shalit for being the inspiration behind this book and to my editor Trevor Dolby for believing in me from the start. My publishers Preface have been fantastic throughout and I would like to thank in particular Richard Cable, Nicola Taplin, Vanessa Milton, Natalie Higgins and my picture researcher Melanie Haselden, you have been a pleasure to work with. Thanks also to Ian Monk for his guidance along the way.

Especial thanks to my esteemed colleague Laura Collins for her invaluable advice, assistance and encouragement and also to my dedicated researchers Helena Pearce and Charlotte Griffiths. I must also thank the Associated Newspapers reference library for all their help and Sian James and Marilyn Warnick at the *Mail on Sunday*. Finally my thanks to Peter Wright for his continued support.

List of Illustrations

Section One

On the steps of St Mary's Hospital © Press Association Images

Mrs Mynors' Nursery © Ron Bell / Press Association Images

Aboard the *Britannia* © Hulton Archive / Getty Images

William's first day at Eton © Stefan Rousseau / Press Association
Images

Kate Middleton at school © Solo Syndication

Diana's last holiday © Eric Ryan / Getty Images

By the River Dee © Mark Cuthbert / Empics / Press Association
Images

Diana's funeral cortege © Mirrorpix

William in Tortel, Southern Chile © UK Press / Press Association
Images

William as superman © Katie Nicholl

Rose Farquhar © Katie Nicholl

Harry at Lesotho Orphanage © AFP / Getty Images

Harry with Chelsy Davy © Jewel Samad / AFP / Getty Images

Don't Walk Fashion Show, St Andrews © M Neilson / Getty Images

Carley Massy-Birch © Katie Nicholl

Surfing in St Andrews © Press Association Images

William and Kate walking in St Andrews © Peter Kelly

Section Two

Kate and friends © Katie Nicholl

William and Kate dancing © Rex Features

William's graduation © Scott Heppell / Press Association Images

Wedding of Prince Charles and Camilla Parker Bowles © Corbis

Sovereign's Parade, Sandhurst © Mark Cuthbert / UK Press / Press Association Images

Harry outside Boujis nightclub © Steve Allen / Rex Features

Skiing in Zermatt © Rex Features

Cheltenham Festival © Mark Cuthbert / UK Press / Press Association Images

The Royal Box at the Concert for Diana © Mirrorpix

William's first solo flight © Mirrorpix

Prince Harry on Patrol © John Stillwell / Press Association Images

RAF Shawbury © Antony Jones / UK Press / Press Association Images

Prince Harry playing polo © Stan Honda / AFP / Getty Images

William and Harry in Lesotho © Chris Jackson / Getty Images

Kate Middleton at a Charity Roller Disco © Dominic O'Neill

William in Melbourne, Australia © Scott Barbour / Stringer / Getty Images

Harry and Chelsy at his graduation © Rex Features

William and Kate at Harry Meade's wedding © Arrow Press / Empics / Press Association Images

Engagement announcement © Rex Features

Bibliography

Berry, Wendy, *The Housekeeper's Diary: Charles and Diana Before the Break-up* (Barricade Books, New York, 1995)

Brandreth, Gyles, *Charles and Camilla: Portrait of a Love Affair* (Century, London, 2005)

Burrell, Paul, *Remembering Diana: The Way We Were* (Harper-Collins, London, 2007)

Hardman, Robert, *Majesty* (Ebury, London, 2007)

Hoey, Brian, *Prince William* (Sutton Publishing, Stroud, 2003)

Jobson, Robert, *Harry's War: The True Story of the Soldier Prince* (John Blake, London, 2008)

Jobson, Robert, *William's Princess* (John Blake, London, 2006)

Joseph, Claudia, *Kate Middleton – Princess in Waiting* (Mainstream, Edinburgh, 2009)

Morton, Andrew, *Diana: Her True Story* (Michael O'Mara, London, 1992)

Pasternak, Anna, *Princess in Love* (Bloomsbury, London, 1994)

Saunders, Mark, *Prince Harry: The Biography* (John Blake, London, 2002)

Seward, Ingrid, *William and Harry* (Headline, London, 2003)

Simmons, Simone with Seward, Ingrid, *Diana: The Last Word* (Orion, London, 2005)

Wharfe, Ken with Jobson, Robert, *Diana: Closely Guarded Secret* (Michael O'Mara, London, 2002)

Index